Christoph W. Keßler (Ed.)

Automatic Parallelization

Informatics

Christoph W. Keßler (Ed.)
Automatic Parallelization
New Approaches to Code Generation, Data Distribution, and Performance Prediction

R. Jungclaus
Modeling of Dynamic Object Systems
A Logic-based Approach

J.M. Schneider
Protocol Engineering
A Rule-based Approach

R. Gotzhein
Open Distributed Systems
On Concepts, Methods, and Design from a Logical Point of View

Spiro N. Pollalis
Computer-aided Project Management
A Visual Scheduling and Management System

W. Bibel
Automated Theorem Proving

E. Eder
Relative Complexities of First Order Calculi

F. Kurfeß
Parallelism in Logic

Vieweg

Christoph W. Keßler (Ed.)

Automatic Parallelization

New Approaches to Code Generation, Data Distribution, and Performance Prediction

vieweg

Die Deutsche Bibliothek – CIP-Einheitsaufnahme

Automatic parallelization: new approaches to code generation, data distribution and performance prediction / Christoph W. Kessler (ed.). – Braunschweig; Wiesbaden: Vieweg, 1994

(Vieweg advanced studies in computer science)

ISBN-13: 978-3-528-05401-4 e-ISBN-13: 978-3-322-87865-6

DOI: 10.1007/978-3-322-87865-6

NE: Kessler, Christoph W. [Hrsg.]

Verlag Vieweg, P.O. Box 5829, D-65048 Wiesbaden

Vieweg is a subsidiary company of the Bertelsmann Publishing Group International.

Printed on acid-free paper

ISBN-13: 978-3-528-05401-4

FOREWORD

Distributed-memory multiprocessing systems (DMS), such as Intel's hypercubes, the Paragon, Thinking Machine's CM-5, and the Meiko Computing Surface, have rapidly gained user acceptance and promise to deliver the computing power required to solve the grand challenge problems of Science and Engineering. These machines are relatively inexpensive to build, and are potentially scalable to large numbers of processors.

However, they are difficult to program: the non-uniformity of the memory which makes local accesses much faster than the transfer of non-local data via message-passing operations implies that the locality of algorithms must be exploited in order to achieve acceptable performance. The management of data, with the twin goals of both spreading the computational workload and minimizing the delays caused when a processor has to wait for non-local data, becomes of paramount importance.

When a code is parallelized by hand, the programmer must distribute the program's work and data to the processors which will execute it. One of the common approaches to do so makes use of the regularity of most numerical computations. This is the so-called **Single Program Multiple Data (SPMD)** or **data parallel** model of computation. With this method, the data arrays in the original program are each *distributed* to the processors, establishing an *ownership* relation, and computations defining a data item are performed by the processors owning the data. Accesses to non-local data must be explicitly handled by the programmer, who has to insert message passing communication constructs to send and receive data at the appropriate positions in the code. The details of message passing can become extremely complex; furthermore, the programmer must decide when it is advantageous to replicate computations across processors, rather than send data.

A major characteristic of this style of programming is that the performance of the resulting code depends to a very large extent on the data distribution selected. It determines not only where computation will take place, but is also the main factor in deciding what communication is necessary. The communication statements as well as the data distribution are hardcoded into the program. It will generally require a great deal of reprogramming if the user wants to try out different data distributions. This programming style can be likened to assembly programming on a sequential machine – it is tedious, time-consuming and error prone.

As a consequence, much research activity has been concentrated on providing high-level languages and programming tools for DMS. The full potential of these systems can only be exploited by a cooperative effort between the user and the language/compiler system: there is a tradeoff between the amount of information provided by a user (interactively or via language extensions in the program) and the effort that has to be spent in the compiler for generating high-performance target code. This has led to a spectrum of approaches to the problem of programming DMS. We mention some of the major research directions below.

- **Semi-automatic parallelization systems** are based on extensions of conventional languages such as Fortran or C which allow the explicit specification and manipulation of data distributions. The compiler uses this information to generate an explicitly parallel program.
  Such systems have been developed since the mid 1980's, and a number of university prototypes as well as commercial systems exist today. They are still limited in their ability to translate "real" programs efficiently and sometimes need a significant amount of user interaction.

- The experience with semi-automatic parallelization and the growing importance of DMS resulted in increased efforts to standardize language features for data distribution. **High Performance Fortran**, based on languages such as CM Fortran, Vienna Fortran, and Fortran D is the most prominent effort in this area. These new languages significantly surpass the capabilities of existing compilation systems, leading to new demands on compiler research for DMS.

- **Fully automatic parallelization systems** attempt to shift the full burden of parallel program generation to the compiler. This includes in particular

  - the automatic generation of data distributions from sequential programs, and
  - the automatic determination of transformation sequences for converting sequential programs to highly efficient explicitly parallel programs.

  For both problems – and a number of related issues – only limited solutions exist today. Successful approaches will have to use a combination of knowledge-based techniques and enhanced analysis methods, with a particular emphasis on performance analysis.

This book presents a collection of articles which illustrate important research directions in all three of these and some related areas. It gives an insight into some successful approaches, identifies a number of unsolved problems, and outlines promising future developments.

It is my hope that the book will contribute to an understanding of the important issues in this exciting and crucial area of current research.

Hans Zima

Contents

1 Preface

The present book emerged from the proceedings of the First International Workshop on Automatic Distributed Memory Parallelization, Automatic Data Distribution and Automatic Parallel Performance Prediction (or short: AP'93) held at the University of Saarbrücken, Germany, in March 1993. This volume contains 11 invited contributions that were presented at the workshop.

Before going *medias in res*, we give a short survey of supercomputer architectures and their impact on optimizing compilers technology. Because of the width of this area, we will only enter into those issues that seem relevant to us in the framework of this book. For a comprehensive survey of available parallel computing systems, we refer to [3]. Then, we will motivate automatic parallelization, consider the state of the art and raise the main problems that have been discussed at AP'93. To the novice reader, we recommend [4] as an excellent textbook.

Why parallel computers? The demand for computational power from natural sciences, engineering, medicine, ecology and other application areas, represented by the so–called "grand challenge" applications, increases rapidly — faster than just technological improvements can fill this gap. As a solution to this dilemma, parallel processing offers — theoretically — a technology–independent *speed–up* over single processor machines scaled by the number of processors.

During the 1970s, a first step towards parallel processing has been made by developing pipelined vector processors (e.g. Cray 1, Fujitsu VP-100). They support the SIMD (Single Instruction, Multiple Data) programming style. Since vector instructions (simple concurrent operations on arrays) can be processed very fast, these computers are very powerful compared to serial machines. However, they have severe limitations: they are not scalable (i.e., the number of pipeline stages cannot be increased arbitrarily), they are often not flexible enough, and they cannot be effectively used for irregular or non–data–parallel programs. Systolic arrays of processors working in a lock–step manner are also SIMD machines and, to some degree, also VLIW (Very Long Instruction Word) architectures.

Since the early 1980's, more and more parallel computers were introduced, at first mostly shared memory multiprocessors (SMS) consisting of a small number of processors connected to a common main memory by a fast interconnection network (e.g. Cray X-MP or Alliant FX/8). Each processor is able to run its own node program, so this corresponds to the MIMD (Multiple Instructions, Multiple Data) programming style: in addition of data parallelism, also task parallelism (parallel threads of program control flow) can be exploited. SMS are handy to program since the global memory structure resembles the sequential view of programming, and the user does not have to worry about communication delays. However, classical SMS are not scalable because the network constitutes a bottleneck that limits the realizable number of processors to an order of 32.

From the middle of the 1980's until today, there is a remarkable trend towards scalable massively parallel architectures consisting of thousands of processing elements. Currently, these are technically realizable only as (physically) *distributed–memory machines* (DMS), either in the form of homogeneous multiprocessors (for instance, Intel iPSC/860, Intel Paragon, NCUBE-2, Thinking Machines CM5 or MasPar MP-2) or as clusters of loosely–coupled workstations (e.g. IBM 9076 SP1). This architecture style is influenced by scalable networks (e.g. hypercubes, trees or tori) connecting the processors, by cheap memory and by cheap, mass–produced standard node processor chips (e.g. Intel i860 or Inmos Transputers). Since there is no longer a global address space, data (especially, arrays) and program code must be distributed over the local memory modules of each processor. Accesses to non-local data must be handled by interprocessor communication, which, implemented as operating system calls, is a time-consuming matter.

Two other architecture models are currently being explored to enhance scalability by using distributed memory modules while maintaining a shared–memory programming view for the user. The first one is the Virtual Shared Memory (VSM) approach which simulates a global main memory by caching. If a processor needs access to data that is not residing in its cache, the memory pages containing these data must be loaded into the cache via the interconnection network. An example machine is the Kendall Square Research KSR-1.

The second approach is still in research: the Parallel Random Access Machine (PRAM) is based on random routing and latency hiding by a sophisticated (but scalable) pipelined network that interconnects processors to memory modules. While the PRAM is really a general–purpose parallel machine, its performance on numerical applications with high locality is beaten by DMS of comparable technology. Both VSM and PRAM hide many implementation details from the user and, unfortunately, also from the compiler. While implicit parallelization is supported, explicit or automatic parallelization is rendered more difficult.

Considering the development of these "supercomputers", we can observe that the gap between peak performance and sustained performance grows, and that it becomes harder and harder to optimize the application towards the hardware.

Not only programming becomes more difficult. For current supercomputers, it is also not easy to predict the performance of a nontrivial parallel program, due to — in general, hardly documented — hardware features like caches, complex message protocols or routing anomalies.

Most numerical applications contain a large amount of grid operations or linear algebra routines. Loops indexing large arrays offer the greatest potential of (data) parallelism. Extracting parallelism thus means converting serial loops to parallel loops without changing the program's semantics by violating *data dependencies*. For a detailed discussion of data dependency theory, the reader is referred to [1].

Another important properties of grid operations and (most) linear algebra routines are *locality* of array references and a low communication–to–computation ratio. A program without these two properties will, in general, not run efficiently on current vector or DMS supercomputers.

Suitable *program transformations* may facilitate data dependency analysis and thus improve the potential for parallelism extraction. Although these transformations are well–

studied (e.g. [2]), automatic guidance in choosing the right sequence of transformations is an unsolved problem. The most sophisticated program transformation we can imagine is locally replacing a complete (sequential) implementation by a parallel algorithm with equal semantics. Many parallel algorithms have been devised within the last decades, but in general, they do not just emanate from their sequential counterparts by simple transformations and loop parallelization.

Parallel code generation for SMS is usually performed by decomposing the program into tasks, scheduling these, and introducing barrier synchronization points to make sure that always the desired version of data is referenced by each task. A good survey of relevant compiler techniques for SMS can be found in [2]. The most important compiler optimizations for SMS address load balancing by decomposing the program into tasks of nearly equal size, and minimizing the number of synchronization points.

Distributed memory multiprocessors are more difficult to program. The decomposition of the program code over the processors is often handled by the SPMD (single program, multiple data) programming paradigm where all processors have the same program, but work on different data sections. Thus, data distribution induces code distribution. An access to nonlocal data results in interprocessor communication. In general, if data has to be transported from one processor's local memory to that of another one, this has to be programmed explicitly as pairs of SEND and RECEIVE instructions (*message passing*). This tedious and error–prone task can be made easier for the user by two different ways: by applying communication libraries for message passing, and by (semi–)automatic parallelization. Message–passing libraries (like PVM, Express, PARMACS, MPI, Linda) contain simple (SEND/RECEIVE) and more higher order (e.g. global collection of array elements) communication primitives. Usage of these libraries also increases portability of the code. Nevertheless, parallelism has to be programmed explicitly by the user, e.g. in the form of parallel loops.

An alternative is offered by *semi–automatic parallelization*: The user determines (manually) how data should be distributed over the processor memories. This may technically be realized either as commands in an interactive system (e.g. SUPERB) or as directives or similar DISTRIBUTE statements in parallel programming languages (e.g. C*, HPF-Fortran, Fortran D, Vienna Fortran, Modula-2*). Moreover, it is often advisable to apply (manually) some suitable program optimizations (e.g. loop transformations, statement reordering or even partial algorithm replacement) at this point to exploit hardware properties such as cache sizes or processor topology. Thereafter, the program is automatically adapted by adding a mask to each instruction that assures that each processor updates exactly those elements that reside in its own local memory (*owner–computes rule*). Furthermore, insertion of the required SEND and RECEIVE instructions into the code is done automatically. The program generated by this method is, in general, not efficient. It has to be further tuned by improving the communication and by simplifying the masks. If the node processors are vector processors themselves (e.g. at CM-5), the parallelized node program should be vectorized to exploit this additional feature.

Although semiautomatic parallelization preserves the user from coding explicit message passing, the user is left alone with the most intellectually demanding steps: determining the data distribution (a hard problem in terms of computational complexity) and applying the suitable sequence of optimizing transformations to the code. Both items are crucial for the efficiency of the generated parallel code. In the worst case, an unsuitable data distribution results in a dramatical speed–*down* (!) of the parallelized program. If the programmer has sufficient knowledge about his data structures and about the target machine, and if he is willing to spend enough time to manually transform thousands of lines of code, then this may be satisfactory for him. But in general, the typical supercomputer user is not a computer scientist and wants to focus on his primary research issues instead of devoting much time to manually tuning a large application towards a machine that may be obsolete a few years later. He just wants to feed in the sequential program into the compiler and get out optimized parallel code. Furthermore, there is an immense potential of dusty deck programs that could be ported to new generations of supercomputers. Even for new programs, application programmers behave reserved towards parallel programming languages since none of them has currently established as *the* standard language.

Despite the fact that recent years have shown several interesting approaches to the problem of automatically determining optimal data distributions and array alignments, semiautomatic parallelization is still the state of the art. *Fully automatic parallelization* is yet a dream, and some people believe it will remain so forever. There are a lot of hard problems involved in it, e.g. obscure and undocumented behaviour of parallel machines, strange properties of the source language, irregular computation structures, important values (loop bounds) that are unknown at compile time, unresolvable alias or pointer references, only exponential–time algorithms available for determining exact data flow information or for computing optimal array alignment and distribution. As fast and complete solutions to these problems seem to be far away, current research on compilers for parallel architectures concentrates more on VSM and on compilers for parallel programming languages — research on automatic methods appears rather at their border. Nevertheless, automatic parallelization is a very important key technology for future use of parallel computers: *Real application programmers do not want to program in parallel — they just want performance.*

It has thus been a major goal of the AP'93 workshop to bring together researchers working on *true* automatic parallelization and to focus on automatic methods rather than on parallel programming languages. In particular, we would like to discuss the following questions:

- Up to which degree is automatic parallelization for DMS possible today, and what is expected to be possible in the near future?
- What are currently the most important problems for automatic parallelization?
- Which new ideas are there, what are their advantages and disadvantages?
- In which cases can knowledge–based methods help? Can they be used in practice?
- Are there promising methods for automatic data distribution and redistribution? What is their computational complexity? Do genetic algorithms offer an alternative?
- Why is performance prediction problematic? What are the actual problems on commercially available DMS machines and on their node processors?

As it is crucial to observe the impact of choosing a special data distribution, or of applying a special code transformation to the program, on the run time behaviour of the parallelized code, automatic parallelization *must* deal with *automatic run time prediction.* Since supercomputer manufacturers hardly publish detailed data sheets of their architecture design, performance prediction must be done indirectly by measuring run times of suitable *benchmark* programs (e.g. the Livermore Loops). From their run times, one tries to verify a simple architecture model for the target machine and to deduce characteristic machine parameters, which, in turn, are the basis for run time prediction. If a compiler and/or the operating system have been used, then also *their* quality is measured. Since the simplified architecture model can not match the target machine exactly, run time prediction by this method can not be exact either.

In the following survey, we shortly present the articles contained in this book. Their order does not impose any precedence relation among them; it is just the order the talks were scheduled at the workshop. In case of several authors, we only mention the name of the speaker. The results of the discussions during the workshop have been incorporated into the final versions of these contributions.

- T. Fahringer presents the Weight Finder, a tool that generates important profile data that is required to predict the run time of parallelized codes in the framework of the Vienna Fortran Compilation System. The derived run time estimates may also be used to limit computationally expensive optimizations to time–critical regions of the program.
- N. MacDonald measures the performance of several microprocessors typically used as node processors in current DMS. It turns out that already predicting the run time of the sequential node programs is a difficult task.
- A. Formella et al. present a set of kernels that are appropriate to explain hardware properties of the parallel machine. They use these insights to predict parallel run times of several well–known numerical algorithms with acceptable accuracy.
- D. Nicole reports on typical compilation problems with INMOS transputers that are designed to be applied as node processors in current massively parallel systems. He suggests optimizing code transformations that should provide better usage of the transputer's hardware properties.
- T. Brandes presents Adaptor, a tool that transforms Fortran programs written in a data–parallel style with parallelization and distribution directives, into a parallel program with explicit message passing that can be run on many current parallel architectures.
- R. Hänisch suggests using genetic algorithms to address the problem of determining good data distributions for DMS.
- C. Keßler works out the PARAMAT system that will be able to parallelize automatically a broad class of sequential numerical application codes. It is based on pattern recognition and on knowledge–based program transformations including local algorithm exchange.

- U. Kremer et al. propose dynamic data distribution by allowing static data redistribution. They embed their distribution algorithm into the Fortran D compiler environment.
- K. Knobe et al. categorize shape–changing operations (scalar and array expansion) on multidimensional arrays and show the impact of optimizing array reshaping on the run time of the parallelized code.
- M. Philippsen et al. address the data alignment problem for the parallel programming language Modula-2* with given directives for data distribution.
- T. Rauber et al. present a research prototype of an automatic parallelization system which applies a branch–and–bound search to determine good data distributions. They also contribute a comprehensive framework for parallel run time estimation.

Finally, we thank all AP'93 participants for their attendance, for their talks and discussion contributions. The AP'93 workshop has been arranged by *Graduiertenkolleg Informatik* at Saarbrücken University. We would like to thank its speaker, Prof. Dr. J. Buchmann, for his greatly appreciated support, and its secretary, Mrs. Monika Fromm, for her assistance in preparing the workshop. We further want to thank our colleagues Arno Formella and Thomas Rauber for taking note of the discussions during AP'93.

According to numerous utterances from all workshop participants, AP'93 has been a great success. For this reason, there is already a successor workshop planned, namely AP'94, in Edinburgh. It is our hope that the AP workshops will continue being a platform to discuss new ideas in automatic parallelization and stimulating future research on this highly interesting area.

Christoph W. Keßler

Saarbrücken, July 1993

References

[1] Utpal Banerjee. *Dependence Analysis for Supercomputing*. Kluwer Academic Publishers, 1988.

[2] Constantine D. Polychronopoulos. *Parallel Programming and Compilers*. Kluwer Academic Publishers, 1988.

[3] Arthur Trew and Greg Wilson (Eds.). *Past, Present, Parallel: A Survey of Available Parallel Computing Systems*. Springer-Verlag, 1991.

[4] Hans Zima and Barbara Chapman. *Supercompilers for Parallel and Vector Computers*. ACM Press Frontier Series. Addison–Wesley, 1990.

2 The Weight Finder - An Advanced Profiler for Fortran Programs

Thomas Fahringer
DEPARTMENT OF SOFTWARE TECHNOLOGY AND PARALLEL SYSTEMS
UNIVERSITY OF VIENNA, AUSTRIA
email: tf@par.univie.ac.at

Abstract: This paper introduces the Weight Finder, an advanced profiler for Fortran programs, which is based on a von Neumann architecture. Existing Fortran codes are generally too large to analyze fully in depth with respect to performance tuning. It is the responsibility of the Weight Finder to detect the most important regions of code in the program, as far as execution time is concerned. Program transformation systems, compilers and users may then subsequently concentrate their optimization efforts upon these areas in code.

Furthermore program unknowns, such as loop iteration counts, true ratios and frequency information, are derived. Analysis and prediction systems require concrete values for these unknowns in order to provide reasonable accurate results.

Animation, simulation, debugging and trace based tools may use the profile data as being derived by the Weight Finder in order to detect program parts which are never executed, simulate the program's control flow, etc.

This tool is based on an optimized instrumented profile run. Several optimizations are shown which eliminate large portions of the instrumentation code, thus decreasing profile run-time and memory requirements, and improving the measurement accuracy. It is shown how the profile data can be adapted for program transformations to the original Fortran program without redoing the profile run.

The *Weight Finder* is a 10000 line software package which is fully integrated under the Vienna Fortran Compilation System.

2.1 Introduction

The *Weight Finder*, an advanced profiler for Fortran77 programs based on a von Neumann architecture, is introduced. The principle aim of this performance analysis tool is to obtain concrete profile data for program unknowns and to find the run-time intensive program portions based on a concrete Fortran77 program for a characteristic set of program input data. The derived profile data provide helpful information about the underlying program to compiler, performance estimation, post-animation, debugging, and trace based tools.

The *Weight Finder* is an integrated tool of the VFCS (Vienna Fortran Compilation System) ([4, 26, 7, 27, 6, 5]), which handles the optimization and parallelization of sequential programs. The *Weight Finder* attributes the internal representation (syntax tree) of a Fortran77 program under the VFCS with the profile data. Consequently, if the program is subsequently parallelized, the profile data, which are valid for both the sequential and the parallel program, can be automatically transferred to the parallel program[1].

The profile data as derived by the *Weight Finder* are useful for following purposes:

- Consider the time consuming and complex task of optimizing either a sequential or a parallel program. There exist well over 100 different program transformations ([28, 5, 18, 24]). For both sequential and parallel programs: statement reordering, scalar forward substitution, loop interchange, loop distribution, constant propagation, etc. For parallel programs only: communication vectorization, communication fusion, loop iteration elimination, optimizing data distribution strategies, etc. The compiler and the user is concerned about what kind of transformation sequences to apply on which portions of the program. The consequence is an enormous search tree for these transformation sequences. Existing Fortran codes are generally too large to analyze fully in depth with respect to all those different transformation sequences. It is the task of the Weight Finder to locate the run-time intensive program portions in the program. Experience indicates that these portions are likely to be from 5 to 10 percent of the original code, leading to a significant reduction in the overall workload for the program optimization process.

- State-of-the-art performance prediction systems — such as the P^3T Parameter based Performance Prediction Tool ([11, 8]) and others ([10, 21, 23]) — which statically predict the performance behavior of parallel programs, are faced with program unknowns, for which concrete values are needed to provide reasonable accurate performance estimates. Mainly loop iteration counts, true-ratios for conditional statements, and frequency information is required by performance estimation tools. The *Weight Finder* obtains concrete values for all of these unknowns. The obtained *Weight Finder* profile data are transferred to a parallel program as indicated above. A performance prediction tool might then use the attributed parallel program to derive estimated performance values based on the parallel program. The P^3T is integrated with the *Weight Finder* and successfully derives accurate performance estimates based on the *Weight Finder* derived profile data (cf. [11]).

- Animation tools might use frequency information and the concrete outcome of IF-expressions specific to a statement instantiation[2] in order to post-visualize the control flow of a program.

- Debugging and trace based tools ([15]) might require frequency information and/or true ratios of program branches in order to detect program portions which are never executed.

Existing profilers ([14, 22, 3, 13, 20]) could not be used for following reasons:

[1] In this paper parallel programs are referred to Single Program Multiple Data parallel programs only

[2] A statement instantiation corresponds to a single statement execution.

- **Most of the existing profilers produce a single output file containing both the original program and the profile data. In order to relate the profile data to specific statements, this file would have to be reparsed. Because both *Weight Finder* and the VFCS use the same program representation (syntax tree), the profile data naturally can be associated to the instrumented program statements.**

- Previous compilers have only very limited support to selectively profile parts of the underlying program for specific data of interest. Conventional profilers derive a vast amount of profile information neglecting the varying needs of different users and tools. This induces unnecessarily long profile times and high profile memory requirements.

- They do not provide any support to transfer the profile data – derived from a Fortran77 program – to a parallel program.

- The profile data required (see below) is usually not supported by existing profilers.

Therefore it was necessary to build the *Weight Finder*, a new and more enhanced profiler, which is based on following design: The original Fortran77 program for which a profile run has to be done, is run through the VFCS frontend. This includes extensive intra- and interprocedural analysis and program normalization and standardization[3] ([12, 25, 28, 26]). The user selectively chooses from a set of *sequential program parameters*: frequency information, true-ratios, loop iteration counts, dynamic outcome of IF-expressions, and timing information for specific program portions or the entire program. The *Weight Finder* then instruments the program according to the chosen parameters, optimizes the instrumented program, compiles and executes it. As instrumentation code may obviously induce a severe overhead in the profile run and, as a consequence, also influence the accuracy of profiled times, strong emphasis was paid to optimize the instrumented program. Three optimization techniques are presented which improve the profile run in terms of instrumentation code, profile memory, and run-time. The obtained sequential program parameters are then visualized together with the original Fortran77 program in a Motif/X11 window. The internal data structures of the program – syntax tree and control flow graph – are attributed with these parameter values.

Program changes, which are induced by applying program transformations, may invalidate the obtained parameter values. In order to prevent re-doing profile runs of a specific program over and over again, it is shown how to adapt the obtained parameter values, in particular for frequency information, true ratios, and loop iteration counts. A single profile for a Fortran77 program is therefore sufficient, even if subsequent program changes are applied.

The paper is organized as follows. First, the sequential program parameters are defined and prerequisites are presented. The next section describes the Weight Finder phases, outlines how to use this tool, explains three optimization techniques which decrease the profiling overhead, and shows a sample session of the *Weight Finder* under the Motif/X11 user-interface. Section 2.4 shows how to adapt the profile data for a variety of program transformations, which prevent redoing the profile run for different program changes. Conclusions and future work are presented in Section 2.5.

[3] This strongly alleviates subsequent compiler analysis

2.2 Prerequisite

The VFCS is the underlying compilation system of the described profiler. It handles the optimization of both sequential and parallel Fortran programs. The *Weight Finder* requires the VFCS's frontend for Fortran77 programs.

For a specific Fortran77 program Q, which has gone through the VFCS frontend, the *Weight Finder* may selectively derive – by incorporating a profile run – the following *sequential program parameters*:

- The loop iteration count of a DO-loop L is specified by the number of times the DO-loop body of L is executed for a single instantiation of L. This is defined by a function $iter : D \rightarrow N_0$, where D is the set of DO-loops in Q and N_0 the set of positive integer numbers including zero.

- The frequency information of a statement $S \in \mathcal{S}$, where $\mathcal{S}$ is the set of statements in Q, specifies how many times S is executed during a single program run of Q. This is defined by a function $freq : \mathcal{S} \rightarrow N_0$

- The true ratio for a conditional statement $S \in \mathcal{S}_{cond}$, where $\mathcal{S}_{cond}$ is the set of conditional statements in Q, determines the probability that the condition of S evaluates to TRUE. This is defined by a function $tr : \mathcal{S}_{cond} \rightarrow [0..1]$, with $[0..1]$ a closed interval of real numbers. $tr(S) = 0$ ($tr(S) = 1$) means that the conditional expression of S never (always) evaluates to TRUE.

- The dynamic outcome of the IF-expression C of a conditional statement $S \in \mathcal{S}_{cond}$, determines whether C evaluates to TRUE or FALSE for a specific instantiation of S during the program run of Q. This is defined by a function $dyn : \mathcal{S}_{cond} \times \Delta_S \rightarrow \{\text{TRUE,FALSE}\}$, where Δ_S is the set of instantiations for statement S and $\mathcal{S}_{cond}$ the set of conditional statements in Q. $dyn(S, i) =$TRUE means that statement S evaluates to TRUE for statement instantiation i.

- The measured time, also denoted as *profiled time*[4] for a set of program statements $\mathcal{U}$, is defined by a function $ptime : \mathcal{U} \rightarrow R_0^+$, where $\mathcal{U}$ may be a DO-loop, a procedure, or the overall program, and R_0^+ is the set of positive real numbers including zero.

Note that all but the last parameter are machine independent. All sequential parameters depend on the user provided set of input data for Q.

2.3 The Weight Finder

In the following, an overview of the six processing phases for a single profile run of the *Weight Finder* as an integrated tool of the VFCS is provided. Thereafter, each of these phases are explained in detail.

[4]The time required to do the profile is denoted as *profile run-time*

1. **Front End Processing**
   In the first phase, the original Fortran77 program Q_1 is run through the VFCS frontend. This includes extensive intra- and interprocedural analysis, normalization and standardization of Q_1, which yields program Q_2. A copy of Q_2, which is further processed in phase-6, is stored.

2. **Choosing Sequential Program Parameters**
   The user selectively chooses the sequential program parameters as described in Section 2.2.

3. **Instrumentation**
   The *Weight Finder* instruments Q_2 based on the chosen sequential program parameters of phase-2, which yields Q_3.

4. **Optimization**
   A series of optimizations are applied on Q_3 in order to reduce the instrumentation overhead in terms of instrumentation code, profile run-time, and memory requirements. Q_4 is the optimized instrumented program.

5. **Compile and Execute**
   Q_4 is then compiled and executed on a von Neumann architecture. The derived *profile data* for the chosen sequential program parameters are written into a set of *profile files*, one for each different sequential program parameter as chosen in phase-2.

6. **Attribute and Visualize**
   The profile data is read from the profile files and the internal data structures of a copy of Q_2 – as created in phase-1 – are attributed with these values. In addition, the derived sequential program parameters are visualized together with Q_2 in a Motif/X11 window.

The user may use the *Weight Finder* in both blocking and non-blocking mode. The non-blocking mode allows the user to work on the optimization of a different program under VFCS during the profile run.

Another facility of the *Weight Finder* enables the user to terminate a profile run before it is finished. The profile run is therefore fully controlled under the X11/Motif user interface of the VFCS.

2.3.1 Choosing sequential program parameters

Based on program Q_2 the user may selectively choose different sequential program parameters to be obtained by the subsequent profile run. Following parameters can be selected:

- *Restricted Frequencies:* Measure the frequency of all procedure calls and all DO-loops. For perfectly nested DO-loops only the outermost loop is measured.

- *All Frequencies:* Measure the frequency of all basic blocks[5], procedure calls and DO-loops. All loops of a perfectly nested DO-loop are measured.
- *True Ratios:* For all conditional statements the overall true ratio is obtained.
- *Dynamic IF-expressions:* Obtain the dynamic outcome of the IF-expression for every conditional statement with respect to all statement instantiations.
- *DO-loop parameters:* Derive the average values for DO-loop upper and lower bounds for all DO-loops. This is only done for non-constant loop bounds.
- *Time measurement (DO-loops):* Acquire the accumulated execution time for every DO-loop. For perfectly nested DO-loops only the outermost loop is considered.
- *Time measurement (Procedures):* Measure the accumulated execution time for every procedure call.

There is an additional option which decreases the amount of instrumentation code and the profile run-time.

- *Loop parameter check:* Instrumentation code is inserted to verify whether or not the loop upper bound is larger than its matching loop lower bound. In such a case, a different instrumentation strategy has to be applied which is more complex and induces higher profile costs in terms of instrumentation code, profile run-time and memory requirements. If the user can guarantee that for all loops in Q_2 the loop upper bound is always larger than its matching lower bound, then a considerable less complex instrumentation policy is utilized by the *Weight Finder* . This option is critical, as instrumentation code inside of nested loops may induce a high profile overhead.

Fig. 2.1 shows a screen snapshot of the *Weight Finder* under VFCS during this phase. The main window shows the main program of the Jacobi relaxation code ([19]) after the VFCS frontend. By selecting the menu item "Information→Weight Finder→Sequential Program Parameters", a selection box ("Select Sequential Program Parameters") allows to choose the sequential program parameters as described above.

For the next *Weight Finder* release it is planned to allow the above parameter selection also on a per statement base. The user will then be able to turn profiling on and off with respect to a specific sequential program parameter for arbitrary statements.

The parameter selection is stored every time the user terminates a session under VFCS. After re-starting, the set of parameters chosen at the most recent *Weight Finder* session is pre-selected by the system per default.

Note that choosing sequential program parameters does not immediately trigger a profile run. After this phase the *Weight Finder* knows which parameters have to be obtained for what program portions.

[5] As a consequence, the frequency of all statements is available

2.3.2 Instrumentation

This section describes the instrumentation policies incorporated in phase-3 of the *Weight Finder* processing phases.

The following terminology is used to describe the instrumentation phase. If, for a specific statement S, a sequential program parameter is to be derived, then S is called the *instrumented statement*. In general, one or several *instrumentation statements* are inserted in Q_2 for every instrumented statement. An instrumentation statement assigns values for sequential program parameters to so-called *instrumentation variables* during the profile run. For all instrumentation code examples, instrumentation variables are prefixed with the $ sign. For the sake of simplicity, instrumentation variables are illustrated as scalar variables. However, in the real implementation, arrays are used instead. This is done to reduce the number of VFCS symbol table entries and to alleviate the administration of instrumentation variables under the *Weight Finder* .

Frequency instrumentation is done based on basic blocks with a single entry and single exit statement as defined in [1].

Instrumentation .1 (Frequency)
Let $B \in \mathcal{B}$, where $\mathcal{B}$ is the set of basic blocks in Q_2.

INPUT: Non-instrumented Basic Block B

```
        B
```

OUTPUT: Instrumented Basic Block B

```
S:      $B_freq = $B_freq + 1
        B
```

S is an instrumentation statement as inserted by the *Weight Finder* . If – before instrumentation – B is a labeled statement, then the label of B is moved to S. $\$B_{freq}$ is set to zero at the beginning of the profile run.

$freq(B)$ is then defined by $value(\$B_{freq})$, the value of variable $\$B_{freq}$ at the end of the profile run.

Instrumentation .2 (DO-loop parameters)
Let $L \in \mathcal{D}$, where $\mathcal{D}$ is the set of DO-loops in Q_2, and $B \in \mathcal{B}$ the predecessor basic block of L.

INPUT: Non-instrumented loop

```
        B
L:      DO I1=LB,UB
```

OUTPUT: Instrumented loop

```
      B
S1:   $LB1 = LB
S2:   $UB1 = UB
S3:   $S_lb = $S_lb + $LB1
S4:   $S_ub = $S_ub + $UB1
L:    DO I1=$LB1,$UB1
```

$S1, \ldots, S4$ are instrumentation statements. In order to prevent side-effects, it is important to assign the loop bound expressions to instrumentation variables. For the sake of simplicity it is assumed that B is the only predecessor basic block of L and L does not have a label.

The average loop iteration count of L is computed by

$$iter(L) = \frac{value(\$S_{lb}) - value(\$S_{ub}) + 1}{freq(B)}.$$

Note that L is assumed to be executed only once for a single instantiation of this statement, rather than once for all of its loop iterations.

In the following, the true ratio instrumentation, which is done for conditional statements, is defined.

Instrumentation .3 (True Ratio)
Let $S \in \mathcal{S}_{cond}$ and S belongs to a basic block $B \in \mathcal{B}$, then the instrumentation for S is done as following:

INPUT: Non-instrumented statement

```
IF (C) S_b
```

where C is an IF-expression and S_b a statement.

OUTPUT: Instrumented statement

```
IF (C) THEN
  $S_freq = $S_freq + 1
  S_b
ENDIF
```

$true(S)$ is then defined by $\frac{value(\$S_{freq})}{freq(B)}$, with $value(\$S_{freq})$, the value of $\$S_{freq}$ at the end of the profile run, and $freq(B)$, the frequency of basic block B. $\$S_{freq}$ is set to zero at the beginning of the profile run.

Instrumentation .4 (Dynamic IF-expression outcome)
Let $S \in \mathcal{S}_{cond}$ and S belongs to a basic block $B \in \mathcal{B}$, then the instrumentation for S is done as following:

INPUT: Non-instrumented statement

```
S:   IF (C) S_b
```

where C is an IF-expression and S_b a statement.

OUTPUT: Instrumented statement

S1: $\$S_{freq} = \$S_{freq} + 1$
S2: $\$C1 = C$
S3: IF ($\$C1$ .NE. $\$C1_{old}$) THEN
S4: call *buffer*($\$S_{freq}, \$C1$)
S5: $\$C1_{old} = \$C1$
ENDIF
S6: IF ($\$C1$) S_b

$S1$ is the frequency instrumentation statement for basic block B. $\$C1$ and $\$C1_{old}$ are instrumentation variables of type boolean.

As the value of C is used in several different statements ($S2, \ldots, S6$), side-effects must be prevented by assigning the boolean value of C to an instrumentation variable $\$C1$, which is done in $S2$.

In $S3$ the current value of $C1$ is compared to the value of $\$C1_{old}$. $\$C1_{old}$ contains the boolean value of C after it changed from TRUE to FALSE or vice versa the last time during the profile run. If the current value of $\$C1$ is different from $\$C1_{old}$, then in a non-optimized profile run, the current value of $C1$ and the current statement instantiation value of $S3$ (which is uniquely defined by $\$S_{freq}$, the current value of the frequency variable of B) are written to a profile file. The *Weight Finder*, however, optimizes this instrumentation by buffering the data to be written to a profile file. This is done in a subroutine with the name *buffer*. In this subroutine the data to be written is buffered in a buffer array. If this array is full, then a write operation to a profile file is executed and the buffer array is considered to be empty again by initializing a buffer pointer. This saves expensive I/O operations during the profile run.

Note that instead of storing the boolean value of C for every instantiation of S, a store operation is launched only when C changes from TRUE to FALSE or vice versa.

Time measurement instrumentation incorporates the insertion of machine independent time measurement calls in Q_2 which are replaced by machine dependent time measurement calls in the backend of the VFCS.

Instrumentation .5 (Time measurement)
Let $L \in \mathcal{U}$, where $\mathcal{U}$ is the set of all DO-loops, procedure calls, and procedures in Q_2, and Q_2 itself.

INPUT: Non-instrumented statement

L

OUTPUT: Instrumented statement

S1: $\$L_{time1}$ = mtime()
L
S2: $\$L_{time2} = \$L_{time2}$ + mtime() - $\$L_{time1}$

$S1$, $S2$ are instrumentation statements as inserted by the *Weight Finder*. $mtime()$ is a machine independent time measurement call. If, before instrumentation, L is a labeled statement, then the label of L is moved to the instrumentation statement $S1$. $ptime(L)$ is then defined by $value(\$L_{time2})$, which contains the accumulated time of L at the end of the profile run. An approximate value for a single instantiation of the computation time of L can then be computed by $ptime(L)/freq(L)$.

2.3.3 Optimization

An instrumented profile run induces overhead with respect to profile memory and profile run-time requirements, which in addition worsens the measurement accuracy of profiled times.

The main objective of the *Weight Finder* 's optimization phase is to reduce the profiling overhead and its associated inaccurate profiled times.

In the following, three different possibilities for such optimizing transformations are described:

2.3.3.1 Equal frequencies beyond basic blocks

Equal frequencies of basic blocks before and after loops may induce the elimination of frequency instrumentation code.

Let $B1$ and $B2$ be two basic blocks and L a loop nest, where $B1$ is the only predecessor and $B2$ the only successor basic block of L, respectively. If for all loops, in which $B1$ is contained, also $B2$ is contained, and vice versa, then $B1$ and $B2$ have the same frequency.

If the above condition is fulfilled for two basic blocks, then only one of them has to be instrumented for frequency information. In the following, a code fragment of the Fast Fourier Transformation ([19]) is shown:

Example 2.3.1

```
S1:   WRK(1)=0.e0
      WRK(N+1) = 0.e0
      W(1)=0.e0
S2:   E(1) = 0.e0
      DO 100 J=2,N
         WRK(J)= (J-1.e0)/sqrt((2.e0*J-1.e0)*(2.e0*J-3.e0))
         WRK(J+N)=0.e0
         E(J) = WRK(J)
         W(J) = 0.e0
  100 CONTINUE
S3:   MATZ = 1
      INDX = 2*N+1
S4:   NP1=N+1
```

Let basic block $B1$ ($B2$) contain all statements between $S1$ and $S2$ ($S3$ and $S4$). Both basic blocks are separated by a DO-loop. It can be easily seen that basic block $B1$ has the same frequency as $B2$. Instead of inserting frequency instrumentation code for both $B1$ and $B2$ only one of these basic blocks has to be instrumented. The same optimization can be frequently done for forward and backward GOTO loops. For further information refer to [9].

2.3.3.2 *Hoisting out frequency instrumentation*

Hoisting out frequency instrumentation code of nested DO loops is in particular critical, because the execution frequency of statements inside of loop nests is very high, which of course also accounts for instrumentation statements. Hoisting out those instrumentation statements significantly reduces the profile run-time and improves the accuracy for profiled times.

The following example illustrates the general policy for a basic block B inside of a loop nest to be frequency instrumented. An instrumentation statement $S1$ is inserted immediately before B, which increments a frequency variable $\$B_{freq}$ by one.

Example 2.3.2 *General frequency instrumentation*

```
        DO I1 = LB1, UB1
          DO I2 = LB2, UB2
            DO I3 = LB3, UB3
S1 :          $B_freq = $B_freq + 1
              B
```

LB1, LB2, LB3, UB1, UB2, and UB3 are constants[6].

If a basic block $B \in \mathcal{B}$ inside of a nested loop has to be instrumented for frequency information, instrumentation code does not necessarily have to be inserted immediately before B. If none of the loop bounds are written inside of the loop nest, then it is possible to hoist instrumentation code out of the loop nest, which can be seen in Ex. 2.3.3. If some of the loop bounds are written inside the loop nest, then only part of the instrumentation code can be hoisted out. For more details on the conditions and algorithms for hoisting out instrumentation code see [9]. In both cases the efficiency of such instrumented program is superior as compared to the general instrumentation policy.

Example 2.3.3 *Hoisting instrumentation code*

```
S1:  $b1 = LB1
S2:  $e1 = UB1
S3:  $b2 = LB2
```

[6] The actual implementation considers loop lower and upper bounds as linearly dependent on all enclosing loop variables.

$S4$: $\$e_2$ = UB2
$S5$: $\$b_3$ = LB3
$S6$: $\$e_3$ = UB3
$S7$: $\$iter_1 = \$e_1 - \$b_1 + 1$
$S8$: $\$iter_2 = \$e_2 - \$b_2 + 1$
$S9$: $\$iter_3 = \$e_3 - \$b_3 + 1$
$S10$: $\$B_{freq} = \$B_{freq} + \$iter_1 * \$iter_2 * \$iter_3$
L_1: DO $I_1 = \$b_1, \$e_1$
L_2: DO $I_2 = \$b_2, \$e_2$
L_3: DO $I_3 = \$b_3, \$e_3$
B

Note that $S1, \ldots, S6$ in Ex. 2.3.3 are necessary to prevent side effects of executing loop lower and upper bounds more than once. The $\$iter$ instrumentation variables evaluate the number of loop iterations for a specific loop header statement. In $S10$ the frequency of basic block B is computed outside of the loop nest. This optimized instrumentation does not contain any instrumentation code inside of the loop nest.

Hoisting instrumentation code out of a loop nest commonly induces more instrumentation code, but depending on the loop iteration count these instrumentation statements are executed only once for every loop nest instance. This is in contrary to the general instrumentation policy, where instrumentation statements are executed for every single loop iteration.

2.3.3.3 Equal true ratios

Recognizing equal true ratios of different conditional statements is important for many compilers, because they normalize and standardize the original input program. This is e.g. done by replacing RETURN, alternate GOTO, arithmetic GOTO, ENTRY statements, etc. by logical IF statements.

If two different conditional statements $S1$ and $S2$ have the same IF-expression and none of the variables in the IF-expression is written between any possible path between $S1$ and $S2$, and whenever $S1$ is executed also $S2$ is executed and vice versa, then for only one of them, true ratio instrumentation code has to be inserted.

In Ex. 2.3.4 instead of all four statements, only $S1$ and $S4$ have to be instrumented for true ratios. Statements $S2$ and $S3$ refer to $S1$ with respect to their true ratio. It is also recognized that the true ratio of $S3$ is the negated true ratio value of $S1$, thus $tr(S3) = 1 - tr(S1)$. In $S3$ variable A might be written. Therefore for $S4$, whose IF-expression contains variable A, a separate true ratio instrumentation is initiated by the *Weight Finder* .

Example 2.3.4

```
S1:  IF (A .AND. B) C = C + 1
S2:  IF (A .AND. B) D = D + 1
S3:  IF (.NOT. (A .AND. B)) A = C + D
S4:  IF (A .AND. B) D = D - C + A
```

The optimization phase yields program Q_4.

2.3.4 Compile and Execute

In this phase the *Weight Finder* compiles and executes Q_4 on a sequential processor machine. For every different sequential program parameter as chosen in phase-2, a unique profile file containing the profile data is created. The profile data for the dynamic outcome of IF-expressions is written to a unique profile file during — for all other sequential program parameters, at the end of — the profile run.

Fig. 2.2 shows a screen snapshot of the *Weight Finder* after this phase. The main window shows Q_4. A Motif information box appears on the screen, which informs the user that the profile run is finished.

The user has the possibility to terminate the profile run by a separate Weight Finder option.

2.3.5 Attribute and Visualize

In order to visualize the derived sequential program parameter values, the *Weight Finder* is loading a copy of Q_2 as stored in phase-1. Then it reads the profile data from the set of profile files, analyzes these data and, if necessary, computes the final values for the sequential program parameters. These values are then visualized together with Q_2 in a Motif/X11 program window. They are shown in the program window at the right hand side of every specific statement for which instrumentation was done.

In addition, the internal data structures of Q_2 (syntax tree and control flow graph) are attributed with sequential program parameters. Thus it is possible for other tools, e.g. performance estimators, to access them.

Fig. 2.3 shows a screen snapshot of the *Weight Finder* after this phase. The sequential program parameters are visualized at the right hand side of each statement of Q_2 for which instrumentation was done in phase-3. FR denotes the frequency parameter, T specifies profiled times in seconds, TR the true ratio and LP the loop parameters. $LP = [/; 10.67]$ means that only the loop upper bound was instrumented for the loop parameters. The average value for the loop upper bound is 10.67. The loop lower bound was not instrumented because it was recognized as a constant.

2.4 Adaptation of Profile Data

In this section the influence of program transformations and different problem sizes on the sequential program parameters, in particular for true ratios, frequencies and loop iteration counts, are analyzed. Profiled times are ignored, as this parameter is used only at the beginning of a program transformation process. Once the performance intensive program parts are detected by the original profiled time values, the transformation process focuses on these parts without reusing profile times again.

2.4.1 Program transformations

For a specific program version Q the user might be interested to apply a series of program transformations ([28, 18, 24, 16]), e.g. loop distribution, interchange, fusion, tiling, skewing, peeling, unrolling and jamming, statement reordering, scalar expansion, constant propagation, etc. A major question arises:

Do program transformations change the outcome of the sequential program parameters, in particular $freq, iter$, and tr ?

In the following, a variety of examples are illustrated which show, that many transformations have only a minor influence on these parameters. For most others, the new parameter value can be re-computed based on the parameter value before applying a transformation.

A major observation is therefore:

A single profile run is sufficient for many important program transformations to provide accurate values for sequential program parameters. Those parameters which change due to a program transformation can be adapted in many cases.

Let the sequential parameter functions $freq, iter$, and tr, specify the function value before the application of a program transformation Tr. $freq', iter'$, and tr' specify the function value after the application of Tr.

Furthermore it is assumed that the loop header statement of a loop L is executed only once for all of its iterations.

2.4.1.1 *Loop distribution and fusion*

Loop distribution ([24],[28]) places each statement in the loop body of a nested loop in a separate loop nest with identical loop header statements. Ex. 2.4.1 shows a loop kernel before loop distribution. From Ex. 2.4.2 it can be easily seen, that none of the frequencies of any statement nor the iteration count of the loop changes after loop distribution.

Example 2.4.1 *before distribution*

```
DO I=3,N
    A(I) = A(I) + 1
    B(I) = A(I-2) - B(I)
ENDDO
```

Example 2.4.2 *after distribution*

```
DO I=3,N
    A(I) = A(I) + 1
ENDDO
DO I=3,N
    B(I) = A(I-2) - B(I)
ENDDO
```

Since loop distribution does not change frequency or loop iteration counts, loop fusion behaves in the same way.

2.4.1.2 Loop Skewing

According to [24] loop skewing does not change the execution order of the loop iterations. It does only change the dependence direction vectors of references inside of the loop nest.

Example 2.4.3 *before skewing*

```
S1:  DO I = 2,N
S2:     DO J = 2,N
S3:          A(I,J) = A(I,J-1) - A(I-1,J)
S4:     ENDDO
S5:  ENDDO
```

Example 2.4.4 *after skewing*

```
S1:  DO I = 2,N
S2:     DO J = I+2,I+N
S3:          A(I,J-I) = A(I,J-I-1) - A(I-1,J-I)
S4:     ENDDO
S5:  ENDDO
```

We see that neither frequencies nor loop iteration counts are changing for any statement. This means that $freq(S1), freq(S2), freq(S3), freq(S4), freq(S5), iter(S1)$, and $iter(S2)$ do not change after loop skewing.

2.4.1.3 Loop interchange

This transformation interchanges the loop header statements of pairs of different loops, without changing the loop bodies ([24],[28]).

Assuming that the loop header statement of a loop L is executed only once for a single instantiation of L, then loop interchange (Ex. 2.4.6) does not change $freq(S3), iter(S1)$, and $iter(S2)$. However, the frequency of the loop header statements and their associated CONTINUE statements change. The new frequency values for $S1, S2, S4$ and $S5$ can easily be adapted as follows: $freq'(S1) = freq(S1) * iter(S2), freq'(S2) = freq(S1)$, $freq'(S4) = freq'(S1)$, and $freq'(S5) = freq'(S4)$.

Example 2.4.5 *before loop interchange*

```
S1:  DO I=2,N-1
S2:     DO J=2,N-1
S3:          A(I,J) = B(I,J) + B(I-1,J)
S4:     ENDDO
S5:  ENDDO
```

Example 2.4.6 *after loop interchange*

```
S2:   DO J=2,N-1
S1:      DO I=2,N-1
S3:         A(I,J) = B(I,J) + B(I-1,J)
S5:      ENDDO
S4:   ENDDO
```

2.4.1.4 *Loop unroll and jam*

Loop unrolling ([17],[28]) unrolls an outer loop in a loop nest by a factor α and jams the resulting inner loops.

Ex. 2.4.8 illustrates the unrolling of loop $S1$ by a factor $\alpha = 2$, which means, that loop $S1$ is unrolled α times. The frequencies of $S1$ and all loop body statements of $S1$ are divided by α, thus e.g. $freq'(S1) = freq(S1)/\alpha$, and $iter'(S1) = iter(S1)/\alpha$. For each statement S in the loop body (before unrolling) a new statement S' is induced after unrolling, for which the following holds $freq'(S') = freq'(S)$. All other sequential program parameters do not change.

Example 2.4.7 *before unrolling and jamming*

```
S1:   DO I=2,N-1
S2:      DO J=2,N-1
S3:         C(I) = C(I) + A(I,J)
S4:      ENDDO
S5:   ENDDO
```

Example 2.4.8 *after unrolling and jamming*

```
S1:   DO I=2,N-1,2
S2:      DO J=2,N-1
S3:         C(I) = C(I) + A(I,J)
S3':        C(I+1) = C(I+1) + A(I+1,J)
S4:      ENDDO
S5:   ENDDO
```

2.4.1.5 *Loop peeling*

Loop peeling ([28]) peels off the first and/or last iteration of a loop.

As can be seen from the example below, $iter(S2)$ and the frequency for all statements inside of the loop (S3,S4,S5) and the loop header statement (S2) is decreased by α, the peeling number. The frequency for those statements (S3'), which are hoisted out of the loop body because of the peeling effect, is equal to $freq(S1)$.

Example 2.4.9 *before peeling*

```
S1:  K = 99
S2:  DO I=1,100
S3:      B(I) = A(K) + C(I+1)
S4:      K = I - 1
S5:  ENDDO
```

Example 2.4.10 *after peeling*

```
S3':  B(1) = A(99) + C(2)
S2:   DO I=2,100
S4:       K = I - 2
S3:       B(I) = A(K) + C(1 + I)
S5:   ENDDO
S1:   K = 99
```

In Ex.2.4.11 scalar forward substitution and statement elimination is applied to $S4$ in that sequence, which yields a more optimized code.

Example 2.4.11 *after forward substitution and statement elimination*

```
S3':  B(1) = A(99) + C(2)
S2:   DO I=2,100
S3:       B(I) = A(I-2) + C(1 + I)
S5:   ENDDO
S1:   K = 99
```

2.4.1.6 Loop tiling

Loop tiling combines strip mining and loop interchange to promote reuse across a loop nest ([24]). The execution sequence of loop iterations is reordered such that iterations from outer loops are executed before completing all the iterations of the inner loop. The tile size TS is chosen to allow maximum reuse for a specific memory hierarchy.

As can be seen from Ex. 2.4.13 the frequency of S3, S4, S5, S6 and S7, and $iter$(S1) do not change. For the outermost loop S1, we derive:
$freq'(S1) = \lfloor iter'(S2)/TS \rfloor * \lfloor iter'(S3)/TS \rfloor * freq(S1)$, and
$freq'(S2) = freq(S2) * \lfloor iter(S3)/TS \rfloor$. Furthermore,
$iter'(S2) \approx TS, iter'(S3) \approx TS, iter'(S2') = \lfloor N/TS \rfloor, iter'(S3') = \lfloor N/TS \rfloor$.
Moreover, $freq'(S8) = freq'(S1)$ and $freq'(S9) = iter(S2')$.

Example 2.4.12 *before tiling*

```
S1:  DO I=1,N
S2:      DO J=1,N
```

```
S3:          DO K=1,N
S4:             C(I,K) = C(I,K) + A(I,J) * B(J,K)
S5:          ENDDO
S6:       ENDDO
S7:    ENDDO
```

Example 2.4.13 *after tiling*

```
S2':   DO J2=1,N,TS
S3':      DO K2=1,N,TS
S1:          DO I=1,N
S2:             DO J=J2,MIN(J2+TS-1,N)
S3:                DO K=K2,MIN(K2+TS-1,N)
S4:                   C(I,K) = C(I,K) + A(I,J) * B(J,K)
S5:                ENDDO
S6:             ENDDO
S7:          ENDDO
S8:       ENDDO
S9:    ENDDO
```

Many other transformations, such as scalar expansion, constant propagation, statement reordering, subscript normalization, etc. do not have any effect on frequency and loop iteration counts.

Based on the above examples another observation can be made: All but *loop unrolling and jam* and *loop peeling* do not influence true ratios at all, because they do not change the frequency of statements other than loop header statements. *Loop peeling* has a negligible influence, because the frequency of a non-loop-header statement is decreased at a maximum by α, the peeling number. *Loop unrolling and jamming* may significantly decrease the frequency of non-loop-header statements. In absolute values this may have a strong influence on true ratios. However, the relative change of a true ratio is reasonably small. This means e.g. that if the true ratio value was small before loop unrolling, then it will be small afterwards.

2.4.2 Problem Size

Choosing a different problem size for a program Q may have a strong influence on frequency and iteration counts. For regular problems mainly loop bounds may depend on the problem size. We believe that, based on initial values for the sequential program parameters as derived by a single profile run, it is possible to incorporate intra- and interprocedural scaling techniques, to scale the initial parameter values for problem sizes. It is in particular important to derive the initial sequential parameter values based on a small problem size. This helps to reduce the profiler runtime. Interprocedural constant propagation ([25],[28]) as implemented in the VFCS, play an important role to scale these parameter values appropriately. Statistical and asymptotic analysis ([2]) methods might be very useful to scale frequency and loop iteration parameters in relationship to the problem size increase. However for cases where the sequential program parameters depend on different array (problem) sizes more advanced techniques are required. This will be addressed in future research.

A considerable effect of varying problem sizes on true ratios with respect to relative changes could not be observed. This can be explained by analyzing the classes of conditional statements frequently occurring in real world programs:

- Conditional exit GOTOs most of the time have a relatively small true ratio.
- Conditions depending on loop iteration counts are rather rare.
- Conditions dependent on the control flow of a program – frequently induced by normalizing and standardizing transformations of the underlying compilation system – are usually independent of the problem size.

We have not yet found a general solution to scale the true ratios for arbitrary conditional statements. However, for simple cases, statistical scaling techniques for different problem sizes should provide reasonably accurate true ratios.

2.5 Conclusion and Future Work

Optimizing and parallelizing a sequential program is a time consuming and complex task. In order to create a performance efficient program, many program transformations, e.g. statement reordering, scalar forward substitution, loop distribution, interchange, fusion, etc., may have to be applied to a program. Existing Fortran codes are generally too large to analyze fully in depth with respect to all different program transformation sequences. In this paper the *Weight Finder*, an advanced profiler for Fortran77 programs based on a von Neumann architecture, is described. It locates the run-time intensive program parts by profiling the underlying program. This allows the user to concentrate program optimization and parallelization efforts on those smaller program sections.

The *Weight Finder* also derives concrete values for program unknowns and symbolics, e.g. frequencies, true-ratios, loop iteration counts, etc. This is a critical requirement for many state-of-the-art performance estimators, which require such data in order to derive reasonable accurate performance predictions. The *Weight Finder* is an integrated tool of the Vienna Fortran Compilation System (VFCS), which handles the optimization of sequential programs as well as parallelizing them. A major advantage of the described profiler is, that the obtained profile data are used to attribute internal data structures (syntax tree) of a given program. If the program is subsequently parallelized, then these values are transferred to the parallel program. Thus the profile data can also be used for performance prediction of parallel programs. The P^3T ([11, 8]) is successfully using the *Weight Finder* profile data to derive accurate performance estimates and to guide the program transformation process under the VFCS.

The *Weight Finder* is able to instrument a program for control flow information, e.g. the concrete outcome of IF-expressions of conditional statements for every statement instantiation. Animation tools may use this data together with frequency information and iteration counts to post-visualize the control flow of a program.

Debugging tools might require the *Weight Finder's* frequency information and/or true ratios of program branches in order to detect program portions which are never executed during a program run.

The user selectively chooses from a set of *sequential program parameters*: frequency information, true-ratios, loop iteration counts, dynamic outcome of IF-expressions, and timing information to be derived by the *Weight Finder* for specific program parts. Based on a Fortran77 program the *Weight Finder* creates an optimized instrumented program, which gets compiled and executed on a von Neumann architecture. The obtained profile data are then visualized on a Motif/X11 window together with the original Fortran77 program.

The *Weight Finder* uses efficient optimization techniques to reduce profile overhead with respect to instrumentation code, profile time and memory requirements.

Furthermore it is shown how to adapt the profile data for a variety of program changes without redoing the profile. This is in particular critical, considering the many transformations a program may undergo until it is reasonably well optimized.

The *Weight Finder* is a 10000 source line (excluding comments) software package developed at the University of Vienna.

Future work will extend the *Weight Finder* to obtain profiles directly from parallel programs. Based on these profile data a trace file will be created, which then serves as input to a visualization tool showing the performance behavior of the parallel program.

References

[1] A. Aho, R. Sethi, and J. Ullman. *Compilers, Principles, Techniques and Tools*. Series in Computer Science. Addison Wesley, 1988.

[2] G. Balbo and G. Serazzi. Asymptotic Analysis of Multiclass Closed Queueing Networks: Multiple Bottlenecks. Technical Report, Dipartimento di Elettronica, Politecnico di Milano, March 1992.

[3] Bell Laboratories, Murray Hill,NJ. *prof command*, January 1979. section 1.

[4] B. Chapman, S. Benkner, R. Blasko, P. Brezany, M. Egg, T. Fahringer, H.M. Gerndt, J. Hulman, B. Knaus, P. Kutschera, H. Moritsch, A. Schwald, V. Sipkova, and H.P. Zima. *VIENNA FORTRAN Compilation System - Version 1.0 - User's Guide*, Jan. 1993.

[5] B. Chapman, T. Fahringer, and H. Zima. Automatic Support for Data Distribution. In *Proc. of the Sixth Annual Workshop on Languages and Compilers for Parallel Computing*, Portland, Oregon, Aug. 1993.

[6] B. Chapman, P. Mehrotra, and H. Zima. *Vienna Fortran - A Fortran Language Extension for Distributed-Memory Multiprocessors*. Elsevier Science Publishers, Amsterdam, 1991. Also: ICASE Report No. 91-72, Contract No. NAS1-18605, NASA, Langley Research Center, Hampton, VA, 1991.

[7] B. Chapman, P.Mehrotra, and H.Zima. Programming in Vienna Fortran. *Scientific Programming*, 1(1):31 – 50, August 1992.

[8] T. Fahringer. Automatic Cache Performance Prediction in a Parallelizing Compiler. In *Proc. of the AICA'93 - International Section*, Lecce, Italy, September 1993.

[9] T. Fahringer. *Automatic Performance Prediction for Parallel Programs on Massively Parallel Computers*. PhD thesis, University of Vienna, Department of Software Technology and Parallel Systems, to appear (1993).

[10] T. Fahringer, R. Blasko, and H. Zima. Automatic Performance Prediction to Support Parallelization of Fortran Programs for Massively Parallel Systems. In *ACM International Conference on Supercomputing 1992*, pages 347 – 356, Washington D.C., July 1992.

[11] T. Fahringer and H. Zima. A Static Parameter based Performance Prediction Tool for Parallel Programs. Invited Paper, in *Proc. of the 7th ACM International Conference on Supercomputing 1993*, Tokyo, Japan, July 1993.

[12] H.M. Gerndt. *Parallelizationfor Distributed-Memory Multiprocessing Systems*. PhD thesis, University of Bonn, December 1989.

[13] S.L. Graham, P.B. Kessler, and M.K. McKusick. gprof: A Call Graph Execution Profiler. In *Proceedings of the SIGPLAN 82 Symposium on Compiler Construction*, pages 120 – 126, June 1982. SIGPLAN Notices, Vol.17, No. 6.

[14] D.E. Knuth. An empirical study of FORTRAN programs. *Software - Practice and Experience*, (1):105–133, 1971.

[15] P. Lenzi and G. Serazzi. ParMon: Parallel Monitor. Technical Report N3/95, Dipartimento di Elettronica, Politecnico di Milano, October 1992.

[16] K.S. McKinley. *Automatic and Interactive Parallelization*. PhD thesis, Rice University, CRCP, Houston, TX, April 1992.

[17] D.A. Padua and M. Wolfe. Advanced compiler optimizations for supercomputers. In *Comm. ACM*, pages 1184–1201, 1986.

[18] C.D. Polychronopoulos. *Parallel Programming and Compilers*. Kluwer Academic Publisher, Boston, MA, 1988.

[19] W.H. Press, B.P. Flannery, S.A. Teukolsky, and W.T. Vetterling. *Numerical Recipes in C; The Art of Scientific Computing*. Cambridge University Press, 1988.

[20] V. Sarkar. Determining Average Program Execution Times. In *ACM International Conference on Supercomputing*, 1989.

[21] V. Sarkar. *Partitioning and Scheduling Parallel Programs for Multiprocessor*. The MIT Press, Cambridge, Massachusetts, 1989.

[22] E. Satterthwaite. Debugging Tools for High Level Languages. *Software - Practice and Experience*, (2):197 – 217, 1972.

[23] K.Y. Wang. A Performance Prediction Model for Parallel Compilers. Technical Report, Computer Science Dept., Purdue University, November 1990. Technical Report CSD-TR-1041, CAPO Report CER-90-43.

[24] M. Wolfe. *Optimizing Supercompilers for Supercomputers*. The MIT Press, Cambridge, Massachusetts, 1989.

[25] H. Zima, H.-J. Bast, and M. Gerndt. SUPERB - A Tool For Semi-Automatic MIMD/SIMD Parallelization. *Parallel Computing*, pages 1–18, 1988.

[26] H. Zima and B. Chapman. Compiling for Distributed-Memory Systems. *Proceedings of the IEEE Special Section on Languages and Compilers for Parallel Machines*, February 1993. to appear.

[27] H. Zima, P. Brezany, B. Chapman, P. Mehrotra, and A. Schwald. Vienna Fortran - a language specification. Technical report, ICASE, Hampton, VA, 1992. ICASE Internal Report 21.

[28] H. Zima and B. Chapman. *Supercompilers for Parallel and Vector Computers*. ACM Press Frontier Series. Addison-Wesley, 1990.

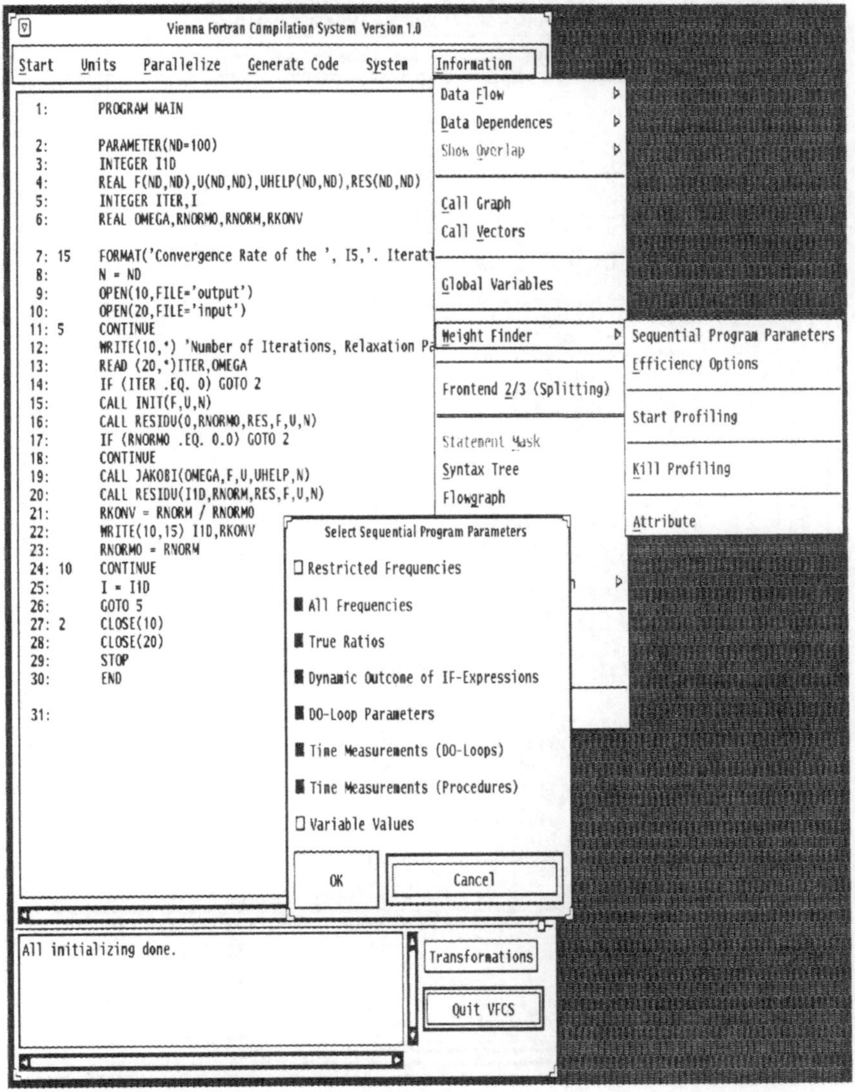

Figure 2.1 Selecting the sequential program parameters using the *Weight Finder*

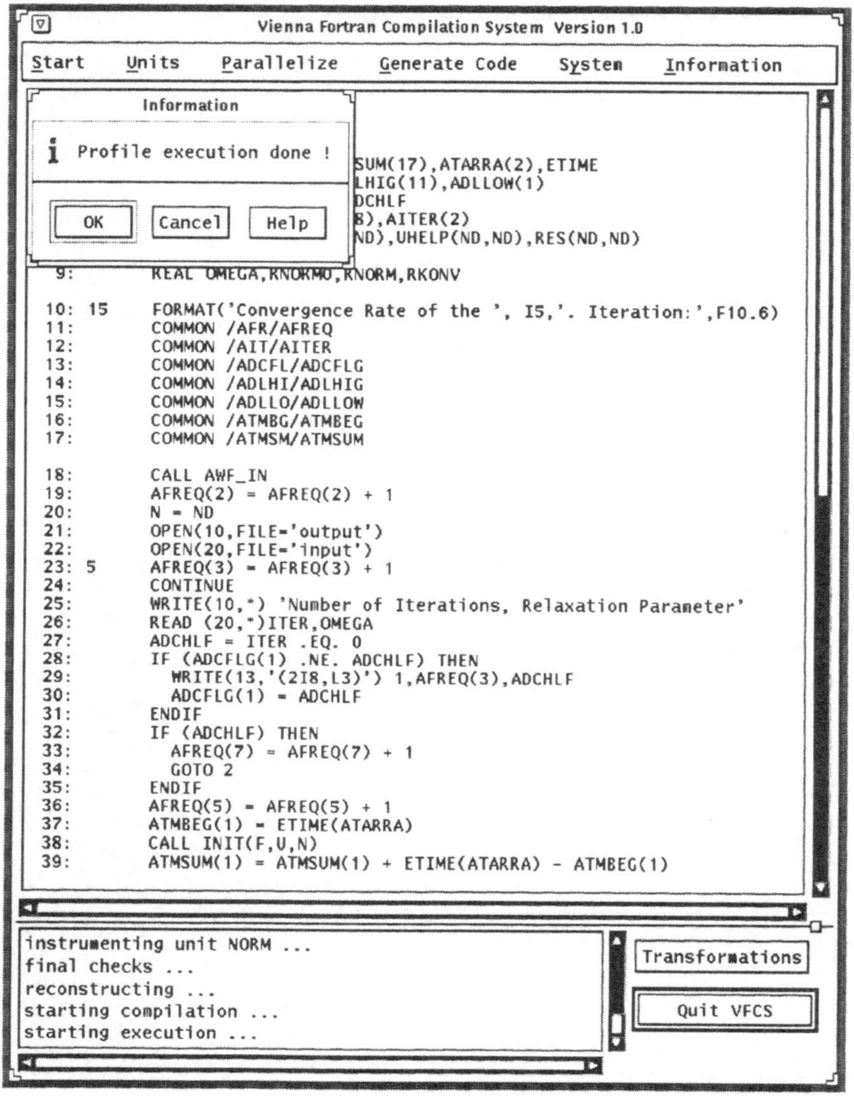

Figure 2.2 After the profile run is finished

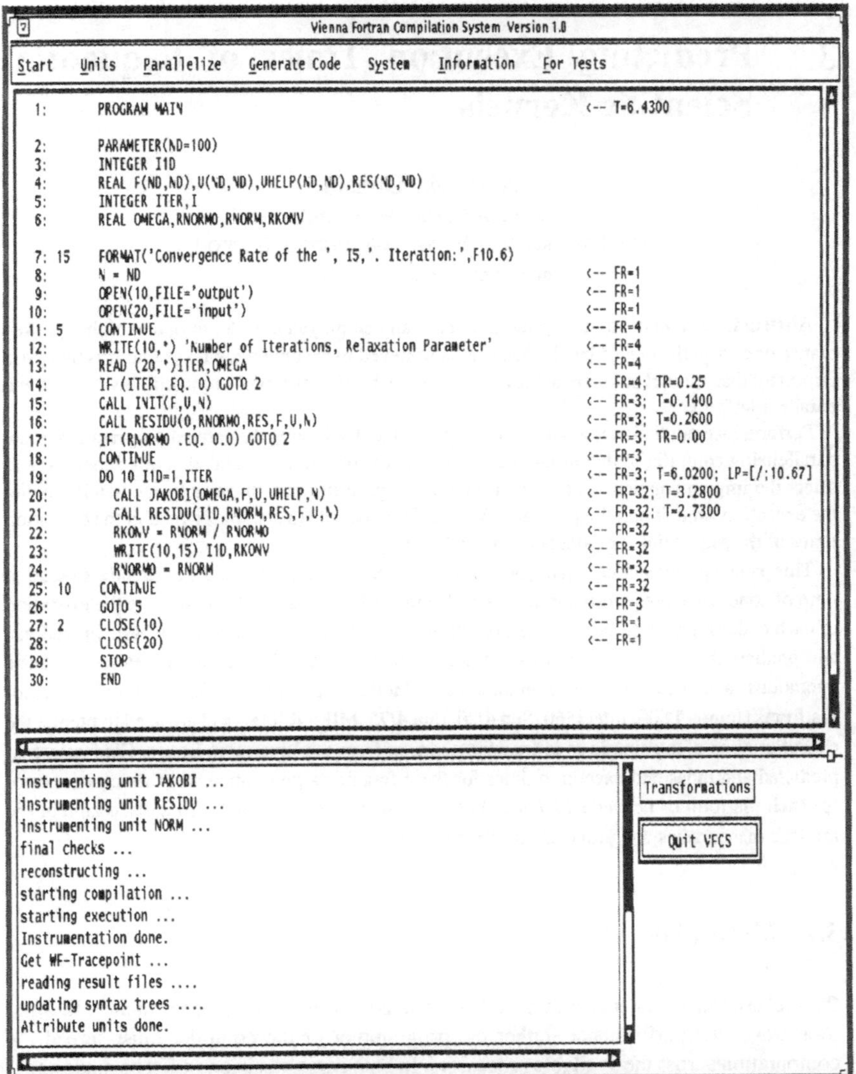

Figure 2.3 Visualizing the sequential program parameters

3 Predicting Execution Times of Sequential Scientific Kernels

N. B. MacDonald
DEPT. OF COMPUTER SCIENCE
THE UNIVERSITY OF EDINBURGH, UNITED KINGDOM
email: nbm@epcc.ed.ac.uk

Abstract: Parallel computer systems are typically employed in order to obtain higher performance or cost-performance levels than can be achieved by a conventional system. It is therefore important that parallel software achieves sufficiently high performance to justify investment in a parallel platform.

Performance prediction is a potentially important tool, allowing the parallel programmer or the parallelising compiler to determine the relative merits of different parallelisation schemes, and select the implementation which offers the highest performance. In order to accurately predict the execution time of parallel programs, we must first be able to accurately predict the execution times of the sequential components of a parallel program.

This paper applies a micro-analysis technique to deriving estimates of the sequential execution time of code fragments written in a subset of Fortran 77. The approach considers the execution of each code fragment to involve the execution of a certain number of various basic operations, and predicts the execution time of the fragment using expected execution times for the basic operations, which can be derived automatically. Models are developed for five microprocessor platforms (Inmos T800, Intel i860, Sun 4/20, Sun 4/75, MIPS R3000) and are used to predict the execution time of six simple code fragments, drawn from the Livermore Loops. Comparison of predicted and measured execution times for these fragments gives an average percentage error for each platform of between 19.7% and 66.1%. The paper concludes with a discussion of the model's inaccuracies and proposals for further work.

3.1 Motivation

Parallel computer systems are typically employed to achieve high performance. In order to achieve that performance, either the programmer or the compiler must spread the computation across the available processors. In both cases, decisions must be made about how to decompose the computation into processes, and then how to assign these processes to the available hardware, in order to minimise execution time. Different decompositions give rise to different sets of processes, and each set of processes can be mapped in many ways, each with different performance characteristics. Performance prediction is an important tool, offering a principled basis on which to select decomposition and mapping techniques.

In order to predict the execution time of parallel programs, there is clearly a need to predict the execution time of the sequential components of parallel programs. A naive

Statistic	T800	i860
Maximum	0.7765	4.5955
Average	0.3303	2.1994
Geometric Mean	0.2953	2.0055
Harmonic Mean	0.2669	1.9285
Minimum	0.1363	1.0066

Table 3.1 Single precision MFlop/s statistics from Livermore Loops

approach might be to seek to determine the MFlop/s rate of the platform, and determine the number of floating point operations performed by the program. Table 3.1 shows various statistical measures of MFlop/s rates obtained from the Livermore Loops [1] on T800 and i860 processors (see Section 3.3 for details of these platforms). The maximum rate is some 5.7 times the minimum rate on the T800, and 4.6 times the minimum rate on the i860. The average rate on the T800 is 2.3 times smaller than the maximum, and 2.4 times larger than the minimum. Hence estimates based on an average MFlop/s rate may be up to a factor of 2.4 away from the actual measured performance. For the i860, Table 3.1 suggests that such predictions could be up to a factor of 2.1 away from reality. Of course, there may be codes which exhibit higher or lower MFlop/s ratings than those included in the Livermore Loops, leading to higher factors. The major problem with this approach is that it takes no account of non-floating point operations, whose execution may comprise a significant proportion of execution time. Since the ratio of floating point calculations to other operations is very program dependent ([2]), a prediction methodology based purely on floating point operations will be unable to distinguish between the performance of programs which have widely different execution times.

A more detailed method, termed "micro-analysis", involves generating a symbolic time-formula for a code (fragment), representing its execution time [3]. The variables occurring in time-formulas represent the time it takes to execute basic operations. The time-formula associated with a code is platform-independent. platform. An estimate of execution time on a particular platform is obtained by substituting the time taken for basic operations on that platform into the time-formula. The use of this technique to estimate the execution times of Pascal or C-like programs is described in [4].

This paper presents current work which seeks to determine the effectiveness of applying similar techniques to Fortran 77 codes, running on a variety of high performance processor platforms. In this environment, the prevalence of sophisticated compiler optimisation and processor technology combine to provide additional challenges to the micro-analysis approach.

3.2 Deriving time formulae for code fragments

A subset of Fortran 77 was identified (Table 3.2). The subset provides only for data-independent code; conditional branches are not supported. The intention is to evaluate

IDENT	::=	SCALARIDENT
	|	ARRAYIDENT
SCALARIDENT	::=	a|...|z
ARRAYIDENT	::=	SCALARIDENT(EXPR)
EXPR	::=	EXPR + EXPR
	|	EXPR − EXPR
	|	EXPR * EXPR
	|	EXPR / EXPR
	|	(EXPR)
	|	IDENT
	|	CONSTANT
STMTLIST	::=	STMT
	|	STMT STMTLIST
STMT	::=	IDENT = EXPR
	|	`do` SCALARIDENT = EXPR, EXPR STMTLIST `enddo`

Table 3.2 Syntax of programs

the degree of accuracy with which the execution time of codes with such completely defined behaviour can be estimated.

Many of the symbols representing basic operation times are subscripted with τ to denote type information. Only `INTEGER` and `REAL` variables are currently supported, represented by the subscripts I and R respectively. We follow the Fortran convention of naming — that variables I through N are `INTEGER` and others are `REAL`.

A mapping from expressions in this language to time-formulae is presented in Table 3.3. A constraint on this translation is that a time formula must be a linear combination of basic operation times. The reason for this restriction will be discussed in Section 3.3.

3.3 Obtaining a platform model

To predict the execution time of codes on a particular platform given their time formulae, we must obtain measurements of the basic operation times on that platform. We do this by measuring the execution time of a number of code fragments and constructing a set

$$T_{\mathrm{EXPR}}(\mathrm{EXPR}_1 + \mathrm{EXPR}_2) = T_{\mathrm{EXPR}}(\mathrm{EXPR}_1) + t_{\mathrm{add}_r} + T_{\mathrm{EXPR}}(\mathrm{EXPR}_2)$$

$$T_{\mathrm{EXPR}}(\mathrm{EXPR}_1 - \mathrm{EXPR}_2) = T_{\mathrm{EXPR}}(\mathrm{EXPR}_1) + t_{\mathrm{sub}_r} + T_{\mathrm{EXPR}}(\mathrm{EXPR}_2)$$

$$T_{\mathrm{EXPR}}(\mathrm{EXPR}_1 * \mathrm{EXPR}_2) = T_{\mathrm{EXPR}}(\mathrm{EXPR}_1) + t_{\mathrm{mult}_r} + T_{\mathrm{EXPR}}(\mathrm{EXPR}_2)$$

$$T_{\mathrm{EXPR}}((\mathrm{EXPR})) = T_{\mathrm{EXPR}}(\mathrm{EXPR})$$

$$T_{\mathrm{EXPR}}(\mathrm{CONSTANT}) = 0$$

$$T_{\mathrm{EXPR}}(\mathrm{SCALARIDENT}) = 0$$

$$T_{\mathrm{EXPR}}(\mathrm{SCALARIDENT}(\mathrm{EXPR})) = T_{\mathrm{EXPR}}(\mathrm{EXPR}) + t_{\mathrm{index}}$$

$$T_{\mathrm{STMT}}(\mathrm{IDENT} = \mathrm{EXPR}) = T_{\mathrm{EXPR}}(\mathrm{IDENT}) + t_{\mathrm{assign}_r} + T_{\mathrm{EXPR}}(\mathrm{EXPR})$$

$$T_{\mathrm{STMT}}\begin{pmatrix}\texttt{do}\ \mathrm{S} = \mathrm{E}_1, \mathrm{E}_2 \\ \mathrm{STMTLIST} \\ \texttt{enddo}\end{pmatrix} = (\mathrm{E}_2 - \mathrm{E}_1 + 1) \times (t_{\mathrm{loopoh}} + T_{\mathrm{STMTLIST}}(\mathrm{STMTLIST}))$$

$$T_{\mathrm{STMTLIST}}([\,]) = 0$$

$$T_{\mathrm{STMTLIST}}\begin{pmatrix}\mathrm{STMT} \\ \mathrm{STMTLIST}\end{pmatrix} = T_{\mathrm{STMT}}(\mathrm{STMT}) + T_{\mathrm{STMTLIST}}(\mathrm{STMTLIST})$$

Table 3.3 Mapping from programs to time formulae

Operation	Time, μs				
	T800	Sun 4/20	Sun 4/75	R3000	i860
t_{loopoh}	2.1662	0.4149	0.3498	0.4161	0.0889
t_{index}	0.4718	0.0626	0.0713	0.0633	0.0953
$t_{\text{assign}\,I}$	0.7418	0.3570	0.2875	0.3553	0.1260
$t_{\text{add}\,I}$	0.7964	0.2968	0.2106	0.2924	0.1972
$t_{\text{sub}\,I}$	0.5952	0.2951	0.2112	0.2908	0.1980
$t_{\text{imult}\,I}$	0.9087	0.9647	0.7761	0.9652	0.4751
$t_{\text{assign}\,R}$	1.0002	0.4034	0.2980	0.4024	0.2266
$t_{\text{add}\,R}$	0.6938	0.2293	0.1952	0.2432	0.1687
$t_{\text{sub}\,R}$	0.5609	0.2304	0.1984	0.2373	0.1683
$t_{\text{rmult}\,R}$	0.3296	0.2300	0.1947	0.2289	0.1683

Table 3.4 Basic operation times

of simultaneous equations in which the predicted execution times, derived the mapping given above, and the measured execution times are equated. The unknowns in this set of equations are the basic operation times for the platform in question. The equations are very unlikely to admit an exact solution, since the model is an approximation. The restriction of linearity which we place on time formulae allows us to use a standard least squares technique to find an approximate solution.

A number of difficulties must be addressed in selecting the set of experiments from which to generate the set of simultaneous equations. We must conduct at least as many experiments as there are basic operations, and in general, the larger the set of experiments the better. Unfortunately, some basic operations will appear disproportionately often in many sets of experiments, and this can lead to a very poorly conditioned matrix of coefficients. Care must also be taken to avoid equations which are almost linearly dependent, since the small differences in basic operation coefficients can lead to a set of equations with a very unstable fit.

Several further issues arise in timing the experiments. In addition to ensuring that the platform is dedicated to the experiment when measurements are made, account must also be taken of the clock resolution. The high clock period on some platforms typically means that a code fragment must be executed many times in order to eliminate significant quantisation errors. It is easy to implement a wrapper which increases the number of iterations and repeats the experiment until the elapsed time is large with respect to the clock period. Finally, it can be important to determine the time taken to read the clock, and to normalise the measured execution times of experiments using this value.

Table 3.4 gives basic operation times obtained using this method on a number of processors[1]

[1] All T800 measurements in this paper refer to an Inmos T800 processor in a Meiko Computing Surface, running code generated by Version 2.12 of Meiko Scientific's mf77 compiler. Code was generated for both Sun 4 workstation platforms using EPC Fortran77 Release 2.6.5.1. The MIPS R3000/3010 processor, in a Silicon Graphics 4D/20G workstation, used Silicon Graphics F77 compiler release 4.0.5. Measurements annotated i860 refer to an i860 processor running in a Meiko Computing Surface executing code generated by Green Hills Fortran-I860 compiler version 1.8.5. Default optimisation levels were used on all platforms.

3.4 Examples

The Livermore Loops [1] are 24 loops from production applications written in Fortran 77 at Lawrence Livermore National Laboratory. In this section, the prediction methodology introduced above is applied to modified versions of six of the Livermore Loops, over a variety of problem sizes. These predictions are then compared with measured execution times on each of the five platforms characterised in section 3.3.

The six codes have been slightly modified in that single precision REALs are used in place of the double precision variables in the original versions.

3.4.1 Fragment A

Fragment A (Loop 1 of the Livermore Loops) is a fragment from a hydrodynamics code:

```
do i=1,n
  x(i) = q + (y(i) * ((r * z(i+10)) + (t * z(i+11))))
enddo
```

The predicted execution time of this code is:

$$\mathrm{n}(t_{\text{loopoh}} + t_{\text{assign}R} + 4t_{\text{index}} + 2t_{\text{add}R} + 3t_{\text{mult}R} + 2t_{\text{add}I})$$

	SGI			i860		
n	Actual	Predicted	Error %	Actual	Predicted	Error %
10	31.67	61.727	+94.9	14.207	19.333	+36.1
100	299.54	617.27	+106.1	135.98	193.33	+42.2
1000	3699.4	6172.7	+66.9	1357.1	1933.3	+42.5
10000	38146	61727	+61.8	14293	19333	+35.3
	T800			Sun 4/20		
n	Actual	Predicted	Error %	Actual	Predicted	Error %
10	72.9	90.231	+23.8	19.185	28.112	+46.5
100	695.6	902.31	+29.7	182.11	281.12	+54.4
1000	6919.0	9023.1	+30.4	1821.4	2811.2	+54.3
10000	69125.0	90231	+30.5	20199	28112	+39.2
	Sun 4/75					
n	Actual	Predicted	Error %			
10	15.592	23.285	+49.3			
100	148.98	232.85	+56.3			
1000	1468.1	2328.5	+58.6			
10000	16393	23285	+42.0			

3.4.2 Fragment B

Fragment B (Loop 3 of the Livermore Loops) is the Inner Product function, which frequently occurs in scientific codes.

```
q = 0.0

do i=1,n
  q = q + (z(i)*x(i))
enddo
```

The predicted execution time is:

$$T = t_{\text{assign}_R} + \text{n}(t_{\text{loopoh}} + t_{\text{assign}_R} + 2t_{\text{index}} + t_{\text{add}R} + t_{\text{mult}R})$$

	SGI			i860		
n	Actual	Predicted	Error %	Actual	Predicted	Error %
10	21.129	27.887	+32.0	5.6267	8.6571	+53.9
100	187.08	274.48	+46.7	50.741	84.531	+66.6
1000	2457.3	2740.4	+11.5	501.89	843.27	+68.0
10000	27295	27400	+0.4	5631.2	8430.7	+49.7
	T800			Sun 4/20		
n	Actual	Predicted	Error %	Actual	Predicted	Error %
10	47.7	52.336	+9.7	12.237	14.432	+17.9
100	441.4	514.36	+16.5	112.84	140.69	+24.7
1000	4375.6	5134.6	+17.3	1120.7	1403.3	+25.2
10000	43712.0	51337	+17.4	12948	14029	+8.3
	Sun 4/75					
n	Actual	Predicted	Error %			
10	10.098	12.100	+19.8			
100	93.055	118.32	+27.2			
1000	918.99	1180.5	+28.5			
10000	10631	11802	+11.0			

3.4.3 Fragment C

Fragment C (Loop 5 of the Livermore Loops) is a fragment of a Tridiagonal Elimination routine.

```
do i=2,n
  x(i) = z(i) * (y(i)-x(i-1))
enddo
```

The predicted execution time of this loop is:

$$T = (\mathrm{n}-1)(t_{\text{loopoh}} + t_{\text{assign}R} + 4t_{\text{index}} + t_{\text{sub}R} + t_{\text{mult}R} + t_{\text{sub}I})$$

	SGI			i860		
n	Actual	Predicted	Error %	Actual	Predicted	Error %
10	22.996	34.124	+48.4	9.3502	11.080	+18.5
100	233.60	375.37	+60.6	97.439	121.88	+25.1
1000	3030.1	3787.8	+25.0	1054.0	1229.9	+16.7
10000	31248	37912	+21.3	11053	12310	+11.4
	T800			Sun 4/20		
n	Actual	Predicted	Error %	Actual	Predicted	Error %
10	53.7	58.855	+9.6	11.878	16.419	+38.2
100	552.7	647.41	+17.1	120.62	180.61	+49.7
1000	5545.6	6532.9	+17.8	1223.2	1822.5	+49.0
10000	55468.8	65338	+17.8	15074	18241	+21.0
	Sun 4/75					
n	Actual	Predicted	Error %			
10	10.098	13.834	+37.0			
100	101.97	152.18	+49.2			
1000	1032.4	1535.6	+48.7			
10000	12987	15370	+18.3			

3.4.4 Fragment D

Fragment D (Loop 7 of the Livermore Loops) is taken from an Equation of State code.

```
do i=1,n
  x(i) = u(i) + (r * (z(i) + (r * y(i)))) +
         (t * (u(i+3) + (r * (u(i+2) +
         (r * u(i+1))))) +
         (t * (u(i+6) + (r * (u(i+5) +
         (r * u(i+4)))))))
enddo
```

The predicted execution time of this loop is:

$$T = n(t_{\text{loopoh}} + 10t_{\text{index}} + 6t_{\text{add}I} + 8t_{\text{mult}R} + 8t_{\text{add}R} + t_{\text{assign}R})$$

	SGI			i860		
n	Actual	Predicted	Error %	Actual	Predicted	Error %
10	58.405	163.90	+180.6	35.166	51.474	+46.4
100	563.98	1639.0	+190.6	346.58	514.74	+48.5
1000	6666.3	16390	+145.9	3548.3	5147.4	+45.1
10000	67329	16390	+143.4	35687	51474	+44.2
	T800			Sun 4/20		
n	Actual	Predicted	Error %	Actual	Predicted	Error %
10	160.5	208.51	+29.9	36.254	69.003	+90.3
100	1571.0	2085.1	+32.7	351.78	690.03	+96.2
1000	15670.4	20851	+33.1	3543.7	6900.3	+94.7
10000	156659.2	208510	+33.1	38517	69003	+79.1
	Sun 4/75					
n	Actual	Predicted	Error %			
10	27.263	57.431	+110.7			
100	267.27	574.31	+114.9			
1000	2686.1	5743.1	+113.8			
10000	29999	57431	+91.4			

3.4.5 Fragment E

Fragment E (Loop 11 of the Livermore Loops) is a First Sum. The value of `x(i)` is set to `y(1) + ... + y(i)`.

```
x(1) = y(1)
do i=2,n
  x(i) = x(i-1) + y(i)
enddo
```

The predicted execution time of the loop is:

$$T = 2t_{\text{index}} + t_{\text{assign}R} + (\text{n} - 1)(t_{\text{loopoh}} + t_{\text{assign}R} + 3t_{\text{index}} + t_{\text{add}R} + t_{\text{sub}I})$$

	SGI			i860		
n	Actual	Predicted	Error %	Actual	Predicted	Error %
10	18.997	26.504	+39.5	7.2444	9.1298	+26.0
100	178.12	280.95	+57.7	72.344	96.255	+33.1
1000	2078.1	2825.5	+36.0	724.23	967.51	+33.6
10000	22221	28270	+27.2	7911.6	9680.1	+22.4
	T800			Sun 4/20		
n	Actual	Predicted	Error %	Actual	Predicted	Error %
10	50.9	54.783	+7.6	10.454	14.304	+36.8
100	509.2	583.18	+14.5	102.96	152.06	+47.7
1000	5092.0	5867.1	+15.2	1022.5	1529.6	+49.6
10000	50905.6	58706	+15.3	12195	15305	+25.5
	Sun 4/75					
n	Actual	Predicted	Error %			
10	8.9066	11.852	+33.1			
100	87.096	125.97	+44.6			
1000	872.16	1267.1	+45.3			
10000	10303	12679	+23.1			

3.4.6 Fragment F

Fragment F (Loop 19 of the Livermore Loops) is a general Linear Recurrence Equation.

```
do i=1,n
  b(i) = t(i) + s * u(i)
  s = b(i) - s
enddo

do i=1,n
  k = n - i + 1
  b(k) = t(k) + s * u(k)
  s = b(k) - s
enddo
```

The predicted execution time of this fragment is:

$$T = n(2t_{\text{loopoh}} + t_{\text{add}I} + t_{\text{sub}I} + t_{\text{assign}_I} + 8t_{\text{index}} + 2t_{\text{add}R} + 2t_{\text{mult}R} + 2t_{\text{sub}R} + 4t_{\text{assign}_R})$$

	SGI			i860		
n	Actual	Predicted	Error %	Actual	Predicted	Error %
10	64.029	101.18	+29.3	26.124	33.783	+29.3
100	623.48	1011.8	+33.5	253.09	337.83	+33.5
1000	7091.8	10118	+28.2	2635.9	3378.3	+28.2
10000	79226	101180	+22.0	27699	33783	+22.0
	T800			Sun 4/20		
n	Actual	Predicted	Error %	Actual	Predicted	Error %
10	157.5	174.10	+10.5	30.593	52.728	+72.4
100	1522.4	1741.0	+14.4	293.93	527.28	+79.4
1000	15167.3	17410	+14.8	2967.2	5272.8	+77.7
10000	151609.6	174100	+14.8	33332	52728	+58.2
	Sun 4/75					
n	Actual	Predicted	Error %			
10	25.729	43.477	+69.0			
100	247.52	434.77	+75.7			
1000	2469.1	4347.7	+76.1			
10000	28055	43477	+55.0			

3.4.7 Summary of results

Tables 3.5 and 3.6 summarise the results by code fragment and platform respectively.

Fragment	Average % Error	Standard Deviation of % Error
A	50.0	20.9
B	27.6	19.5
C	30.0	15.8
D	88.2	49.8
E	31.7	13.3
F	46.1	24.8

Table 3.5 Summary of results for each code fragment

Platform	Average % Error	Standard Deviation of % Error
T800	19.7	8.3
i860	36.6	14.7
Sun 4/20	51.5	25.3
Sun 4/75	54.6	33.0
R3000	66.1	51.7

Table 3.6 Summary of results for each platform

3.5 Discussion and Further Work

All of the predictions are higher than the corresponding measured execution time. This suggests either that the basic operation times are too high, or that the time formulae are ascribing too many operations to code fragments. The code fragments currently used in experiments to determine the basic operation times for each platform are very simple, and only a small set of experiments are conducted. It is possible that these experiments are not representative of larger codes, in terms of instruction mix, and that this is leading to erroneously high values of basic operation times. Although not modelled explicitly, load costs appear in the time taken to perform arithmetic operations. The time model used in this paper has a very naîve view of the memory hierarchy: variables referenced several times in a statement will incur the corresponding number of load costs. This can clearly lead to overestimation of execution time. Significantly, Fragment D, by far the least-well modelled of the example codes, has the highest number of repeated references to objects. Furthermore, the best results overall were obtained for the T800, which probably makes significantly less use of registers than the other platforms. However, extending the model to include loads explicitly is not straightforward. Firstly, the strong correlation between the number of loads and the number of arithmetic operations in a statement can make determining the basic operation times a very badly conditioned fitting problem which does not readily admit a stable solution. Secondly, iterating code fragments many times to obtain measurements of execution time tends to hide the cost of bringing data up the memory hierarchy, which can be a significant proportion of execution time when the code fragment is executed only once. It may be the case that using larger set of more complex fragments to determine the basic operation times will be a more fruitful approach.

A second striking feature of the results is that those for the T800 and i860 platforms are significantly better than the others. These two platforms are dedicated processors in a multicomputer, running only a run-time kernel in addition to the code fragments, whereas the others are all workstations running a full operating system implementation. While the workstations were otherwise idle when measurements were taken, further investigation of hidden interference is necessary.

If the difficulties with the current language can be adequately resolved, it would become important to extend the domain of the technique to include other language features, such as branches, multi-dimensional arrays, procedure calls, I/O and a wider range of operations and data types. This would necessitate careful choice of the code fragments used in obtaining basic operation times, in order to avoid unstable solutions. It would also be worthwhile to explore the robustness of the approach on a wider range of platforms, and with aggressive compiler optimisation enabled.

Acknowledgements

The author was supported by a Research Studentship from the UK Science and Engineering Research Council.

The work presented in this paper was performed on the facilities provided by the Edinburgh Parallel Computing Centre (EPCC). EPCC is a multidisciplinary centre supported by major contracts from European industry and grants from the Advisory Board for the Research Councils, the Department of Trade and Industry, the Joint Informations Systems Committee, the Science and Engineering Research Council, Scottish Enterprise Software Group, Lothian and Edinburgh Enterprise Ltd., the Commission of the European Communities, the Department of Transport and the Economics and Social Sciences Research Council. It is a pleasure to acknowledge substantial additional support from the University of Edinburgh and from the Industrial Affiliates of the centre.

References

[1] F. H. McMahon. L.L.N.L FORTRAN kernels: MFLOPS. Lawrence Livermore National Laboratory, 1986.

[2] J. L. Hennessy and D. A. Patterson. *Computer Architecture: A Quantitative Approach.* Morgan Kaufmann, 1990.

[3] J. Cohen. Computer-Assisted Microanalysis of Programs. *Communications of the ACM*, 25(10):724–733, October 1982.

[4] J. Cohen and A. Weitzman. Software Tools for Micro-analysis of Programs. *Software — Practice and Experience*, 22(9):777–808, September 1992.

4 Isolating the Reasons for the Performance of Parallel Machines on Numerical Programs

Arno Formella Silvia M. Müller Wolfgang J. Paul Anke Bingert[1]
COMPUTER SCIENCE DEPARTMENT
SAARBRÜCKEN UNIVERSITY, GERMANY
email: {formella, smueller, wjp}@cs.uni-sb.de

Abstract: In this paper we present a nontrivial set of modules which measure performance parameters of node processors and interconnection networks. With the help of these parameters we explain the run time of the following algorithms *conjugate gradient method, one–dimensional partial differential equation solver* and *two–dimensional partial differential equation solver* on the parallel machine Ncube–2. The iPSC/860 Hypercube and the vector machine VP100 are analyzed in an other paper (see [3]). Our explanations are sometimes within 0.5 % and almost always within 5 % of the measured run times.

4.1 Introduction

Benchmark programs come in four flavours: (i) small loops designed to measure machine parameters [4], (ii) inner loops of algorithms [6], (iii) whole applications [11] and (iv) synthetic benchmarks [10]. Benchmark suites may include modules of several flavours [9], [11]. In such cases one sometimes wishes to explain results of higher–order modules by results of lower–order modules [9].

Such an explanation would amount to isolating the reasons why an algorithm or an application runs well or poorly on a particular machine. It should be of considerable interest for two reasons: on the one hand designers of machines are given direct information which parameters of the machines are responsible for the performance delivered, on the other hand prospective buyers of machines can analyze their own algorithms and applications and check if the reasons for a machine's performance on the benchmark apply to their own program.

Unfortunately, we have been unable to find any such explanation whatsoever in the literature, and it has been stated that often it cannot be given at all [4]. This is obviously true, because any such explanation would have to involve some kind of analysis of algorithms which is not feasible if the flow of control depends too heavily on the input data (e. g. *Livermore loop 15* [6]) and in general, of course, because of the unsolvability of the halting problem. On the other hand one would hope that there are relevant situations where such an explanation can be given, although it might be a tricky task to arrive at that explanation.

[1]This research is part of the PARANUSS–project, which is funded by BMFT and DLR.

In this paper we present a nontrivial set of micro benchmarks which measure performance parameters of node processors and interconnection networks. With the help of these parameters we explain the run time of the following algorithms (i) *conjugate gradient method*, (ii) *one–dimensional partial differential equation solver* and (iii) *two–dimentional partial differential equation solver* on an Ncube–2 parallel machine. The iPSC/860 hypercube and the VP100 vector processor are analyzed in an other paper (see [3]). Our explanations are sometimes within 0.5 % and almost always within 5 % of the measured run times.

Our goal is it to extract the features of a machine concerning both the hardware, i. e. the functional units and the data paths, as well as the compiler, i. e. code generation strategies. Built–in libary functions exploiting the underlying hardware are examined, too. In the end, we are able to model the machine based on the gathered information in a such way that the run time prediction is close to the measured run time even for parallel algorithms. At the start of the analysis we only know the machine's cycle time. Then we gradually build a model of the machine we benchmark. We do not pretend that the machine actually *is* like the model. We only claim that it *behaves* like the model.

Section 4.2 discribes the micro measurements we have implemented in order to measure the parameters of the node processor and those of the communication network. Section 4.3 summarizes the tests we have performed and the features we have inferred from the tests. In section 4.4 we present the algorithms under consideration both in serial and parallel versions. In section 4.5 we predict the run time of the algorithms on the Ncube and compare our modelled time with the measured run times. Finally, section 4.6 gives a brief conclusion about the presented benchmarking and prediction method.

4.2 Micro Measurements

This section has two parts. In the first part we describe test routines for node processors. In the second part we describe routines which exercise the interconnection network of parallel machines.

From the run time of the test routines described in the sequel we try to infer the presence or absence of certain hardware features and how the compiler makes use of them. We are interested in the performance characteristics of arithmetic units, the addressing modes supported, the processor's memory hierarchy and the bandwidths within this hierarchy. We are interested in the compiler's capabilities to perform vectorization, strip mining and loop optimization under the most simple circumstances.

Similar to the *Livermore Loops* ([6], [2]), our test routines for the node processors consist of a few lines of FORTRAN code inside two nested loops with loop variables i and j which range from 1 to n or L, respectively. In general n is the upper bound for the loop variable of the inner loop and denotes something like vector length. The outer loop serves both to increase the accuracy of timer measurements and to distinguish between encached ($L \geq 20$) and non–encached ($L = 1$) performance.

4.2.1 Micro Measurements for a Node Processor

We arrange our test routines in groups g. Within each group g there are several routines $r(g,j)$, $j = 1,2,\ldots$. We denote by $\hat{t}(g,j,L,n)$ the run time of routine $r(g,j)$ started with parameters L and n, by $\bar{t}(g,j,L,n)$ the run time of one pass of the outer loop and by $t(g,j,L,n)$ the run time of one pass of the inner loop, respectively. If no confusion is possible we will drop arguments g, j or L in order to simplify notation.

We are interested in large problem sizes, so it would seem natural to take measurements for large values of n only. In general this does not suffice because parallelization decreases the problem size, which must be handled by a node processor. Run time curves depending on n characterize the memory's hierarchy, its type (e. g. register file, vector register or cache) and strip mining strategies of the compiler. This paper focuses on the Ncube, which is a scalar machine, so our model can be held very simple. For a more detailed description for a vector machine or a processor with a cache see [3], where we extended this approach for the VP100 and iPSC/860–Hypercube.

If routine $r(g,j)$ consists of a fixed number of operations, then for large n we expect to observe run times of the form

$$\bar{t}(L,n) \approx \alpha + \beta n \qquad (= \frac{1}{r_\infty}(n_{1/2} + n))$$

(see [5], [4]) or

$$t(L,n) \approx \frac{\bar{t}(L,n)}{n} = \frac{\alpha}{n} + \beta$$

On a scalar machine we expect the operation time, i. e. β, to be much greater than α/n, even for small n. We took measurements for $n = 10,\ldots,1910$ with step 100 and $L = 1$ as well as $L = 20$.

4.2.1.1 Details of the Implementation

In order to simplify notation we often will not write complete FORTRAN–sequences. A vector statement (or an inner loop) will just express the block of the DO–loop without the surrounding control statements. Thus the line

```
A[i] = B[i] + C[i]
```

is an abbreviation for the full loop:

```
      DO 88  J=1,L
        DO 88  I=1,N
88        A(I) = B(I) + C(I)
```

The outer loop simply iterates on the same vector. A smart compiler will drop the outer loop and we can not rely on the measured data. Therefore we used always two–dimensional implementations of the vector statements. The following example shows how the vector addition given above might be written

```
      DO 77  K=1,L
         DO 77  I=1,N
77          A(I,K) = B(I,K) + C(I,K)
```

However, this would increase the memory space needed to store all variables of the benchmark. Moreover, caching strategies of the hardware can not be observed, because no data is referenced twice. Finally we chose the following version:

```
      DO 66  J=1,L
         K = IND(J)
         DO 66  I=1,N
66          A(I,K) = B(I,K) + C(I,K)
```

Vector IND contains only values 1 and 2, thus addressing two rows of a matrix. During compile time the array is not known to the compiler, so it is not possible to eliminate the outer loop in J. A reference to the same data word is now performed at least $L/2$ times. The inner loop still can be vectorized, because K appears as a constant. In order to verify that we do not loose to much while addressing in this way, we have implemented the simple vector statement, too. We have not detected a significant loss of performance ([1]).

4.2.1.2 group 0. scalar loops, simple scalar–vector operations

```
1)  an empty statement within the 2 nested do-loops
2)  A[i]=a0
3)  A[i]=B[i]
4)  A[i]=a0+B[i]
5)  A[i]=a0*B[i]
```

Routine $r(0,1)$ measures the time for the loop overhead T_{ov}. It is

$$T_{ov} = \frac{\hat{t}(0,1,L,n)}{Ln + L}$$

and should be more or less independent of L and n. T_{ov} cannot be optimized away completely because after the loops the variables k and i should have values L and n. A smart compiler should replace this loop by two assignments, but we have not encountered this. Routine $r(0,2)$ gives a first hint if loop control and store operations can be overlapped. If $t(0,1) = t(0,2)$ this clearly can be done. In the other case at least the bandwidth to store a vector can be calculated as

$$b^s_{mm} = \frac{Ln}{t(0,2,L,n)}$$

Yet, b^s_{mm} does not reflect the real bandwidth, because the degree of overlapping is still not known. It is assumed that a0 is held in a register and not loaded in every loop body. Routine $r(0,3)$ copies a vector from one location to another, which can be done bypassing the functional units. Similar to routine $r(0,3)$ the bandwidth and the overlap facilities can be examined. In routines $r(0,4)$ and $r(0,5)$ additional arithmetical operations are performed. Their influence on the run time and possible overlaps (e. g. $t(0,3) = t(0,4)$) can be detected.

4.2.1.3 *group 1. scalar recursive* $(+,*)$*–expressions*

```
1)   a0= a0+a1
2)   a0=(a0+a1)*a2
3)   a0=(a0+a1)*a2+a3
     ...
j)   a0=(...(a0+a1)*a2+a3)*a4+...
```

These loops are supposed to measure scalar encached performance even if $L = 1$, because the number of operands is very small. If a compiler knows how to pull statements out of loops at least the first two of the routines will run in constant time. (This violates the FORTRAN expression evaluation scheme). Otherwise for odd j and large n the difference

$$d(j,n) = t(1,j,1,n) - t(1,j-1,1,n)$$

should be independent of j and n. It should be the time as for a scalar addition performed on the fastest level of the processor's memory hierarchy. For even j one should get the time for a scalar multiplication.

4.2.1.4 *group 2. scalar recursive* $(-,/)$*–expressions*

Same as above with subtraction and division.

4.2.1.5 *group 3. simple vector operations*

```
1)   A[i]=B[i]+C[i]
2)   A[i]=B[i]*C[i]
3)   A[i]=B[i]/C[i]
```

These loops measure performance of vector operations in the spirit of HOCKNEY ([4], [5]). For large n, $t(3,j,L,n)$ is the time needed to perform a vector operation out of main memory. For small n but large L it is the time to perform a vector operation out of a fast memory, like a cache or vector memory. Naturally, all loads, stores and computes can possibly be overlapped, so the different times for one type of operation can not be extracted. However, every version needs three operands out of main memory, thus a first estimation for the effective bandwidth to main memory can be done: $b_M = 3/t(3,j,L,n)$ for large n. If $t(3,j) \leq t(0,1)$ it can be assumed that the machine operates with real (hard wired) vector operations instead of scalar loop constructs. Since the operations on parts of the operands are independent, strip mining compilers can yield a higher performance if the hardware has more than one arithmetic pipe.

4.2.1.6 *group 4. one–vector* $(+, *)$*–expressions*

```
1)   A[i]= A[i]+A[i]
2)   A[i]=(A[i]+A[i])*A[i]
3)   A[i]=(A[i]+A[i])*A[i]+A[i]
     ...
j)   A[i]=(...(A[i]+A[i])*A[i]+A[i])*A[i]+...
```

The measurements done in group 1 for scalar variables which are held probably within the register set of a machine are performed in this group for components which are addressed out of a vector. Every pass through the inner loop needs one operand out of main memory, which has to be loaded before and must be stored afterwards. Thus the expected run time $t(4, j, L, n)$ should differ from $t(1, j, L, n)$ according to the additional transfer operations. For a well–designed system with an optimizing compiler the differences $t(4, j) - t(1, j)$ should be constant, because main memory must be accessed only twice, once to load `A[i]` and once to store it. Increasing differences for larger j can be interpreted in two ways: more than two accesses to a lower memory in the hierarchy are performed or the fastest memory (or register file) cannot be accessed by three–address–operations specifying the same address (or register) more than once. Decreasing differences may be due to hiding load and store operations behind arithmetical operations.

4.2.1.7 *group 5. vector* $(+, *)$*–expressions*

```
1)   A[i]= B[i]+C[i]
2)   A[i]=(B[i]+C[i])*D[i]
3)   A[i]=(B[i]+C[i])*D[i]+E[i]
     ...
j)   A[i]=(...(B[i]+C[i])*D[i]+E[i])*F[i]+...
```

The vector operations of group 4 are implemented in this group on a set of different operands. Thus the transfer rate to main memory is much higher. Each additional operation requires a load out of main memory. Therefore, $(j+2)/t(5, j, L, n)$ for large n gives a next estimation for the effective bandwidth to main memory. If $t(5, j) \approx t(5, j-1)$ for odd (or even) $j \geq 3$ (or $j \geq 2$) addition and multiplication can be chained. If there is no loss of cycles for large n and for large L the effective bandwidth to main memory is high enough to support fully chained operations. For large L and strip mining compilers the bandwidth to main memory is no longer the bottleneck. The bandwidth to a vector memory or a vector register file dominates the run time.

4.2.1.8 *group 6. one–vector recursive* $(+, *)$*–expressions*

```
1)  X[i]= X[i]+X[i-1]
2)  X[i]=(X[i]+X[i-1])*X[i-2]
3)  X[i]=(X[i]+X[i-1])*X[i-2]+X[i-3]
    ...
j)  X[i]=(...(X[i]+X[i-1])*X[i-2]+X[i-3])*X[i-4]+...
```

The vector components of the expressions within this group are addressed in a recursive manner out of one operand vector. The required bandwidth to main memory is similar to the bandwidth needed in group 4. To evaluate the expressions more scalar registers are necessary. A very sophisticated compiler can use a parallel prefix method or a recursive doubling method to avoid bubbles in a pipe, at least for the smaller expressions. Once again, constant differences $t(6,j) - t(4,j)$ can be attributed to the additional address calculation.

4.2.1.9 group 7. simple addressed vector expressions

```
1)  A[i]= B[i]+C[i-1]
2)  A[i]=(B[i]+C[i-1])*D[i-2]
3)  A[i]=(B[i]+C[i-1])*D[i-2]+E[i-3]
    ...
j)  A[i]=(...(B[i]+C[i-1])*D[i-2]+E[i-3])*F[i-4]+...
```

The same address calculations as in group 6 are necessary in group 7. But here, different operands are used in the expression. If the run times are equal to those in group 5, addressing is not the bottleneck of an operation, in the other case, its influence can be documented. Because there are no data dependencies, we expect almost the same run time as for group 5.

4.2.1.10 group 8. dot product and matrix product

```
1)  Q=Q+A[i]*B[i]
2)  P[i,j]=P[i,j]+A[i,k]*B[k,j]
3)  P[i,j]=P[i,j]+A[i,k]*B[j,k]
4)  P[i,j]=P[i,j]+A[k,i]*B[k,j]
```

In this group the dot product $r(8,1)$ and the matrix product are implemented. Routine $r(8,2)$ addresses one matrix column wise and one matrix row wise, $r(8,3)$ addresses both operands column wise and $r(8,4)$ addresses both matrices row wise. A matrix product can be implemented just as a sequence of dot products. If a dot product, can profit from previously loaded operands a speed–up is possible. On the other hand one matrix is row wise addressed, so addressing with constant stride may increase the time to load the operands. Differently declared sizes of the matrices are used to measure the run times belonging to different stride sizes. In the case that $t(8,2) \approx t(8,3) \approx t(8,4)$ addressing of main memory does not slow down the load or store time.

4.2.1.11 group 9. more complex vector expressions

```
1)  X[i,k]=X[i,k+1]+a0*X[i,k+2]
2)  X[i,k]=X[i,k+1]+a0*X[i,k+2]+a1*X[i,k+3]
3)  X[i,k]=X[i,k+1]+a0*X[i,k+2]+a1*X[i,k+3]+a2*X[i,k+4]
    ...
j)  X[i,k]=X[i,k+1]+a0*X[i,k+2]+a1*X[i,k+3]+a2*X[i,k+4]+...
```

This group contains a set of more complex expressions. The operands are addressed as columns out of a matrix. Parallel operations are possible, because subexpressions are independent from each other. All in all the routines are used to verify the model generated so far by the analysis of the first eight groups.

4.2.1.12 group 10. more complex constant stride vector expressions

```
1)  X[k,i]=X[k+1,i]+a0*X[k+2,i]
2)  X[k,i]=X[k+1,i]+a0*X[k+2,i]+a1*X[k+3,i]
3)  X[k,i]=X[k+1,i]+a0*X[k+2,i]+a1*X[k+3,i]+a2*X[k+4,i]
    ...
j)  X[k,i]=X[k+1,i]+a0*X[k+2,i]+a1*X[k+3,i]+a2*X[k+4,i]+...
```

The routines are similar to those of group 9, but the operands are taken as the rows of a matrix, which leads to a more complex addressing scheme. So especially preloading of consecutive elements of a vector can not be used to reduce the run time, as it is often done by caches equipped with a block wise access strategy.

4.2.2 Micro Measurements for Communication Networks

The test routines in this section are arranged in groups, too. They measure the network performance and the speed at which global functions are computed. We do not specify the exact code of these routines. It is machine dependent but quite obvious.

We will use the same notation we have introduced in the last section. g indicates the group number and j stands for the routine. L denotes the outer loop length and m the message length in *byte*. We denote by $n = m/8$ the message length in words (8 *byte* floating point format). A new parameter d is introduced to denote the distance or the direction between two nodes according to the network's architecture.

4.2.2.1 group 11. simple unidirectional node to node communication

The routines in this group test the communication between two processors i and j while no other communication is performed. In routine $r(11,1)$ an arbitrary processor i sends a block of m bytes to one of his neighbors. We assume that the neighbors are ordered in a hypercube structure, where the numbers of two nodes just differ in the appropriate bit which defines the dimension. Processor i sends its data while processor j is waiting. After j has received all data, the data block is sent back to i. Parameter d specifies in what direction, dimension resp., the communication is performed. If the underlying hardware system is a symmetric hypercube the communication time $t(11,1,d,L,m)$ for communication in *one* direction (not round trip) should be independent of d. We expect the time $t(11,1,d,L,m)$ to run this program to be of the form

$$t(11,1,d,L,m) = S(i,j) + m/B$$

where $S(i,j)$ is the startup time for the communication (roughly the time to transmit the first byte) and B is the bandwidth of the links of the communication network. Startup time $S(i,j)$ should be independent of L and m. The bandwidth B can depend on m if messages are transmitted in blocks with fixed sizes. Routine $r(11,2)$ is similar to routine $r(11,1)$ but the sending and the receiving node are selected as members of a GRAY–code chain embedded on a hypercube structure. Parameter d reflects the distance of i to j on the chain. The run time $t(11,2,d,L,m)$ may increase for larger d, but for large m and blockwise parallel data transfer on all of the links between i and j we expect the time to be of the form

$$t(11,2,d,L,m) = S(i,j,d) + m/B$$

where $S(i,j,d)$ is the startup time.

4.2.2.2 group 12. simple bidirectional node to node communication

Both routines in this group are similar to those of group 11. But now processor j is not waiting to receive the data. In contrast i and j are exchanging their data blocks simultaneously. For bidirectional communication channels we expect half the communication times, because sending and receiving of both messages can be done in parallel.

4.2.2.3 group 13. simple parallel node to node communication

In group 13 we test parallel communication speed when more than two processors are sending/receiving data simultaneously. In routine $r(13,1)$ all processors send their messages in the same dimension using the hypercube structure. The direction is indicated by the parameter d. We expect the same communication speeds between any pair of processors as we measured in group 11 or 12, which should be independent of d. Routine $r(13,2)$ deals with a one dimensional exchange communication. We create as many processes as there are processors. We arrange them on a GRAY–code chain and each process exchanges m bytes with his neighbor on the chain (according to group 11). In

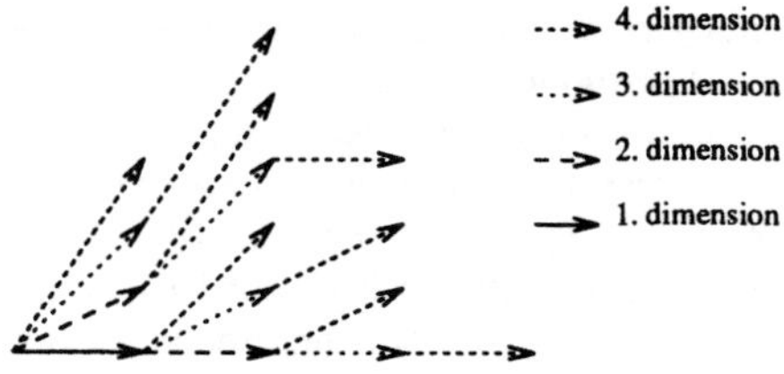

Figure 4.1 Broadcast on a 4–dimensional hypercube

a well designed system the measurements should not be worse than measurements from group 11 or 12 above. In routine $r(13,3)$ the mapping of the processors on the chain remains the same as in routine $r(13,2)$. Now, the processors send their data not to their neighbors, but to a processor being in distance d on the chain.

4.2.2.4 group 14. one to all communications

Group 14 tests the speed of broadcast, of synchronization and of global sum computations within clusters of p processors. We do not give a general formal definition of clusters. On a hypercube a cluster is a subcube. Routine $r(14,1)$ measures for an arbitrary processor i as a member of a cluster with p processors (p is a power of two) the time $b(i,m,p)$ to broadcast n bytes from processor i to all processors of the cluster. Generally, we would expect run times of the form

$$b(i,m,p) = S_{total} + m/B_{eff}$$

independent of i, where S_{total} is the total startup time and B_{eff} is the effective bandwidth of the chained links in the network. There are a lot of ways to implement a broadcast on a network. One simple approach on a hypercube would use something like a tree embedded on the network. The root sends the data block to its sons and they send the block to their sons and those to their sons etc. In each stage the direction is switched into another dimension (see figure 4.1). This algorithm needs $d(p)$ stages where $d(p)$ is the diameter of the cluster.

We expect the total start–up time to be composed of two terms:

$$S_{total} = S_0 + S(p)$$

S_0 is independent of p and represents the overhead at the beginning of the transfer. $S(p)$ reflects the start–up times of every node encountered on the longest path of the embeded communication graph. In the example given above we have

$$S(p) = S_p \, d(p)$$

where $d(p)$ is the diameter of the hypercube and S_p is the time spent on one node.

We expect the effective bandwidth B_{eff} to be independent of n. We suppose B_{eff} to be composed of a bandwidth B_V due to the physical limitations of the network and of a bandwidth B_S due to software overhead, e. g. copying the message from user to system space.

$$\frac{1}{B_{eff}} = \frac{1}{B_V} + \frac{1}{B_S}$$

On a hypercube with all links having the same bandwidth B we expect for the described broadcast algorithm

$$B_V = B/d(p)$$

Finally we have for a symmetric hypercube

$$b(i, m, p) = S_0 + S_p\, d(p) + m(\frac{d(p)}{B} + \frac{1}{B_S})$$

Routine $r(14, 2)$ measures the time $sy(p)$ spent to synchronize p processors of a cluster. This requires the computation of a boolean OR. With very little extra hardware this can be achieved in constant time for machines with moderate numbers of processors [7]. Routine $r(14, 3)$ measures for p processors of a cluster the time $gs(p)$ spent to compute and distribute to all processors the sum of p data, where each of the data is contributed by a different processor. We expect run times

$$gs(p) = S + \sigma\, d(p)$$

S stands for a start–up time and σ is the time spent in one node while the message travels through the diameter $d(p)$ of the network.

4.2.2.5 group 15. global collection

The routine, named `gcol()`, in this group updates a vector of length n which is known to every processor of a cluster but which has been modified partially on each one, i. e. each processor i within the cluster of size p has to broadcast its portion of length n/p of the vector to all other processors in the cluster. This can be achieved in $\log(p)$ communication steps. In each step s ($s = 1, \ldots, \log(p)$) processor i sends a block of length $2^{s-1} * n/p$ to processor j with

$$j = i \begin{cases} +\,2^{s-1} & \text{if} \quad i \bmod 2^s < 2^{s-1} \\ -\,2^{s-1} & \text{if} \quad i \bmod 2^s \geq 2^{s-1} \end{cases}$$

The received block is copied to the left or to the right side of the recently updated part of the vector. The appropriate side is determined according to the same condition as given above.

	1	2	3	4	5	6	7	8	j
0	19	23	24	34	35				
1	26	36	43	53	60	70			
2	26	58	65	97	104	136			
3	34	36	33						
4	31	41	50	58	67				
5	34	44	53	61	70				
6	28	43	52	64	72				
7	33	45	52	62	69				
8	43	54	54	53					
9	45	63	80	97	131	165	189	208	
10	57	74	93	123	157	179	204	230	
g									

Table 4.1 Operation times in *cc* for Ncube's node processor on micro kernels

4.3 Measurements

In this section we summarize the data we got while executing our micro kernels on an Ncube–2 parallel machine. We try to model the performance of the node processor as well as the behavior of the communication network.

It is more convenient to use the number of clock cycles as unit for the run times rather than absolute times if we deal with a node processor. Therefore, we will denote with *cc* as unit length one clock cycle of the machine. The abbreviation *dpc* (datawords per clock cycle) is used to express the bandwidth in terms of clock cycles within the node processor's memory hierarchy. If one knows the clock cycle time the bandwidth in *MByte/s* can easily be calculated. For the communication network we will keep the unit *MByte/s* to measure the bandwidth.

4.3.1 Measurements of the Serial Kernels

We benchmarked an Ncube–2 Parallel Computer with 64 nodes. The node processor is clocked with 50 ns cycle time and it is equipped with 4 *MByte* local memory. In total the Ncube has a distributed main memory of 256 *MByte*. The node processors are connected in a six–dimensional hypercube structure.

All programs are written in FORTRAN under *Ncube Development Environment 3.0 Beta 11/01/91*. The FORTRAN–compiler was started with the `-O` optimization option. A peak performance of 2.4 *MFlop/s* and a communication bandwidth of 80 *MByte/s* between two nodes are announced by the manufacturer. The communication in FORTRAN is done using library functions (see section 4.3.2).

We used the library function `dclock()` to measure the execution times. This timer returns the elapsed time since the start of the program. A call to that function requires at least 33 μs and at most 64 μs, so we have an accuracy of 31 μs for the timer.

In the data set that we obtained for $L = 1$ and $L = 20$ (see [1]), there is almost no difference due to L. In table 4.1 the operation time β is summarized for all groups of the

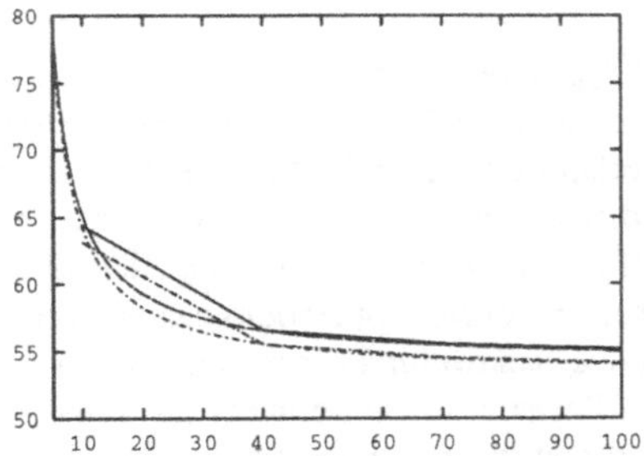

Figure 4.2 Measured run time in *cc* versus modelled run time of group 8, routines 2, 3 and 4, of the Ncube node processor

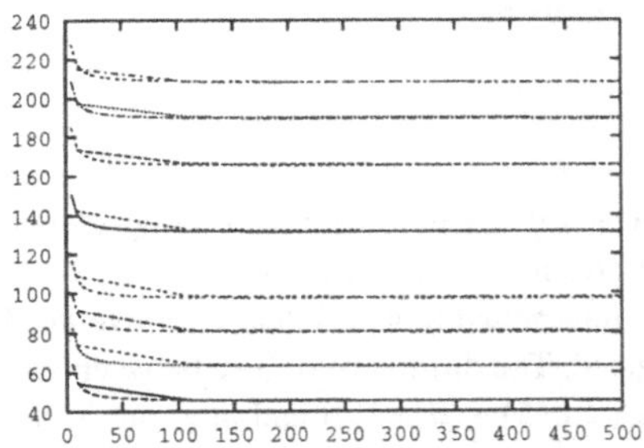

Figure 4.3 Measured run time in *cc* versus modelled run time of group 9 of the Ncube node processor

micro kernels ($L = 20$). With start–up time $\alpha = 100\,cc$ (see section 4.2.1), which we will write as T_{in} (loop initialization time) the run times of all routines can be modelled closely. In figure 4.2 and 4.3 the measured run time and the modelled run time $t(g, j, n, 20)$ are given for group 8 (routines 2, 3 and 4) and group 9, respectively.

Because there is almost no difference in the run times due to L, it can be concluded that the Ncube's memory hierarchy is very simple, consisting of a register file for scalar values (high performance in group 1) between functional units and main memory. In the following only large L will be discussed.

We observed the highest performance of 1.70 *MFlop/s* (not considering divide operations) in $r(1, 6)$, where a large scalar expression has to be evaluated a lot of times. This is 71 % of the peak performance. Because divide operations are counted as four *Flop*, a higher performance is reached, e. g. in $r(3, 3)$ almost 2.40 *MFlop/s* have been measured. In $r(1, 6)$ a floating point multiplication or addition is executed in a mean time of at least 580 ns or more than 11 cc, so we can conclude that the processor works like a scalar machine and not like a vector machine.

Now we will discuss the different groups in detail and derive the parameters of the Ncube.

4.3.1.1 group 0.

Routine $r(0,1)$ implies a loop overhead of $T_{ov} = 19$ *cc*. Initializing a vector $r(0,2)$ with a value probably held in a register requires additional time $T_{asg} = 4$ *cc* $(= t(0,2) - t(0,1))$. These cycles are due to a non–overlapped store or due to the additional address calculation, which can not be overlapped with the loop control maybe there is only one integer unit, or due to the reloading of the constant out of memory. The difference $t(0,3) - t(0,2)$ of one cycle shows that load and/or store operations can be overlapped. With 24 *cc* for a vector move the effective bandwidth to main memory is at least $b_{mm} \geq 2/24 = 0.083$ *dpc* (13.3 *MByte/s*). Because it is more likely that rather a store than a load can be overlapped, we assume that the additional time is due to the load whereas the store is hidden or at least reduced to one *cc* needed to initialize the transfer. An additional add operation in $r(0,4)$ increases the run time by 10 *cc*, a multiplication by 13 *cc*. Thus adding is 3 *cc* faster than multiplying.

4.3.1.2 group 1.

The differences $t(1,j) - t(1,j-1)$ for even $j \geq 2$ and for odd $j \geq 3$ imply run times for a scalar multiplication $T_{mul} = 10$ *cc* and for a scalar addition $T_{add} = 7$ *cc*. The difference $t(1,1) - t(0,1) = 7$ *cc* can be interpreted in a way that loop overhead and floating point operation can not be overlapped. The difference of 3 *cc* between addition and multiplication is equal to the difference $t(0,5) - t(0,4)$ found in group 0. No load or store is encountered, we assume that all operands are held in registers.

4.3.1.3 group 2.

Analogously to group 1 we get $T_{sub} = 7$ *cc* for a scalar subtraction and $T_{div} = 32$ *cc* for a scalar division by inspecting the corresponding differences in group 2. The time T_{ov} for loop overhead derived in groups 0 and 1 can be observed, too.

4.3.1.4 group 3.

In group 3 the vector division $r(3,3)$ has the smallest run time, which is quite astonishing. But if we assume that a divide operation can be overlapped with the loop control, then 32 *cc* (derived in group 2) still fit into $t(3,3)$. The effective bandwidth to main memory is at least $b_{mm} \geq 3/33 = 0.091$ *dpc* (14.5 *MByte/s*) because three data words have to be transmitted in 33 *cc*. The difference $t(3,2) - t(3,1)$ of 2 *cc* reflects not the encountered difference of 3 *cc* which we have assumed as the difference between an addition and a multiplication. But the missing cycle may be hidden in an overlap. The time $t(3,1)$ for a vector addition is equal to the time $t(0,4)$ for an addition of a vector with a scalar value. Thus in group 0 the scalar value is loaded every time. Let us assume that a store can be hidden, that all arithmetical operations are performed with scalar operation time, and that the time T_{ld} to load a value is equal to 4 *cc* (a value suggested by $T_{asg} = t(0,2) - t(0,1)$ or $t(0,3) - t(0,1)$). Loop overhead T_{ov} is fixed with 19 *cc*. Thus we can model the

	g							
j	4	Δ%	5	Δ%	6	Δ%	7	Δ%
1	30	-3.2	34	0.0	30	7.1	34	3.0
2	40	-2.4	44	0.0	40	-7.0	44	-2.2
3	47	-6.0	51	-3.8	47	-9.6	51	-1.9
4	57	-1.7	61	0.0	57	-10.9	61	-1.6
5	64	-4.5	68	-2.9	64	-11.1	68	-1.5

Table 4.2 Modelling run times of groups 4, 5, 6 and 7 for the Ncube in *cc*

operation time per element of a vector addition with $T_{ov} + 2T_{ld} + T_{add}$ resulting in $19 + 2 * 4 + 7 = 34$ *cc*. A vector multiplication needs 37 *cc* by replacing T_{add} with T_{mul}.

Up to now no loop unrolling techniques have been detected. The loop overhead of 19 *cc* appears for each inner loop.

4.3.1.5 group 4, group 5, group 6 and group 7.

These groups are analyzed simultaneously. The maximal bandwidth occurs in $r(5,5)$ with $b_{mm} \geq 7/70 = 0.1$ *dpc* (16 *MByte/s*). The differences $t(5,j) - t(4,j)$ are equal to 3 *cc* for all j. Thus, addressing different operands in a loop body increases the run time of the loop only by 3 *cc* independent of the number of operands. If we assume that calculating the address of an operand and loading it can be hidden almost entirely behind the arithmetical operation, we have to count the load time only at the beginning of the expression evaluation for the first and second operand. The second load is only counted if it is a different operand. Even in group 7, where all operands are taken from different vectors with different indices, no large increase of the run time can be detected, which depends on the number of operands. Addressing and loading an operand seems not to be the bottleneck of an operation. Thus the evaluation of the simple vector expressions can be closely modelled with the following assumptions: arithmetical operations take times according to group 1 and 2, loop overhead $T_{ov} = 19$, loading an operand $T_{ld} = 4$ at the beginning of the expression evaluation. Further we count the time T_{ld} to load an operand only if the operand has not been calculated or loaded previously in the same basic block, because it otherwise apparently would be held in a register. Storing and addressing is hidden. We get the modelled run times for the groups 4, 5, 6 and 7 given in table 4.2. The absolute error is often less than 2 *cc*, the relative error is less than 4 %.

In group 6 the run time for small expressions is less than the run time in groups 4, 5 or 7; for large expressions it is greater. On the one hand there is a data dependency in group 6 between each pass of the loop and its following one, but on the other hand the large loop overhead should make it possible that no wait is necessary over loop boundaries (there seems to be no loop unrolling). We note at this point that addressing the same vector in a recursive manner leads to slightly different run times than we have modelled so far.

The machine seems to be able to overlap parts of the operations both on integer operands (addresses) and floating point values and memory accesses.

group		$j=1$	$j=2$	$j=3$	$j=4$	$j=5$	$j=6$	$j=7$	$j=8$
9	measured	45	63	80	98	127	165	189	208
	approximated	44	61	78	95	112	129	146	163
	Δ%	-2.3	-3.2	-2.5	-3.1	-13.4	-27.9	-29.5	-27.6
10	measured	57	74	93	124	157	180	207	231
	approximated	54	71	88	105	122	139	156	173
	Δ%	-5.3	-4.1	-5.4	-18.1	-28.7	-29.5	-32.7	-33.5

Table 4.3 Run time approximation of group 9 and 10 for the Ncube

4.3.1.6 group 8.

This group measuring inner loops for dot product and matrix product shows two facts. On the one hand there is almost no difference in the run time for row or column wise addressing. But on the other hand one pass through the inner loop of a dot product is about 20 % faster than one pass through the inner loop of a matrix product, although, naively spoken, both inner loops should have nearly equal run time. Possibly, the compiler is not able to pull the address multiplication out of the inner loop, if two loops are nested and the address calculation depends on both loop variables. Addressing a vector out of a matrix seems to add $T_{adr} = 10$ *cc* to the run time inner loop. However, $t(8,1)$ is equal to $t(5,2)$ where the same types of operations are performed. So we can model the run time of the dot product simply in the way introduced in group 5 leading to a run time for one pass of the inner loop of the dot product of 44 *cc* and of the matrix product of 54 *cc*.

4.3.1.7 group 9 and group 10.

The last two groups are discussed together. Looking at the differences $t(g,j)-t(g,j-1)$ for both $g = 9$ and $g = 10$ we find a quite unstructured list of values. But if we choose the modelling derived so far with increasing j the run time $t(9,j)$ should increase by 17 *cc*:

$$t(9,j) = (T_{add} + T_{mul}) * j + 2T_{ld} + T_{ov}$$

In group 10 we have an additional time T_{adr} for addressing out of a matrix. In table 4.3 we have listed the approximated run times using this formulae as far as the modelling ranges within 5 % of the measured run time. Larger expressions take more time to get evaluated. It is easy to see that the run time seems to be faster if we split the expression in the high level language. But the compiler has not detected this possibility. Thus exact, simple modelling is impossible. Almost 30 % of the performance are lost because the compiler does not find a good way to evaluate the more complex expressions.

We summarize the properties and parameters of an Ncube's node processor (in conjunction with this particular compiler):

	T_{in}	T_{ov}	T_{add}	T_{mul}	T_{div}	T_{ld}	T_{adr}
cc	100	19	7	10	32	4	10

Table 4.4 Run times of inner loops for the Ncube in *cc*

- There is no data cache. The memory hierarchy is very simple. It consists of a register file between main memory and the functional units. Its size has not been detected by the test routines. It seems to be large enough to avoid any bottleneck.
- The processor behaves like a scalar machine, because no vector operations, i. e. the generation of a result every clock cycle, could be encountered.
- Dividing is pretty fast. Probably there is a special dividing routine, which allows for more overlapped work of the functional units of the processor.
- Load and store operations can be overlapped with address calculation and arithmetical operations. The time to load an operand occurs only at the beginning of the expression evaluation, if the operand has not been loaded beforehand in the expression (or basic block).
- The effective bandwidth b_{mm} between functional units and main memory through the register file is ≥ 0.1 *dpc*, which is about 16 *MByte/s*. However, the time to load for one item can be modelled with 4 *cc*, which is about 50 *MByte/s*.
- Addressing of main memory keeps almost pace with floating point performance, but multi–dimensional addressing adds a constant term T_{adr} to the run time of the inner loop.
- We can model the run times of all test routines sufficiently by using the parameters given in table 4.4.
- The compiler has difficulties with common subexpression elimination.
- The compiler does not optimize beyond DO–loop bounderies.
- The loop overhead T_{ov} is quite large compared with the time to perform a floating point operation. One should avoid simple inner loops.
- The compiler does not use loop unrolling techniques to reduce the run time due to loop overhead.
- The sustained performance on expression evaluation ranges from 25 to 63 % of the peak performance (excluding divide operations, see discussion in group 3 above).

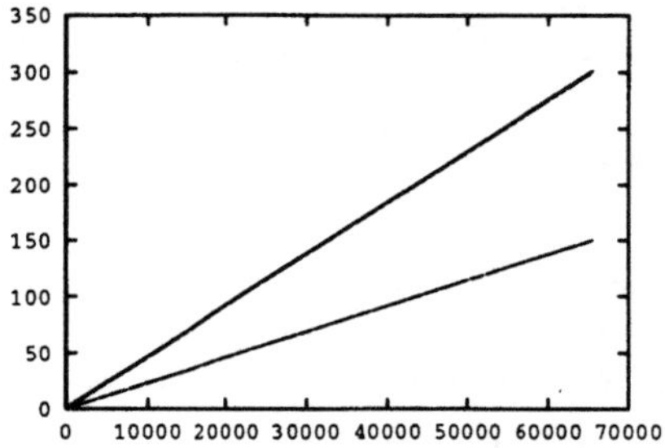

Figure 4.4 Measured run time in ms versus modelled run time of group 11 (upper curve) and group 12 (lower curve)

4.3.2 Measurements of the Parallel Kernels

A brief description of the Ncube's architecture is given in section 4.3.1. We used the two communication routines `nwrite` and `nread`, which are provided by the FORTRAN library, to perform the data transfer. `nwrite(b,l,n,t)` sends a data block `b` with length `l` to a node `n` in context `t`. `nread(b,l,t)` receives a data block `b` with length `l` in context `t`, which can be sent by any other node. Corresponding calls to `nread` and `nwrite` have equal block lengths and the same context.

4.3.2.1 group 11.

The test routines in this group are started using the whole 64 node Ncube. The communication is performed only between directly connected nodes. Because the run time appeared to be independent of the direction in which the communication takes place (see [1]), d occurs not as a parameter. The run time $t(11,1)$ in μs can be modelled with

$$t(11,1,8n) = \begin{cases} 290 & \text{if } n \leq 3 \\ 354 + 8n/1.75 & \text{if } n > 3 \end{cases}$$

In figure 4.4 (upper curves) the run times of routine $r(11,1)$ for two outer loop lengths L and the modelled run time are plotted. The difference $t(11,1,d,1,8n) - t(11,1,d,10,8n)$ is almost constant. The error between modelled run time and measured run time with $l = 10$ is always less than 1 %. Thus the bandwidth between any two connected nodes is about 1.75 *MByte/s* (or 0.011 *dpc*) with a startup time of about 354 μs (or 7080 *cc*). Small packets of less than 32 *Byte* are transmitted in a constant time of 290 μs (or 5800 *cc*). For $L = 1$ the startup time increases by about 900 μs (or 18000 *cc*) independent of n.

For routine $r(11,2)$ we measured the same run times as in routine $r(11,1)$, although now the distance between two nodes increases with d. Thus, the node to node communication time on the Ncube seems to be independent of the distance of the two nodes which participate on the data transfer. Note that no other communication takes place simultaneously.

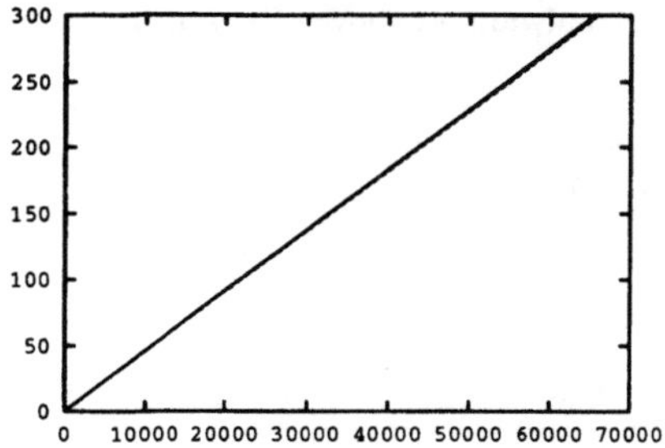

Figure 4.5 Measured run time in ms versus modelled run time of group 13, routine 1

4.3.2.2 group 12.

Similar to group 11 the run times of routine $r(12,1)$ are independent of the direction in which the communication takes place, so d occurs not as a parameter. The run time $t(12,1)$ in μs can approximated by

$$t(12,1,8n) = \begin{cases} 289 & \text{if } n \leq 3 \\ 289 + 8n/3.5 & \text{if } n > 3 \end{cases}$$

which is shown in figure 4.4 (lower curve). Again the error made is always less than 1 percent. Thus the bandwidth between any two connected nodes is about 3.5 *MByte/s* (or 0.022 *dpc*) — twice as high as in group 11 — with a startup time of about 289 μs (or 5780 *cc*). Small packets of less than 256 *Byte* are transmitted in a constant time of 289 μs (or 5780 *cc*). For $L = 1$ the startup time increases by about 900 μs (or 18000 *cc*) for small block sizes n, but in this routine the additional term vanishes for larger ones.

For routine $r(12,2)$ we measured almost the same run times as in routine $r(12,1)$, although now the distance between two nodes increases with d. Thus, the node to node communication time on the Ncube seems to be independent of the distance of the two nodes, which participate on the data transfer, even if it is bidirectional. Note, that no other communication takes place simultaneously.

4.3.2.3 group 13.

In this group all nodes participate in the communication.

For routine $r(13,1)$ the run times in different directions d are almost equal (see [1]). They differ by less than 1 percent The outer loop length L has no noticeable influence on the run times neither. Therefore, those two parameters do not occur in the run time formula. The run time $t(13,1)$ in μs is modelled with

$$t(13,1,8n) = \begin{cases} 232 & \text{if } n \leq 4 \\ 236 + 8n/1.76 & \text{if } n > 4 \end{cases}$$

which is shown in figure 4.5. The error is in all cases less than 1.6 %.

Routine $r(13,2)$ shows the expected behavior, too. The run time is independent of L and can be modelled with almost the same bandwidth as above. The startup times have been chosen differently:

$$t(13,2,8n) = \begin{cases} 230 & \text{if } n \le 2 \\ 216 + 8n/1.75 & \text{if } n > 2 \end{cases}$$

The maximal error is about 4.3 %.

4.3.2.4 group 14.

All of the routines in this group were started with an appropriate cluster of p processors which had been allocated before the program was started.

Routine $r(14,1)$ deals with a broadcast of a message from one node of a cluster to all other nodes. The FORTRAN library provides a routine `bcast()` to perform such an operation. According to section 4.2.2 we can model the run time $b(i,n,p)$ in μs with

$$b(i,n,p) = S_0 + S_p\, d(p) + 8n(\frac{d(p)}{B} + \frac{1}{B_S})$$

where n denotes the message length in words, $d(p)$ denotes the diameter of the network, i. e. the longest path from the source node to the destination node used by `bcast()`, B denotes the bandwidth on the links in *MByte/s*, which we assume to be equal on all links, and B_S denotes the bandwidth due to software overhead. With $S(p) = S_0 + S_p\, d(p)$ and $1/B(p) = d(p)/B + 1/B_S$ this can be written as

$$b(i,n,p) = S(p) + 8n/B(p)$$

The run times of broadcast from node 0 to $p-1$ nodes within a cluster are not listed here, because the data set is quite large. The length of a message varies from 1 to 65536 words. In table 4.5 those run times are approximated with the two parameters $S(p)$ and $B(p)$ according to the formula given above for all p. The difference between the approximation and the measurement is less than 1 percent, if n is larger than the value listed in the fourth column of the table.

Now, we want to derive the parameters $d(p)$, S_0, B_S, S_p and B required by our model. The differences $1/B(p') - 1/B(2p')$ and the differences $S(2*p') - S(p')$ are almost constant ($\approx$ 0.46 for $B(p)$ and $\approx$ 50 for $S(p)$) for all $2 \le p' < 64$. So the routine `bcast()` exploits the hypercube structure of the Ncube, the diameter $d(p)$ is equal to $\log(p)$ and the parameter S_p is equal to 50 μs. α can be set to 185 μs. If we solve the equation

$$1/B(p) = d(p)/B + 1/B_S$$

in B and if we use $d(p) = \log(p)$ we get

$$B = \frac{\log(p)B(p)}{1 - B(p)/B_S}$$

p	$t_s(p)$	$B(p)$	$n_\leq$	$t_s(p)$	$B(p)$
2	235	1.96	8	235	1.96
4	285	1.04	2	285	1.04
8	335	0.71	4	335	0.71
16	380	0.54	4	385	0.54
32	435	0.43	2	435	0.43
64	485	0.36	2	485	0.36
	approximated			modelled	

Table 4.5 Modelling the run time in μs and the bandwidth in *MByte/s* of broadcast on the Ncube

p	$sy(p)$	
2	25190	503800
4	25343	506860
8	50663	1013260
16	101299	2025980
32	102571	2051420
64	205126	4102520

Table 4.6 Run time in μs and cc to synchronize a cluster on the Ncube

Now we have a set of equations for B with parameter B_S, which we both expect to be constant. The values $B = 2.22$ *MByte/s* and $B_S = 16.7$ *MByte/s* give a good approximation, which is documented in the last column of table 4.5, where $B(p)$ has been recalculated.

Finally, we have the run time formula for broadcast (in μs)

$$b(1, 8n, p) = 185 + 50\log(p) + 8n * (\frac{1}{16.7} + \frac{\log(p)}{2.22})$$

for the Ncube. This run time formula can be interpreted in the following way. The startup time for a broadcast, which is independent from the size of the cluster is about 185 μs (3700 cc). In order to copy the message from user space to system space on the first node and to copy it from system to user space on all receiving nodes 0.06 μs (12 cc) are used for each word. The effective bandwidth on a link is about 2.22 *MByte/s* (0.014 *dpc*). The software uses a tree–like transfer scheme on the hypercube with an additional startup time of about 50 μs (1000 cc) on each branch.

Routine $r(14, 2)$ measures the time $sy(p)$ to synchronize p processors within a cluster. We used the library function `nodesy()` to perform synchronization. In table 4.6 this time is listed as the maximum over all participating nodes of the cluster.

The measured time is incredibly large. Before the loop, which just calls `nodesy()`, is entered all processors have been synchronized by another call to `nodesy()`. Thus, the large run time should not be caused by non–synchronized nodes at the beginning of the measurement.

p	$gs(p)$		
	minimal	maximal	modelled
2	278	282	278
4	444	450	444
8	611	689	610
16	777	842	776
32	942	951	942
64	1109	1118	1110

Table 4.7 Run time in μs to compute the global sum in a cluster on the Ncube

Routine $r(14,3)$ measures the time $gs(p)$ to build the global sum of p values and distribute the sum to all processors within the cluster. Initially, every processor owns his part of the sum. We used the library function `dsum()` to perform the calculation. Table 4.7 summarizes the minimal and maximal measured run times $gs(p)$.

If we treat the two maximal values for 8 and 16 processors as exceptions, we have almost constant differences $gs(2 * p') - gs(p')$ ($\approx 166\mu s$) for all $2 \leq p' < 64$. Thus the software exploits the hypercube structure with diameter $d(p) = \log(p)$ and implements a tree–like structure to evaluate the global sum. The run time can be approximated with

$$gs(p) = 112 + 166\log(p)$$

which is listed in the last column of table 4.7, too.

4.3.2.5 Remark.

Because `gsum()` also has to synchronize the nodes, one should prefer this routine, instead of `nodesy()`, which is provided by the library, if the program needs an explicit synchronization point.

4.3.2.6 group 15.

Until now the data set is much too small, so we are still not able to give a model for the run time. Most of the time is spent in start up time and loop control. The maximal length of the vector distributed over the cluster has been set to 256 elements, thus, in a cluster of 64 nodes there are only 4 words located on every node. The run times must be taken as they are, a simple extrapolation for greater vector lengths should not be performed. In table 4.8 the measured data is summarized. The difference between minimal and maximal value is not very large, so we will use the averaged value later. Nevertheless, the data set is sufficient for use in later sections.

n/p	p	gc_{min}	gc_{max}	gc_{avg}
32	2	551	556	553
64	2	830	836	833
128	2	1420	1430	1425
16	4	920	925	923
32	4	1340	1363	1351
64	4	2228	2248	2238
4	8	881	943	932
8	8	1146	1205	1185
16	8	1670	1730	1714
32	8	2731	2751	2740
4	16	1379	1453	1428
8	16	2000	2028	2015
16	16	3062	3120	3103
2	32	1599	1675	1648
4	32	2166	2263	2227
8	32	3323	3415	3378
1	64	1790	1895	1862
2	64	2385	2481	2447
4	64	3553	3647	3614

Table 4.8 Run time in μs of global collection on the Ncube

4.4 Algorithms

This section contains the description of serial and parallel programs of a (i) conjugate gradient method for dense arrays (CG–method), and (ii) of an explicit solver for a partial differential equation with one (PDE1–method) respectively (iii) two (PDE2–method) spatial dimensions.

4.4.1 CG–method

The conjugate gradient method [8] is an iterative method for solving linear systems of equations $Ax = b$. For vectors u and v we denote by $\langle u, v\rangle$ the scalar product of u and v. The conjugate gradient method iteratively computes vectors x_t, d_t and g_t. In one iteration the following computations are performed:

$$
\begin{aligned}
\alpha &= \langle g_t, g_t\rangle / \langle d_t, Ad_t\rangle \\
x_{t+1} &= x_t + \alpha d_t \\
g_{t+1} &= g_t + \alpha A d_t \\
\beta &= \langle g_{t+1}, g_{t+1}\rangle / \langle g_t, g_t\rangle \\
d_{t+1} &= -g_{t+1} + \beta d_t
\end{aligned}
$$

The following segment of FORTRAN code for p processors performs a certain number it of the above iterations. Vectors x_t, d_t and g_t are computed in local arrays `vx(mp)`, vd(m) and vg(mp); local arrays vh(mp) store intermediate results. The symmetric $m \times m$ matrix A is stored in local arrays ma(m,mp). In general each processor stores m_p consecutive rows of A and m_p consecutive elements of the vectors. The conjugate gradient algorithm accesses the matrix by rows, but, because in FORTRAN arrays are stored by columns and because A is symmetric, the program accesses columns instead.

```
        t1 = secnd()
1000    CONTINUE
          CALL gcol(vd,m,mp,me)
          ab = 0.0
          DO 20  i=1,mp
            vh(i) = 0.0
            DO 21  j=1,m
              vh(i) = vh(i) + ma(j,i) * vd(j)
21          CONTINUE
            ab = ab + vh(i) * vd(i+u-1)
20        CONTINUE
          CALL gsum(ab)
          IF(ab.NE.0.0)  ab = nga/ab
          err = 0.0
          ngn = 0.0
          DO 30  i=1,mp
            vg(i)  = vg(i) + ab * vh(i)
            vh(i)  = ab * vd(i+u-1)
            vx(i)  = vx(i) + vh(i)
            err    = err + vh(i) * vh(i)
            ngn    = ngn + vg(i) * vg(i)
30        CONTINUE
          CALL gsum(err)
          CALL gsum(ngn)
          IF(nga.NE.0.0)  ab = ngn/nga
          nga    = ngn
          nsteps = nsteps + 1
          DO 40  i=1,mp
            vd(i+u-1) = ab * vd(i+u-1) - vg(i)
40        CONTINUE
          IF(nsteps.LT.it)  GOTO 1000
        t2 = secnd() - t1
```

At the end of each iteration, each processor knows his section of length mp of vector vd. At the beginning of each iteration, procedure gcol() performs a multicast where each processor me broadcasts his segment of vector vd (length m) to all other processors (see group 15 in section 4.2.2). Procedure gsum() computes the global sums necessary for the computation of the global scalar products (see group 14 in section 4.2.2).

Most of the time the sequence stays in the inner DO–loop 21 within the DO–loop 20. The body of the loop is similar to the routines of group 8: in vh(i) the dot product of row i of matrix ma with vector vd is accumulated. A dot product $r(8,1)$ follows this loop and a scalar assignment $r(0,2)$ precedes it. DO–loop 30 consists of an assembly of vector operations and dot products (group 4 to 8). DO–loop 40 is similar to routine $r(9, 1)$. The three loops are embedded in an outer loop (labeled with 1000) which performs the iterations. The version for one processor is obtained by setting mp=m and eliminating all calls to procedures gcol() and gsum().

4.4.2 PDE1–method

This kernel deals with an explicit solver for a partial differential equation for one spatial dimension.

$$\begin{array}{rcll} u_t(t,x) & = & \sigma u_{xx}(t,x) & t > 0, x \in [0,1] \\ u(0,x) & = & \phi(x) & x \in]0,1[\\ u(t,0) & = & u(t,1) = 0 & t \geq 0 \end{array}$$

Solving such an inital boundary value problem often leads to explicit iterative formulae like

$$\begin{array}{rcl} u_{k+1,i} & = & u_{k,i} + \frac{\sigma \Delta t}{\Delta x^2} * (u_{k,i-1} - 2u_{k,i} + u_{k,i+1}) \\ u_{0,i} & = & \phi(i \Delta x) \\ u_{k,0} & = & u_{k,m+1} = 0 \end{array}$$

The forward differential quotient is used to approximate u_t and a central differential quotient to approximate u_{xx}.

The following segment of FORTRAN code for p processors performs a certain number it of the above operations. The vectors u_i and u_{i+1} are computed in local arrays u0(mp+2) and u1(mp+2). The new result is stored alternately in u0 and u1. Each processor stores m_p consecutive elements of both vectors. To update all local values the processors also need one value from both of their neighbors. These data are transferred after every time step and are stored in the vector elements u[0] and u[mp+1]. Element u[0] of processor $me = 0$ and element u[mp+1] of processor $me = p-1$ contain the boundary values.

The version for one processor is obtained by setting mp=m and eliminating all calls of the procedure exchlr(). The iteration does not converge, because the constant value have been chosen in a way that the initial configuration is repeated every second time step.

```
      t1 = secnd()
      DO 20  lp=1,it,2
        DO 21  i=1,mp
21        u1(i) = u0(i) + c0 * (u0(i-1)-2*u0(i)+u0(i+1))
      CALL exchlr(lp,u0,m,mp);
        DO 22  i=1,mp
22        u0(i) = u1(i) + c0 * (u1(i-1)-2*u1(i)+u1(i+1))
      CALL exchlr(lp,u1,m,mp);
20    CONTINUE
      t2 = secnd() - t1
```

4.4.3 PDE2–method

This routine solves an initial boundary value problem for two spatial dimensions

$$\begin{aligned} u_t(t,x,y) &= \sigma\Delta u(t,x,y) && t>0,(x,y)\in\Omega \\ & && \Omega\equiv[0,1]\times[0,1] \\ u(0,x,y) &= \phi(x,y) && (x,y)\in\Omega \\ u(t,x,y) &= 0 && t\geq 0,(x,y)\in\partial\Omega. \end{aligned}$$

The LAPLACE operator Δu is approximated by a five point central differential quotient and the time derivation by a forward differential quotient. This leads the following explicit time stepping method

$$\begin{aligned} u_{k+1,i,j} &= u_{k,i}+\frac{\sigma\,\Delta t}{\Delta x\Delta y}*\left(u_{k,i,j-1}+u_{k,i-1,j}-4u_{k,i,j}+u_{k,i+1,j}+u_{k,i,j+1}\right) \\ u_{0,i,j} &= \phi(i\Delta x,j\Delta y) \\ u_{k,0,j} &= u_{k,m+1,j}=0 \\ u_{k,i,0} &= u_{k,i,m+1}=0 \end{aligned}$$

There are two ways to distribute the matrices over the set of processors. In the first parallelization method every processor participating the computation holds one stripe of the matrices. Communication is performed on the boundaries of the stripes, thus leading to a neighbor–to–neighbor communication on a chain. The second method gives every processor a squared part of the matrices, so data exchange is done in four directions.

The following segment of FORTRAN code for p processors performs a certain number it of the above iterations (loop labeled with 1000). For technical reasons two iterations are done in this loop. The matrices u_i and u_{i+1} are computed in local arrays u0(mp+2,m+2) and u1(mp+2,m+2). The new result is stored alternately in u0 and u1. Each processor holds $m_p = m/p$ columns of the matrix with range m. We have listed the program for the first data distribution (stripes). The code for the second possibility is quite obvious. After every iteration one colum is exchanged both to the right and to the left neighbor. These data are received in column 0 and mp+1. The boundary values are stored in row 0 and m+1. The constant values have again been chosen in a way that the initial configuration is repeated every second time step.

```
      t1 = secnd()
      DO 1000  lp=1,it,2
        DO 20  j=1,mp
          DO 20  i=1,m
            u0(i,j) = u1(i,j)+c0*(u1(i,j+1)+
     &        u1(i-1,j)-4*u1(i,j)+u1(i+1,j)+u1(i,j-1))
20    CONTINUE
      CALL exchlr(lp,u0,m,mp)
        DO 30  j=1,mp
          DO 30  i=1,m
            u1(i,j) = u0(i,j)+c0*(u0(i,j+1)+
     &        u0(i-1,j)-4*u0(i,j)+u0(i+1,j)+u0(i,j-1))
30    CONTINUE
      CALL exchlr(lp,u1,m,mp)
```

```
1000      CONTINUE
          t2 = secnd()
```

The version for one processor is obtained by setting mp=m and eliminating all calls of procedure exchlr().

4.5 Analysis of the Programs

We will map the test routines described in section 4.2.1 in an almost systematic way to the expressions of the algorithms. The run time is predicted using the node parameters derived in section 4.3.

The measured run time curves are always step wise linear curves, because the data points are connected by lines. In the diagrams the predicted run time curve is the smoother one, so we have omitted any labeling of the curves.

4.5.1 Serial Versions

4.5.1.1 CG–method

The local problem size m_p is kept in the run time formulae, so we can apply the formulae later in the parallel run time prediction. The run time of the inner loop 21 is

$$t_{21} = m * (T_{mul} + T_{add} + T_{adr} + 2T_{ld} + T_{ov}) + T_{in} = 54m + 100$$

The DO–loops 20, 30 and 40 have run times

$$\begin{aligned} t_{20} &= m_p * (t_{21} + T_{mul} + T_{add} + 2T_{ld} + T_{ov}) + T_{in} = 54mm_p + 144m_p + 100 \\ t_{30} &= m_p * (4T_{mul} + 4T_{add} + 5T_{ld} + T_{ov}) + T_{in} = 107m_p + 100 \\ t_{40} &= m_p * (T_{mul} + T_{add} + 2T_{ld} + T_{ov}) + T_{in} = 44m_p + 100 \end{aligned}$$

with the following explanations.

In loop 20 the constant and vd are loaded. In loop 30 the scalar ab and the elements of the vectors vh, vg, vd and vx are loaded. In loop 40 the scalar and the elements of the vector vd are loaded.

We add all times of the inner loops and do not consider the simple assignments within the iteration DO–loop 1000. The number of iterations it has been chosen as 10. We get as predicted run time ts^p_{CG} (in cc) of the serial CG–program

$$T^s_{CG} = it * (t_{20} + t_{30} + t_{40} + T_{ov}) + T_{in} = 540mm_p + 2950m_p + 3290$$

Figure 4.6 shows the predicted run time versus the measured data. The relative error is always less than 1.4 %.

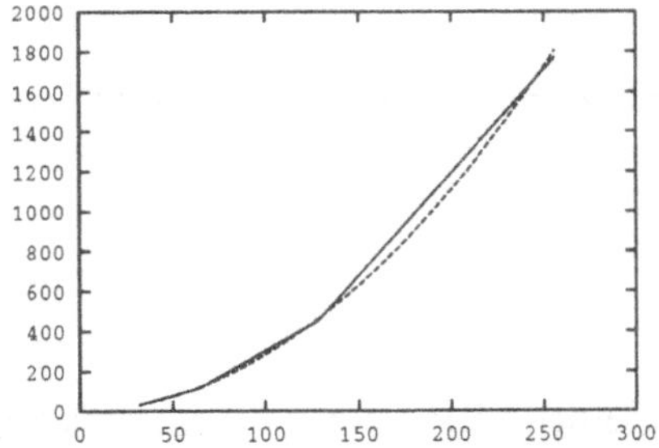

Figure 4.6 Measured run time in ms versus modelled run time of serial CG–program for the Ncube ($it = 100$)

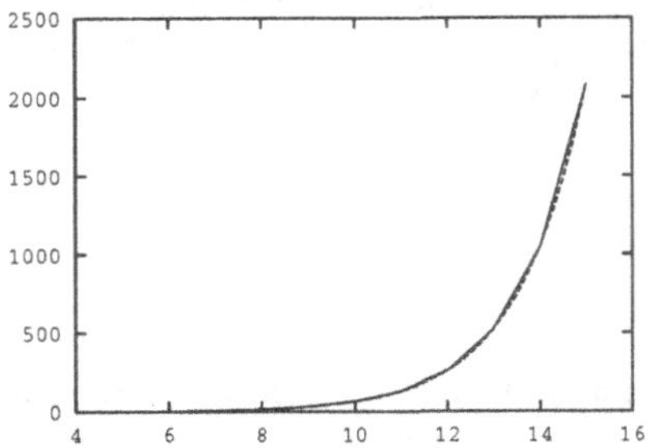

Figure 4.7 Measured run time in ms versus modelled run time of serial PDE1–program for the Ncube ($it = 10$, x–scale logarithmical with base 2)

4.5.1.2 PDE1–method

In order to allow for a later usage in the parallel run time prediction the parameter m_p as local problem size is kept in the run time formulae. The run time of both loop `21` and loop `22` is

$$t_{22} = t_{21} = m_p * (2T_{mul} + 3T_{add} + T_{ld} + T_{ov}) + T_{in} = 64m_p + 100$$

Only the load of `u0(i)` can not be overlapped with an arithmetical operation, if we suppose that both `c0` and the value 2 are held in registers. The multiplication `2*u0(i)` can be started during the load of `u0(i-1)`. The run time of both the iterated loops is then

$$T^s_{PDE1} = it * (t_{21} + t_{22} + T_{ov}) + T_{in} = it * (128m_p + 219) + 100$$

The predicted run time for different problem sizes m and the measured data are shown in figure 4.7. The error is for $m \geq 128$ always less than 1 %.

4.5.1.3 PDE2–method

In order to allow for a later usage in the parallel run time prediction the parameter m_p as local problem size is kept in the run time formulae. The run time of both loop `20` and loop `30` is

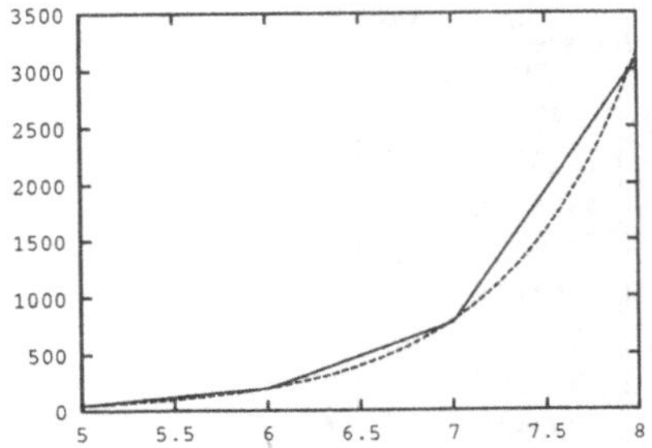

Figure 4.8 Measured run time in ms versus modelled run time of serial PDE2–program for the Ncube (it = 10, x–scale logarithmical with base 2)

$$\begin{aligned} t_{20} &= m_p * (m * (5T_{add} + 2T_{mul} + T_{adr} + 3T_{ld} + T_{ov}) + T_{in} + T_{ov}) + T_{in} \\ &= m_p * (m * (5 * 7 + 2 * 10 + 10 + 3 * 4 + 19) + 100 + 19) + 100 \\ &= 96mm_p + 119m_p + 100 \end{aligned}$$

Only three operands, namely the first three vector components, have to be loaded without the possibility to overlap the load with an arithmetical operation. We suppose `c0` and `4` are held in registers. The addresses of the components depend on both indices `i` and `j`, so we have to add T_{adr} to perform the address multiplication. The run time of both the iterated loops as predicted run time T^s_{PDE2} of the serial PDE2–algorithm is then

$$\begin{aligned} T^s_{PDE2} &= it/2 * (2t_{20} + T_{ov}) + T_{in} \\ &= it/2 * (2 * (96mm_p + 119m_p) + 100 + 19) + 100 \\ &\approx it * (96mm_p + 119m_p + 60) + 100 \end{aligned}$$

The predicted run time of the serial version for different problem sizes m $(= m_p)$ and the measured data are shown in figure 4.8.

4.5.2 Parallel Versions

The abbreviations introduced in the previous sections concerning run times of operations or communication routines are used in this section without any further reference.

4.5.2.1 CG–Method

In section 4.5.1 we have derived the formula

$$T^s_{CG} = it * (54mm_p + 295m_p + 319) + 100$$

in order to predict the run time in *cc* of the serial version of the conjugate gradient method. m was the problem size and m_p was the local problem size. Within the outer iterating loop a global collection is performed once and three times a global sum is distributed. This leads to the following formula which predicts the run time in *cc* of the program with parameters p as size of the cluster and n as size of the problem

m_p	p	T^m_{CG}	T^p_{CG}	Δ%	
32	4	27000	30806	14.10	*
64	4	50600	52722	4.19	
128	4	138000	142306	3.12	
256	4	478000	487672	2.02	
32	8	31300	31830	1.69	
64	8	43900	45318	3.23	
128	8	89700	93260	3.97	
256	8	264000	271768	2.94	
32	16	37000	39748	7.43	*
64	16	44600	45226	1.40	
128	16	69600	72422	4.06	
256	16	161000	167426	3.99	
32	32	44000	45916	4.35	*
64	32	48700	48656	-0.09	
128	32	63400	65108	2.69	
256	32	114000	118680	4.11	
32	64	47100	52530	11.53	
64	64	54700	53900	-1.46	
128	64	64400	65082	1.06	
256	64	93900	97782	4.13	

Table 4.9 Run time prediction in μs for parallel CG–method on the Ncube ($it = 100$)

$$T^p_{CG} = it * (54n^2/p + 295n/p + 319 + gc(p) + 3gs(p)) + 100$$

The modelling of the run time of the parallel functions is taken from section 4.3.2. The run time $gc(p)$ of globel collection `gcol()` is taken directly from table 4.8 and the run time $gs(p)$ of global sum `gsum()` in μs is modelled with

$$gs(p) = 112 + 166\log(p)$$

In table 4.9 the predicted run times T^p_{CG} are listed. The error is for $m_p > 32$ in all cases less than 5 %. The marked lines in the table are predicted without correct global collection times. We have taken the values in table 4.8 of the next larger local problem size.

4.5.2.2 PDE1–Method

In section 4.5.1 we have derived the formula

$$T^s_{PD1} = it * (128m_p + 219) + 100$$

in order to predict the run time in cc of the serial version of the one–dimensional differential equation. m_p was the local problem size. After every iteration one item is exchanged both to the right and to the left neighbor. We have to add two times the run time of the exchange routine $r(13, 2)$ taken from section 4.3.2.

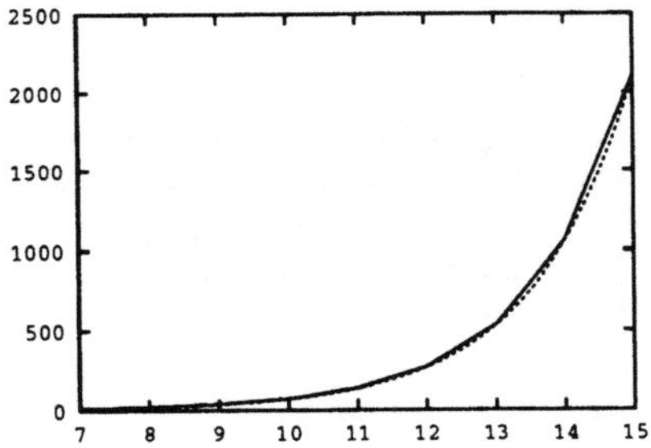

Figure 4.9 Run time prediction in ms for parallel PDE1–method on the Ncube ($it = 10$, x–scale logarithmical with base 2, local problem size m_p)

$$T^p_{PD1} = it * (128m_p + 219 + 2t(13, 2, d, p, 1)) + 100$$

Because only one item is exchanged, $t(13, 2, d, p, 1)$ is equal to 230 μs. This modelling leads to the prediction shown in figure 4.9, where for $p = 2$ and $p = 32$ the measured run time is compared to the modelled run time. The curves are almost identical, because we have chosen the local problem size as x–axis.

4.5.2.3 PDE2–Method

In section 4.5.1 we have derived the formula

$$T^p_{PD2} = it * (96mm_p + 119m_p + 60) + 100$$

in order to predict the run time in cc of the serial version of the program to solve a two–dimensional differential equation.

In the **first partitioning method** each processor holds one column with width $m_p = m/p$ of the matrix with rank m. After every iteration the borders are exchanged both to the right and to the left neighbor. Thus we have to add two times the run time of the exchange routine $r(13, 2)$ taken from section 4.3.2.

$$T^{p1}_{PD2} = it * (96mm_p + 119m_p + 60 + 2t(13, 2, d, p, m)) + 100$$

with

$$t(13, 2, 8n) = \begin{cases} 230 & \text{if } n \le 2 \\ 216 + 8n/1.75 & \text{if } n > 2 \end{cases}$$

This modelling leads to the prediction shown in figure 4.10

The **second partitioning method** divides the matrix in squares. Each processor holds a problem size of $m_p \times m_p$ with $m_p = m/\sqrt{p}$. The code is not given in section 4.4 but quite obvious: the outer loop is now also limited by m_p and the exchange routine transfers data to four neighbors. So we get

$$T^{p2}_{PD2} = it * (96m_p^2 + 119m_p + 60 + 4t(13, 2, d, p, m_p)) + 100$$

This modelling leads to the prediction shown in figure 4.11. A larger error occurs when merely four processors are used for parallelization. In that case, the communication of every node takes place just in two directions, which probably is a reason for the better run time.

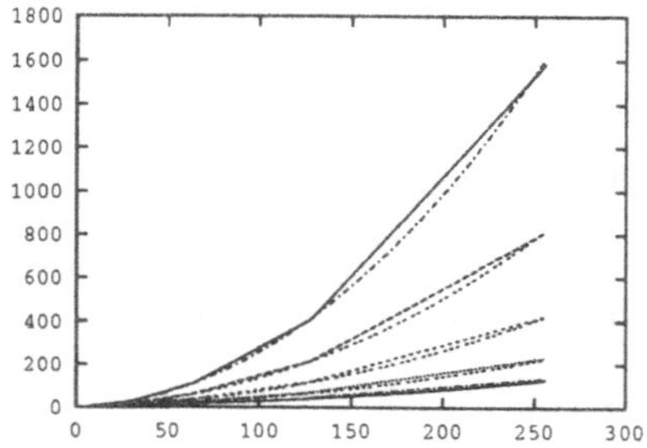

Figure 4.10 Run time prediction in ms for parallel two–dimensional differential equation solver using data partitioning in stripes on the Ncube ($it = 10$, local problem size m_p)

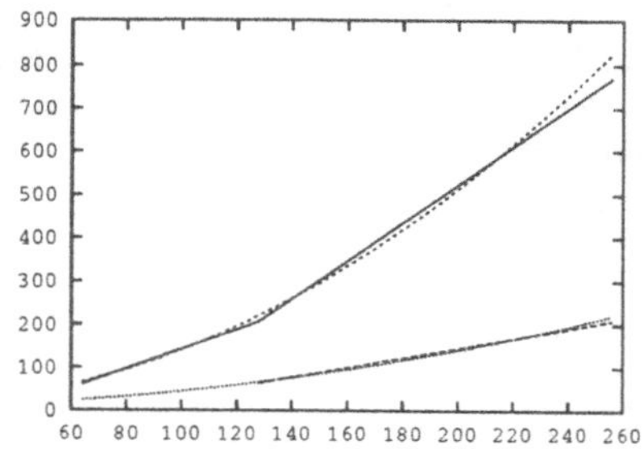

Figure 4.11 Run time prediction in ms for parallel two–dimensional differential equation solver using data partitioning in squares on the Ncube ($it = 10$, local problem size m_p)

4.6 Conclusion

In this paper we presented a set of test routines which has been designed to measure both features of the node processor of a parallel architecture as well as features of the communication network. Based on the measured data set we have derived a relatively small set of parameters for the Ncube–2, which allows for a consistent modelling of the behavior of the machine on the test routines. Moreover, we have shown that the model can be used to predict the run time of a set of algorithms (CG–method and one– and two–dimensional partial differential equations solver) with high accurracy.

In particular we have seen that an Ncube–2 parallel machine can be modelled in a way that a prediction of the performance even for moderate problem sizes can be done with an error of less than a few percent.

References

[1] A. Bingert and A. Formella. Results and Data Sets benchmarking the iPSC and Ncube. Technical report, Universität des Saarlandes, 1992.

[2] J.T. Feo. An Analysis of the Computational and Parallel Complexity of the Livermore Loops. In *Parallel Computing*, volume 7, pages 163–185, 1988.

[3] A. Formella, S.M. Müller, W.J. Paul, and A. Bingert. Isolating the Reasons for the Performance of Parallel Machines on Numerical Programs II. In A.J.G. Hey, editor, *Portability and Performance for Parallel Processors*. John Wiley & Sons, Ltd., 1993.

[4] R. Hockney. Performance parameters and benchmarking of supercomputers. *Parallel Computing*, 17:1111–1130, 1991.

[5] R. W. Hockney and C. R. Jesshope. *Parallel Computers 2*. Adam Hilger, Bristol, 2nd edition, 1988.

[6] F.H. McMahon. The Livermore Fortran Kernels Test of the Numerical Performance Range. Technical report, Livermore National Liboratory, 1988.

[7] W.J. Paul and D. Scheerer. The DATIS–P parallel machine. In *Proceedings of HICSS–24*, volume I, pages 560–571, 1991.

[8] J. Stoer and A. Bulirsch. *Einführung in die Numerische Mathematik*, volume I/II of *Heidelberger Taschenbücher*, chapter 2, Das CG–Verfahren. Springer, 1972.

[9] A.J. Van der Steen. The benchmark of the EuroBen group. *Parallel Computing*, 17:1211–1221, 1991.

[10] R. Weicker. Dhrystone – a synthetic systems programming benchmark. In *Communications of the ACM 27*, volume 10, pages 1013–1030, Oct. 1984.

[11] R.P. Weicker. A detailed look at some popular benchmarks. *Parallel Computing*, 17:1153–1172, 1991.

5 Targeting Transputer Systems, Past and Future

Denis A. Nicole[1]
DEPARTMENT OF ELECTRONICS AND COMPUTER SCIENCE
UNIVERSITY OF SOUTHAMPTON
SOUTHAMPTON SO9 5NH, UNITED KINGDOM
email: dan@ecs.soton.ac.uk

Abstract: We discuss some features of three generations of INMOS transputer: the 32 bit T800 family, the 64 bit T9000 family, for which early Silicon is now available, and the recently initiated *Chameleon* programme. The impact of these features on automatic high-performance compilers is discussed.

5.1 Introduction

INMOS, which is now one of the SGS-Thompson group of companies, introduced a family of *transputer* components in the mid 1980s. These transputers were complete single-chip computers which, by analogy with *transistors*, were intended to be used as components for parallel computers. Each transputer included a RISC-like CPU, microcoded scheduler, on-chip RAM and four high-speed (20M bit/s) bidirectional serial communication links.

The initial transputer was the 32 bit T414 component; this was rapidly followed by the T212 16 bit part and the T800 [4], developed under Esprit project 1085 "Supernode", which featured fast on-chip floating point arithmetic support. For a while, the T800 could reasonably be described as the "fastest single-chip computer in the world." Along with these components, INMOS developed the occam language to provide the primary programming environment for transputers.

After a considerable period of definition, design, and development, β versions of one of the next family of transputers, the T9000 component are now (September 1993) with some manufacturers and will be demonstrated publicly this month. The T9000 is largely software compatible with the T800 family; the influence of occam continues to show clearly in the design.

Work is also just starting on the specification of a third generation of transputer components, the *Chameleon* family. It is believed that the parallel processing facilities of these new components will be extended to include support for a single global address space; it is known that the design has been substantially influenced by Valiant's "Bridging Model" [1].

[1]This work is being conducted as part of Esprit collaboration 5404, "GPMIMD" funded by the Commission of the European Communities.

5.2 The T800 family

INMOS made a remarkable achievement in squeezing a complete parallel processing component, the T414, onto a single die in the mid 1980s. In part this was achieved by a very compact CPU design, occupying only about ten percent of the chip area. Much of the rest of the space was taken up by the four kilobyte internal RAM and the four communications link engines. The need to preserve chip area, and to provide support for very fast interrupt handling, demanded that the CPU maintain only a very simple context. It also encouraged the use of a simple RISC-like load-store instruction set to minimise decoder and address generator complexity.

As well as the hardware imperatives to conserve space and minimise interrupt latency for embedded applications, there was a software imperative to provide a programming environment which would support the development of reliable and predictable codes for use in critical embedded systems. The difficulty of adding secure parallel constructs to existing languages such as `C` and `FORTRAN`, coupled with recent theoretical progress in the development of the CSP and CCS models at Oxford, Edinburgh and Warwick Universities, led INMOS to propose a new language, `occam` to form the core of the principal programming interface to the transputer.

Following these twin imperatives, a novel and effective register organisation was selected for the T9000.

- The operand (`O`) register served to accumulate long operands using a special opcode prefixes. A basic instruction, eight bits long, contained a four-bit operand. Longer operands were built up four bits at a time in the `O` register using special prefix instructions.

- The instruction pointer (`IP`) was a conventional pointer into the instruction stream.

- The workspace pointer (`WP`) served as combined frame/stack pointer and process identifier. This setup is quite natural in `occam`, a language in which each line of code is potentially a separate process, but introduces considerable difficulties for more conventional schemes.

- The evaluation stack consisted of three registers `A`, `B` and `C`. It was intended to be used, in the manner of a Hewlett Packard (HP35) calculator, to hold temporaries during expression evaluation. It was not preserved across context switches which, for transputers, could occur at most communication and control flow instructions. The T800 had a corresponding, separate, floating-point evaluation stack.

The performance of the T800 using `occam` was very good; over one megaflop could easily be sustained on interesting scientific codes. The performance from `C` and `FORTRAN` was considerably worse, perhaps a quarter to a third of a megaflop. In retrospect, several reasons can be found for this disappointment:

- The principal problem was the poor quality of available compilers. It would be possible to generate good code for the three register stack, but a code generator for this purpose would bear little resemblance to that used by, for example, the freely distributed *GNU* compilers to target processors with conventional register sets. Considerable investment would be required to build new high quality back-ends for the new processor and, for a new processor from a new manufacturer, that investment was not forthcoming.

- The C and FORTRAN languages require access to global variables defined at the outermost scope of the program. These are the C statics and the FORTRAN commons. FORTRAN arrays and SAVE variables may also be addressed in this way. Unfortunately, the T800 provides no spare register which can be set up to point to these globals. The hardware also provides no direct support for relocation; compiler vendors found that they needed to pass the global pointer as an additional parameter into each subroutine. A surprising proportion of FORTRAN instructions are associated with passing and with indexing from this parameter.

- The addresses around the workspace pointer, including the global pointer, are accessed frequently. It is thus desirable to ensure that they, and other highly used locations, are in fast internal memory. Indeed, internal memory needs to be treated as a precious and scarce resource, with careful compiler optimisation of its use. In practice, language systems, at best, allowed the user to allocate internal memory by hand and to place the first workspaces there.

- The T800 contained, in addition to an unconditional jump and subroutine calls, two rather strange control flow instructions:

Loop End This instruction was set up with an IP offset in the A register and took as operand a pointer to a two word loop control block. Its approximate action may be summarised as

```
if ((--(O[1]))>0) {
    O[0]++;
    goto (IP-A); }
```

This was used to implement the occam equivalent of FORTRAN DO-loops, but is of little value to an optimising compiler. It is improbable that the offset in the A register could have been placed there other than by an explicit load. Furthermore, this instruction can deschedule and thus no useful information can be held in the evaluation stack.

Conditional Jump At first sight a straightforward instruction, the conditional jump, which does not deschedule, should have permitted interesting values to be retained in the evaluation stack around loop iterations. This instruction, which takes an IP offset as operand, jumps if the A register is zero. Unfortunately, if the jump is taken, it leaves the uninteresting zero in the A register while if it is not taken, it pops the potentially interesting A value.

The form of these loop control instructions made it very difficult to preserve any useful context on the evaluation stack around loop iterations. As far as the author can determine, no compilers do so.

- The small evaluation stack and its floating point equivalent combine with the awkward behaviour of the control flow instructions to give an enormous incentive for loop unrolling. The inner SAXPY loop of LINPACK can, for instance, be unrolled so that all temporaries and loop variables are held in registers; the processor then need only resort to memory for the source and destination vectors and a better than factor of two speed-up is achieved. Again, these possibilities are not exploited by current compilers.

- A transputer process has its workspace pointer as its "handle". This can be very inconvenient for conventional operating systems.

  Firstly, this "handle" changes when a subroutine is called. Secondly, the "handle" can be held in many different places by the transputer scheduler: on an execution queue, in a link engine, in an internal channel, on a timer queue, etc. Compilers to be used with a conventional OS need, as a result, to restrict their use of transputer instructions in order to fit a conventional OS model. As the T800 family provides no relocation support, it is also difficult for the Unix `fork()` call to be implemented.

Overall, the T800 has been poorly supported by FORTRAN and C compilers. Parallel programming support, intrinsic to the occam programming system has typically been provided by simple message-passing libraries such as PARMACS, supported by message-passing software capable of routing messages between transputers that are not directly connected [6].

5.3 The T9000 family

The T9000 transputer [5] is, in most respects, a compatible upgrade of the T800 series. Several of the limitations of the T800 family have been eliminated by new architectural innovations.

- The internal memory can be organised as a sixteen kilobyte unified cache. This completely eliminates the need to manage internal memory explicitly and provides other performance advantages.

- A thirty-two word workspace cache effectively provides a register set for use by high level languages. Its presence, however, worsens the surge in cache activity at each subroutine call.

- Half-word instructions considerably accelerate certain codes.

- The main integer CPU is organised as a seven deep, four wide superscalar pipeline. This mitigates against the complex evaluation stack manipulations of the SAXPY example above and rewards straightforward code generation. It also demands that addresses be generated using proper address generation instructions, evaluated early in the pipe, rather than arithmetic instructions. Furthermore, it is necessary to devote effort to maintaining good instruction grouping in the four wide pipe.

On the other hand, some microcoded instructions carried over from the T800 have proven difficult to implement efficiently on the T9000 pipeline. Architectural trade-offs in design have been influenced by code generated by the old, naive, T800 compilers and have thus tended to freeze code quality. Overall, for FORTRAN and C the T9000 appears to be ten times faster than the T800, with about a factor of five enhancement coming from the architectural improvements. Unfortunately, this performance in 1993/1994 does not appear as impressive as that of the T800 when it appeared.

Operating system support in the T9000 is limited. Minimal address mapping is provided in order to support the Unix `fork()`. Unfortunately, operating systems have evolved during the gestation of the T9000 and modern operating systems such as Unix SVR4 and Microsoft Windows NT expect full virtual memory support.

Parallel programming support is also problematic. The T9000 has a hardware *Virtual Channel Processor* which implements an elaborate `occam` channel model. The VCP, in conjunction with the C104 router, offers effectively unlimited `occam` channels between any processors in a network. This is, however, provided at a considerable cost; each incoming packet from the network consumes memory bandwidth in manipulations of the *Virtual Link Control Blocks* and communications start-up times are not improved over the T800.

The main problem with T9000 communications is, as with OS support, that the needs of language and embedded systems have evolved during its development. Systems such as *High Performance Fortran* do not need `occam`'s elaborate synchronisation mechanisms but they do need lightweight remote read and write facilities. On the embedded front, support for protocols such as ATM would be eased if the T9000 supported a slightly larger maximum packet size, able to contain an ATM frame and routing information.

5.4 The Chameleon family

Comments about the Chameleon are bound to be speculative. It is, however, expected that this processor will support a global address space like that of the Stockholm *Data Diffusion Machine* [3], the Stanford *DASH* [2] or the *Kendall Square Research* computers but implemented scalably using some of Valiant's [1] ideas. With such architectures, the complex data placement information provided by HPF is of little direct value; it can, however, be used to maintain processor load balance via the "owner computes" rule. A more important requirement is to restructure accesses to write-shared variables, such as reduction variable `sum` below:

```
for(i=0; i<100000; i++)
    sum += array[i];
```

These operations would otherwise produce severe cache thrashing or network loading.

A variety of investigations involving hashing strategy, shared cache line detection and reduction variable detection are ongoing in the GPMIMD collaboration.

References

[1] L G Valiant. *A bridging model for parallel computation.* Communications of the ACM 33,8 p103 (1990).

[2] D Lenoski, J Laudon, T Joe, D Nakahira, L Stevens, A Gupta and J Hennessy. *The DASH prototype: Logic overhead and performance.* IEEE Transactions on Parallel and Distributed Systems 4 p41 (1993).

[3] E Hagersten, A Landin, S Haridi and D Warren. *Moving the shared memory closer to the processors—DDM.* Submitted to IEEE Computer.

[4] M Homewood, D May and D Shepherd. *The IMS T800 Transputer.* IEEE Micro 7,5 (1987).

[5] *The T9000 transputer product manual.* INMOS Ltd (1993).

[6] M Debbage, M Hill, D Nicole and A Sturgess. *The virtual channel router.* Transputer Communications 1 p3 (1993).

6 Adaptor: A Compilation System for Data Parallel Fortran Programs

Thomas Brandes
GERMAN NATIONAL CENTER FOR COMPUTER SCIENCE (GMD)
ST. AUGUSTIN, GERMANY
email: brandes@gmd.de

Abstract: Data parallel programming stands for single threaded, global name space, and loosely synchronous parallel computation. This kind of parallel programming has been proven to be very user-friendly, easy to debug and easy to use. But this programming model is not available for most message passing multiprocessor architectures.

Adaptor (Automatic Data Parallelism Translator) is a compilation system that transforms data parallel programs written in Fortran with array extensions, parallel loops, and layout directives to parallel programs with explicit message passing. Therefore it does automatic partitioning directed by user specified data distributions . The current version supports especially the translation of Connection Machine Fortran and High Performance Fortran programs to message passing programs.

After a short description of the system it will be shown how efficient the compilation is. Therefore many results about speed-ups and efficiencies of real codes are presented. Furthermore, the automatically generated message passing programs are compared with hand written message passing programs. The results will show that data parallel programs will be competitive to hand written message passing programs if the data parallelism in the program can be recognized and utilized by the compiler.

6.1 Introduction

MIMD (multiple instruction, multiple data) architectures with distributed memory are the kind of parallel machines that are scalable and can be used for a wide range of scientific applications. Usually, these architectures are programmed with explicit message passing between the processes running on the different processors. As the message passing programming model is very error prone and difficult to use, many efforts have been made to offer other programming models that are easier to use.

These difficulties are not given when using the data parallel programming model. This model stands for single threaded, global name space, and loosely synchronous parallel computation.

Language extensions and modifications for Fortran 90 have been defined by the High Performance Fortran Forum [15] to take advantage of data parallelism. This language High Performance Fortran (HPF) allows code tuning for various architectures and should guarantee top performance on MIMD and SIMD (single instruction, multiple data) computers with non-uniform memory access costs. Many large scientific applications are expected to be programmed in this data parallel language.

The Adaptor system (Automatic Data Parallelism Translator) makes it possible to translate these programs to message passing programs already now. It transforms data parallel programs written in Fortran 77 with array extensions, parallel loops, and layout directives to parallel programs with explicit message passing.

Therefore the code with global data references together with a user specified or implicitly defined data distribution is translated into a program with local and non-local references, where the latter are satisfied by automatically inserting message-passing statements.

Experiments with many sequential programs and their Fortran 90 counterparts have shown [6] that automatic methods could not parallelize the sequential version where it is possible for the version with explicit array operations. In Adaptor only the inherent parallelism of the array operations and of parallel loops is used. Local array operations will be distributed among the available nodes, for non-local array operations efficient communication is generated as these operations have mostly regular communication patterns (e.g. global reductions, shift and spread operations).

In the following the Adaptor system is described. Results of benchmark and real application codes are presented and useful optimization issues will be discussed.

6.2 The Adaptor Compilation System

The Adaptor system transforms Fortran 77 or Fortran 90 programs with explicit data parallelism into parallel programs for MIMD architectures with explicit message passing. Together with a run time system these programs can run on most available parallel architectures. The current version has been designed especially to translate data parallel Connection Machine Fortran (CMF) [4] programs to message passing programs, but it supports also features of High Performance Fortran (HPF) [15].

6.2.1 Properties of Adaptor

The central idea of an automatic translation is to distribute the large data structures like arrays among the available processors. This should be done in such a way that most operations can be done locally without any need of communication. Where global operations are necessary the corresponding message passing statements are inserted automatically.

Though the user will need to understand some issues of parallelism and has to know for efficiency reasons where message passing will be generated, the effectiveness of Adaptor is based on the fact that the user has not to know any message passing command and not to manage the control of the data partitioning. He can change types of variables (e.g. single to double precision) and data distributions without rewriting any other statement in his program. He has not to write two versions of code (host and node program) and many global array operations are translated to the most efficient code for the underlying architecture.

The parallel program can be written in such a way that it can be developed on a serial machine and is also suitable for vector machines or parallel machines with shared memory. Many features supported by Adaptor result also in good execution times for these architectures. By this way, it helps to design programs that run efficiently on nearly all architectures.

Adaptor takes only advantage of the parallelism in the array operations and of the parallel loops. It has no features for automatic parallelization.

The generated code of Adaptor should be as efficient as possible and competitive to a hand-coded Fortran program with message passing. Otherwise the acceptance of such a tool cannot be expected.

Adaptor supports the development of parallel codes that scale with the number of processors. No support is given for any kind of programming where the number of processors is fixed in any way. It makes heavy use of dynamic arrays and the executable version of the generated program can run for any number of processors without any recompilation.

6.2.2 Overview of Adaptor

Figure 6.1 gives an overview of the Adaptor compilation system. The essential parts are the interactive source-to-source transformation (fadapt) and the run-time system DALIB (distributed array library). For compiling and linking of the generated programs, the available Fortran compiler of the parallel machines is utilized.

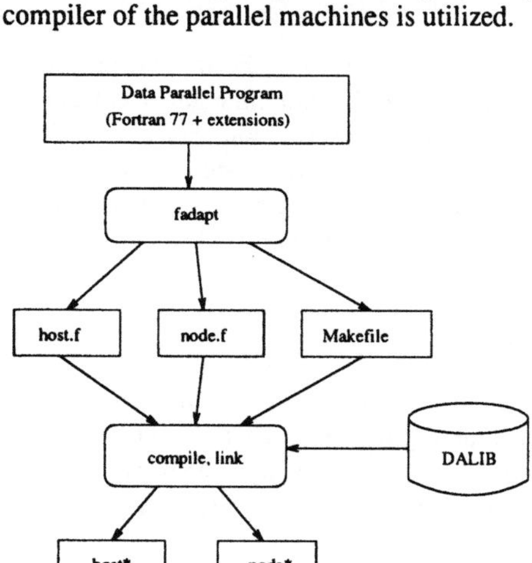

Figure 6.1 Overview of Adaptor

6.2.3 The Input Language

The input language of Adaptor can be defined as Fortran 77 with some restrictions, but with many extensions like dynamic arrays, array operations, parallel loops and layout directives of CMF, HPF and Fortran 90 [1].

The user can define host arrays, replicated arrays and distributed arrays. For the specification of data layouts in Adaptor similar directives as in CMF or HPF are used. Also the parallel FORALL statement supported by Adaptor has the same syntax and semantic as proposed in these data parallel languages.

Many features of Fortran 90 and HPF cannot be used with Adaptor. The most serious restrictions are that Adaptor supports no modules, no pointers, no array-valued functions and no assumed-shaped arrays.

In contrary to many other systems [19, 22, 7, 10] Adaptor supports only block distributions along one dimension. More distributions will be supported in future releases.

In CMF and HPF explicit alignment can be used to reduce communication [17] especially for a given program. For Adaptor this feature is not supported until now, but of course there is an implicit alignment of arrays that are declared and distributed in the same way.

6.2.4 Programming Models for the Generated Programs

The user can select between the following three programming models:

- If the *HOST-NODE* programming model is selected, Adaptor will generate a host program and a node program. The node program runs on all available nodes of the parallel machine, while the host program contains all I/O operations that will be executed on the front end system.
- In the *ONLY-NODE* programming model only one program will be generated that runs on all available nodes. There is no host program. The first node takes care of all I/O operations.
- A program that runs only on a single node is generated when using the *UNIPROC* programming model. The program has no communication and therefore it ought to be faster than the previous one running on a single node. By choosing this model programs with array operations that are not available in Fortran 77 can be translated to sequential Fortran 77 programs.

6.2.5 Interactive Source-to-Source Transformation

The translation of the input file can be done as a batch job, but an interactive translation is also possible. A graphical environment allows the user to select units of the source program (program, functions, subroutines) or variables in a unit to get information about them (see figure 6.2).

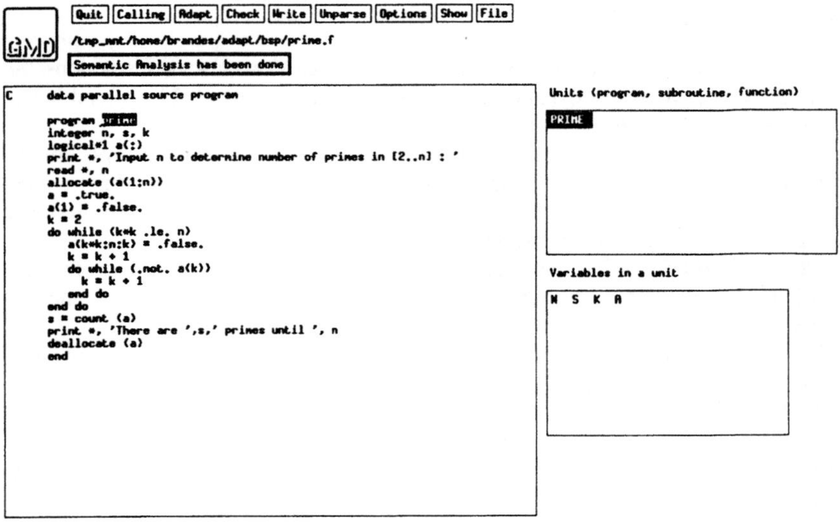

Figure 6.2 fadapt: Interactive Source-to-Source Transformation

6.2.6 Realization of the Translation

The following steps are done during the source to source transformation of Adaptor:

1. The source program is parsed and an abstract syntax tree will be generated.

2. Symbol tables are created and used for a semantic analysis.

3. The program (abstract syntax tree) is normalized to reduce the complexity of the translation.

4. The real translation on the internal abstract syntax tree and symbol tables has four phases:

   (a) In the *analysis phase* the code is checked to verify that there are no violations of the current restrictions.

   (b) In many cases array assignments need communication. In this case Adaptor tries to split up the assignment in primitive array assignments with communication and local array assignments. Sometimes new temporary arrays have to be created.

   (c) In the *initial transformation phase* local array operations will be translated to parallel loops, the forall statement will be translated to equivalent do loops. After this phase only parallel loops without communication will exist.

   (d) In the *final translation* loops will be restricted to the part of the arrays that is owned by one processor and communication statements or movements are translated to corresponding subroutine calls of the underlying run time system.

5. The new internal abstract syntax tree is unparsed back to source text.

Except the graphical interface, the whole source-to-source transformation of Adaptor is generated with a toolbox for compiler construction [12]. These tools have a great flexibility and can generate very efficient code. For the intermediate language, abstract syntax trees will be used where the program module that defines the structure of the abstract syntax trees and provides general tree manipulating procedures is also generated by a tool.

For the analysis and transformation components the compiler tool *Puma* is utilized [11]. This tool cooperates with the generator for abstract syntax trees and supports the transformation and attribution of attributed trees. It is based on pattern-matching, unification and recursion. The flexibility of this tool allows not only to have a modular design but also to extend it in a way as one would expect from a knowledge-based system [2].

6.2.7 Distributed Array Library

For the realization of the communication needed for global operations on distributed arrays, many library functions will be used that build the DALIB (distributed array library). This library contains

- low level communication (send, receive, wait, ...),
- high level communication (broadcast, reduction, barrier, ...),
- data movements based on regular and irregular communication patterns,
- timing functions and tracing facilities,
- and a parallel random number generator.

The DALIB, which can be considered as the runtime system of the whole compilation system, is implemented in C. Most part of this library is portable between the different parallel machines. Only the low level message passing commands, the timing functions and the random number generator have to be adapted to the hardware architecture.

Though the realization of the high level communication routines is based on the low level routines, these functions should be tuned for the underlying hardware architecture. As e.g. the CM-5 [5] has an own control network, broadcasts and reductions are more efficient when using this network than using the data network by message passing.

One version of the DALIB is implemented upon the public domain software PVM [21]. PVM is a software system that enables a collection of heterogeneous computers to be used in parallel. It includes libraries of user-callable functions and a daemon program which coordinates inter-machine activity. PVM guarantees the portability of the generated parallel programs to all machines where it is available. Another version of the DALIB exists for shared memory and virtual shared memory systems where the message passing is realized via a shared memory segment.

At the moment the DALIB has been implemented and tested for iPSC/860, net of SUN or IBM workstations, Alliant FX/2800, Parsytec GC, CM-5, KSR 1 and SGI multiprocessor machines. Versions for the Intel Paragon and IBM SP1 are in development.

6.2.8 Visualization of the Run Time Behavior

If the generated parallel program is started with the trace flag switched on, a tracefile will be generated that gives information about the behavior of the parallel program. The information of the tracefile can be visualized and animated with the public domain software ParaGraph [14]. Especially the information about the utilization and communication can be used for further optimizations.

6.2.9 Availability

The source files of Adaptor, documentation files in PostScript and a number of example programs are available via 'anonymous ftp' from:

```
ftp.gmd.de         (129.26.8.90)
in subdirectory    gmd/adaptor
```

The latest version of June 1993 has more functionality, stability and more supported features than the first version that has been released in September 1992.

6.2.10 Related Work

Many other systems have been developed during the last time that also support SIMD or data parallel programming for MIMD architectures. A SIMD program is translated into an equivalent SPMD program (single program, multiple data stream). This has been done for C* [13] or for Fortran 90 with additional layout directives [19, 23]. Though the latter systems are very similar to Adaptor there is no information about the efficiency of the generated message passing programs and about their availability.

Due to the introduction of High Performance Fortran, many compilers will be available in the next future and compiler optimizations are goals of some other projects [16].

Further developments have been made to support data parallel programming in an object-oriented language like C++ [3, 18]. This approach has the great advantage that no additional preprocessor or compiler is necessary. But due to the lack of efficiency there is not a great acceptance for scientific applications until now.

6.3 Results of Benchmark Codes

For testing the Adaptor system the High Performance Fortran Benchmark Suite has been utilized [20] where many data parallel programs are given in different versions. The Purdue set (J.R. Rice set) with 14 simple data parallel problems has been used to test the efficiency of the generated message passing programs.

6.3.1 The Purdue Set

In the Purdue Set many different kernels of data parallel algorithms have been put together. Table 6.1 shows what kind of algorithms on which problem sizes have been tested.

no	short description of the problem	problem size
1	Trapezoidal rule	1048576
2	reduction function 1	1024 x 1024
3	reduction function 2	1024 x 1024
4	reduction function 3	524288
5	simple search	128 x 4096
6	tridiagonal set.of lin. equations	65536
7	Lagrange interpolation	10 x 32768
8	divided differences	65536 x 8
9	finite differences	512 x 512
11	Fourier's moments	262144
12	array's construction	1023 x 511
13	floating point arithmetic	262144
14	Simpson's and Gauss' integration	262144
15	Chebyshev interpolation	16384

Table 6.1 Problems of the Purdue Set

Three different versions of the programs have been considered:

- the Fortran 77 version can be translated for one node and is used to measure real speed ups,
- the CMF version gives results for the Connection Machine and is used for Adaptor with slightly changes to get automatically generated message passing programs for different parallel machines,
- the parallel version, Fortran 77 with explicit message passing based on PICL [9], is used to compare the results of Adaptor with a hand-coded message passing program. PICL is a subroutine library that implements a generic message-passing interface for a variety of multiprocessors.

6.3.2 Comparison of Sequential and Parallel Version

Table 6.2 shows the results of the sequential Fortran 77 version running on one node of the iPSC/860 compared with the generated message passing program of the hostless programming model. The parallel program is only running on one node.

The results show that the Adaptor version is faster than the sequential Fortran 77 counterpart for the problems 2, 3, 4, 12, 14 and 15. The following reasons are responsible for this effect:

no	sequential version	parallel version	ratio
1	284.7 s	290.6 s	0.98
2	45.9 s	33.8 s	1.36
3	47.0 s	10.3 s	4.56
4	222.1 s	185.5 s	1.20
5	175.9 s	209.3 s	0.84
6	414.7 s	1008.9 s	0.41
7	131.1 s	143.4 s	0.91
8	104.8 s	186.5 s	0.56
9	46.2 s	46.2 s	1.00
11	289.7 s	289.1 s	1.00
12	182.6 s	21.9 s	8.34
13	588.4 s	555.9 s	1.06
14	35.5 s	25.2 s	1.41
15	133.2 s	92.0 s	1.45

Table 6.2 Comparison of sequential and parallel version on one node

- In problem 2, 3 and 12 Adaptor generates a different loop nesting (innermost loop is always for the first index that results in stride 1 for the loop iterations). After loop interchanging and loop distribution the sequential version was as fast as the Adaptor version.
- In problem 4 only one loop fusion makes the sequential version as fast the generated parallel one.
- For problems 14 and 15 the Adaptor version has a vector version of the function that is integrated. By this way there is only one subroutine call instead of a call for every point.

But usually the Adaptor version is a little bit slower due to the generated communication and due to additional memory movements. Especially the problems 6 and 8 require much communication.

6.3.3 Efficiency and Scalability

Table 6.3 shows the speed ups and efficiencies for the generated message passing programs on the iPSC/860 for 8, 16 and 32 nodes. On other parallel machines similar results were achieved. Also on a net of workstations there were reasonable speed-ups for large problem sizes.

These results verify that the scalability of the data parallel programs results also in scalability of the automatically generated message passing programs.

no	8 nodes	16 nodes	32 nodes
1	7.96 (99.5 %)	15.79 (98.7 %)	31.25 (97.6 %)
2	7.41 (92.6 %)	14.08 (88.0 %)	28.17 (88.0 %)
3	6.44 (80.5 %)	12.88 (80.5 %)	25.75 (80.5 %)
4	6.08 (76.0 %)	13.16 (82.2 %)	26.13 (81.6 %)
5	7.12 (89.0 %)	14.14 (88.4 %)	27.91 (87.2 %)
6	4.86 (60.7 %)	8.75 (54.7 %)	16.17 (50.5 %)
7	7.97 (99.6 %)	15.76 (98.5 %)	31.17 (97.4 %)
8	7.61 (95.2 %)	13.92 (87.0 %)	25.90 (80.9 %)
9	7.97 (99.6 %)	15.40 (96.3 %)	28.88 (90.2 %)
11	7.94 (99.3 %)	14.90 (93.1 %)	29.20 (91.3 %)
12	6.84 (85.5 %)	10.95 (68.4 %)	16.85 (52.6 %)
13	7.91 (98.9 %)	15.80 (98.7 %)	31.71 (99.0 %)
14	7.20 (90.0 %)	14.00 (87.5 %)	25.20 (78.8 %)
15	7.48 (93.5 %)	14.84 (92.7 %)	28.75 (89.8 %)

Table 6.3 Speed-Up and Efficiency of Adaptor generated parallel programs

6.3.4 Adaptor vs. hand-coded message passing programs

The parallel programs based on PICL stand for portable hand-coded message passing programs. The most interesting results came up when comparing these programs with the automatically generated message passing programs of Adaptor.

Both versions are portable parallel programs. Both versions are able to run on different number of processors. The hand-coded version realizes this by having the whole data structure replicated on all arrays but every node works only on a subset of the arrays. This has the disadvantage that for bigger problems the code has to be rewritten completely. The Adaptor version can also be used for bigger problems with the only restriction that the program will not run on smaller machine sizes.

- A hand-coded message passing program of problem 6 was not available.
- For problem 2, 3, 4, 14 Adaptor was much more faster,
- for all other problems a little bit faster or nearly the same (problems 5, 8, 11, 12, 13).

As a hand-coded program should always be faster than an automatically generated message passing program, the results show in any case that Adaptor can generate more efficient programs than just straightforward hand written message passing programs. In section 6.4.3 more reliable results on a real application code are given.

6.3.5 Full vs. Loosely Synchronous Execution

The Connection Machine CM-5 [5] of Thinking Machines Corporation offers the data parallel programming model by using CMF and the message passing model by using Fortran 77 and the CMMD message passing library.

no	PICL: hand-coded	Adaptor: automatic
1	25.4 s	18.4 s
2	5.2 s	2.4 s
3	7.1 s	0.8 s
4	24.3 s	14.1 s
7	9.0 s	9.1 s
9	5.3 s	3.0 s
14	11.6 s	1.8 s
15	14.6 s	6.2 s

Table 6.4 Comparison with hand-coded message-passing programs

The 14 CMF applications have been compiled with the CM Fortran compiler (SIMD model). The runtimes have been compared with the runtimes of the by Adaptor automatically generated message passing programs (MIMD model). The vector units of the CM-5 nodes have not been utilized.

Table 6.5 shows the results on a CM-5 with 64 nodes. These results are preliminary as an early version of the CMF Compiler has been used and the programs have been slightly modified for the translation with Adaptor. But it shows that the execution of data parallel programs in MIMD mode is more favorable than the execution in SIMD mode, which requires more synchronization.

no	SIMD execution	MIMD execution
1	16.8 s	8.8 s
2	6.2 s	1.0 s
3	14.6 s	0.6 s
4	25.8 s	6.3 s
5	43.4 s	19.2 s
6	98.7 s	n.a.
7	24.8 s	2.7 s
8	22.8 s	10.1 s
9	8.4 s	1.7 s
11	34.2 s	15.9 s
12	28.1 s	4.8 s
13	56.0 s	21.5 s
14	4.9 s	1.8 s
15	14.1 s	3.5 s

Table 6.5 SIMD and MIMD execution on a CM-5 (64 nodes, no vector units)

If the vector units are used, both versions will be faster. But the advantages of MIMD are lost as every single node works in SIMD mode.

6.4 Results of Application Codes

6.4.1 HYDFLO: a CM Fortran Code for Fluid Dynamics

HYDFLO is a three-dimensional compressible hydrodynamics code based on an explicit two-step Lax-Wendroff finite difference scheme on a regular Eulerian mesh in a regular domain. Such a scheme operates on a compact stencil and is therefore particularly simple for parallel computing.

The given code has run efficiently on a CM and could successfully be translated by Adaptor. In general case it can be assumed that data parallel Fortran programs that run efficiently on SIMD architectures like CM or MasPar should run efficiently on MIMD architectures.

6.4.2 ESM: a Fortran 90 Code for Circulation

The Earth System Model (ESM) is part of a three-dimensional atmospheric general circulation model. This code is a finite difference approximation to the equations of hydrodynamics following the potential enstrophy conserving methods of Arakawa (UCLA). It is based on a grid-point based scheme rather than the more standard spectral decomposition schemes and uses a hydrostatic approximation.

Though the Fortran 90 version of ESM can run on MIMD architectures after using Adaptor, there have been no speed-ups. This is due to the fact that the data decomposition was not conform to the parallel loops in the code.

This effect can be explained with the following example. The code is very inefficient as the parallelism is given for the first dimension of the array, but the distribution is along the second one.

```
      real A(N,N), B(N)
!hpf$ distribute A(*,BLOCK)
!hpf$ distribute B(BLOCK)
      ....
      do J = 1, N
         A(1:N,J) = B(J) * A(1:N,J)
      end do
```

Acceptable results for the ESM code could be achieved after introducing better parallel loops.

6.4.3 IFS: a Fortran 77 Code for Weather Prediction

In a cooperation between GMD and ECMWF (European Center for Medium-Range Weather Forecasts) it is intended to parallelize the ECMWF's production code for medium-range weather forecasts, the IFS (Integrated Forecasting System). For a evaluation of Adaptor a sequential program of the 2D model of the IFS has been investigated. This version contains already all relevant data structures and algorithmic components of the corresponding 3D model.

Results on a CM-5 (without VU)	1 node	4 nodes	16 nodes	32 nodes
hand-written message passing	71.3 s	24.9 s	7.8 s	4.8 s
Adaptor generated version	64.5 s	34.0 s	4.6 s	2.6 s

Table 6.6 Comparison of hand-written and automatically generated MP programs

The same distribution and parallelization strategy has been used as proposed in a parallelization by hand [8]. Though the data structures of the code must be rearranged for Adaptor and the runtime is higher, the effort for parallelization was much less. Table 6.6 shows the runtimes on a CM-5 for a problem with 63 wave numbers, the vector units are not used.

The experiences with the IFS code have shown that Adaptor can also deal with coarse-grained parallelism from parallel loops and not only with fine-grained parallelism from array-operations. The potential of fine-grained parallelism was very low in the given code.

6.5 Summary

Adaptor is a prototype of a compilation system for High Performance Fortran that has given very useful insights how far it is possible to translate efficient data parallel programs to efficient message passage programs for MIMD architectures and in which situations hand-written message passing programs can be faster.

With these insights Adaptor itself can and will be used to implement different optimization strategies for High Performance Fortran compilers. Adaptor will also be used to define and test language extensions of interest that could be part in one of the next versions of High Performance Fortran. Especially features that deal with sparse matrices and parallel I/O are of great interest.

Acknowledgements

I thank the Central Institute for Applied Mathematics at the research center in Jülich for providing the iPSC/860 and Renate Knecht for her user support.

The following people have influenced this work by valuable discussions: James Cownie (Meiko, Bristol), Clemens-August Thole (GMD), Rolf Hänisch (GMD), Michael Gerndt (ZAM, Research Center Jülich), John Merlin (University of Southampton), and Dave Watson (NA Software, Liverpool). Many improvements of the current release have been proposed by the Adaptor users.

Many thanks are also due to Falk Zimmermann for his implementation work and for the discussions about proving correctness of the transformations realized within Adaptor.

References

[1] T. Brandes. ADAPTOR Language Reference Manual (Version 1.0). Internal Report ADAPTOR-3, GMD, June 1993.

[2] T. Brandes and M. Sommer. Realization of a Knowledge-Based Parallelization Tool in a Programming Environment. In *International Conference on Supercomputing*, Athens, Greece, June 1987.

[3] C. Chase, A. Cheung, A. Reeves, and M. Smith. Paragon: A Parallel Programming Environment for Scientific Applications Using Communications Structures. In *Proc. of 1991 International Conference on Parallel Processing*, St. Charles, Illinois, August 1991.

[4] Thinking Machines Corporation. Connection Machine Model CM-2. Technical Summary Version 6.0, TMC, November 1990.

[5] Thinking Machines Corporation. Connection Machine Model CM-5. Technical summary, TMC, November 1992.

[6] G. Fox. Achievements and prospects for parallel computing. *Concurrency: Practice and Experience*, 3(6):725–739, December 1991.

[7] G. Fox, S. Hiranandani, K. Kennedy, C. Koelbel, U. Kremer, C. Tseng, and M. Wu. Fortran D language specification. Technical Report TR90079, Department of Computer Science, Rice University, April 1991.

[8] U. Gärtel, W. Joppich, and A. Schüller. Parallelizing the ECMWF's Weather Forecast Program: The 2D Case, Technical Documentation and Results for the IFS-2D Model. Arbeitspapiere der GMD 740, Gesellschaft für Mathematik und Datenverarbeitung mbH, March 1993.

[9] G.A. Geist, M.T. Heath, B.W. Peyton, and P.H. Worley. PICL: A Portable Instrumented Communication Library, C Reference Manual. Technical report, Oak Ridge National Laboratory, 1990.

[10] H.M. Gerndt. *Automatic Parallelization for Distributed-Memory Multiprocessing Systems*. PhD thesis, University of Bonn, 1989.

[11] J. Grosch. Puma - A Generator for the Transformation of Attributed Trees. Compiler Generation Report 26, GMD, Forschungsstelle an der Universität Karlsruhe, 1991.

[12] J. Grosch and H. Emmelmann. A Tool Box for Compiler Construction. *Lecture Notes of Computer Science*, 477:106–116, October 1990.

[13] P. Hatcher, A. Lapadula, R. Jones, M. Quinn, and R. Anderson. A production quality C* compiler for hypercube machines. In *3rd ACM SIGPLAN Symposium on Principles Practice of Parallel Programming*, pages 73–82, April 1991.

[14] M. Heath and J. Etheridge. Visualizing the Performance of Parallel Programs. *IEEE Software*, pages 29–39, September 1991.

[15] High Perforamnce Fortran Forum. High Performance Fortran Language Specification. Final Version 1.0, Department of Computer Science, Rice University, May 1993.

[16] S. Hiranandani, K. Kennedy, and C.-W. Tseng. Compiler Optimizations for Fortran D on MIMD Distributed-Memory Machines. Technical report, Department of Computer Science, Rice University, 1991.

[17] K. Knobe, J. Lukas, and G. Steele. Data Optimization: Allocation of Arrays to Reduce Communication on SIMD Machines. *Journal of Parallel and Distributed Computing*, 8:102–118, 1991.

[18] M. Lemke and D. Quinlan. P++, a C++ Virtual Shared Grids Based Programming Environment for Architecture-Independent Development of Structured Grid Applications. In Springer Verlag, *Lecture Notes in Computer Science, No. 634*, CONPAR/VAPP V, Lyon, France, September 1992.

[19] J. Merlin. ADAPTing Fortran 90 Array Programs for Distributed Memory Architectures. In *Proc. 1st International Conference of the Austrian Center for Parallel Computation*, Salzburg, October 1991.

[20] A. Mohamed, G. Fox, G. Laszewski, M. Parashar, T. Haupt, K. Mills, Y. Lu, N. Lin, and N. Yeh. Applications Benchmark Set for Fortran-D and High Performance Fortran. Technical Report 327, Northeast Parallel Architectures Center, 1992.

[21] V. Sunderam. PVM: a Framework for Parallel Distributed Computing. *Concurrency: Practice and Experience*, 3(10), December 1990.

[22] Thinking Machines Corporation. CM Fortran Programming Guide, Version 1.0. Manual, TMC, January 1991.

[23] M. Wu and G. Fox. Compiling Fortran 90 programs for distributed memory MIMD parallel computers. Technical Report No. SCCS-88, Syracuse Center for Computational Science, 1991.

7 SNAP! Prototyping a Sequential and Numerical Application Parallelizer

Rolf Hänisch
GMD–FIRST
BERLIN, GERMANY
email: Rolf.Haenisch@gmd.de

Abstract: In the PACE Project we will construct and implement parts of a software system for a distributed–memory MIMD architecture. These parts are the higher system levels and comprise autoparallelizing compilers for FORTRAN, Lisp and the operating system components for Virtual Shared Memory. This article describes our approach for automatic parallelizing sequential FORTRAN programs for distributed–memory MIMD architectures. Annotations are not needed and data distribution is done automatically at compile time.

7.1 Introduction

One of the most interesting parallel architectures are MIMD systems. In the MANNA Project (Multiprocessor Architecture for Numerical and Non numerical Applications) a distributed–memory MIMD system will be built with an operating system that provides virtually shared memory (VSM).

In many numerical applications there exists a certain amount of potential parallelism. The obvious thing in programming such parallel systems is to use a language or its extensions providing a parallel concept.

Unfortunately the user has not only to deal with parallelism in the program but also with data distribution. In some newer language extensions [1, 8] this can be expressed.

However, the users of parallel architectures want to take advantage of the computational power provided by them and want to avoid being confronted with the problems of programming parallel systems [19].

While parallelism is a language issue, *data distribution* is an optimization problem and, for this reason, should not be included in a programming language. This means that data distribution is architecture dependent and will often change during the life time of the program.

For this reason we will try to automate data distribution in our approach. But unlike to [9] we do not think that data distribution can be done by a simple preprocessor.

If a sequential program implements a mathematical method that contains a certain amount of parallelism, this parallelism must be reflected in the concrete implementation, whether the actual language supports parallelism or not.

For vector supercomputers the user has come to write programs in a *vectorizable* style long before languages like Fortran 90 where defined. We believe that it will be equally possible for users to write programs in a *parallelizable* style.

Therefore we assume that parallelism can easily be detected, and describe a compilation approach for automatically generating data distribution. We will address three levels of parallelization:

1. procedural level (functional)
2. loop level (data parallel)
3. instruction level (vectorization)

For the second and third level of parallelism, we use a SPMD computational model as used in shared memory systems except that we deal with locality of data access. Thus, there are two major issues involved in data distribution: *partitioning* and *separation* into local and distributed data, as we base our approach on VSM. VSM systems are usually based on caching memory pages. So arrays and scalars have to be mapped onto memory pages. To avoid page threshing and other conflicts that reduce performance, one has to be very careful in mapping objects into the memory. This paper focuses on techniques for finding an efficient data partitioning.

7.2 Compiler

Fortran has several advantages for a parallelizing compiler. Fortran programs are storage oriented and for that all data accesses can – more or less – be determined. It belongs to the class of imperative languages having built-in notions of globally updatable variables which tends to make them superior to functional languages for parallel processing. In the first phase of our project we will implement only a subset of `FORTRAN 77` that is sufficient for compiling real programs. In this paper we describe the prototype compiler called SNAP!.

In addition we are working on a compiler system with more functionalities accepting **Fortran 90** and **HPF**. Functional parallelism will only be exploited in the advanced compiler system.

The user interface is window–based and uses the X-Windows system. The whole prototype system is implemented using the compiler specification language *gentle* which provides a common notation for a high-level description of analysis, transformations, and synthesis. It is based on the calculus of Horn logic [21, 22]. The GNU-C compiler is used for a highly optimizing back-end, which also gives us great portability.

Fig. 7.1 shows the passes and function of the prototype compiler system.

7.2.1 Front-End for `FORTRAN`

The front-end normalizes `FORTRAN` programs to an intermediate language which looks like a subset of an Algol–type language. Actually, a subset of *C* is used with special

Prototype System
Normalizer
simple control flow analysis and transformation
loop start value 0 and step size +1
inline expansion of heavy procedures
dead code elimination
ordering of expressions
integer expression evaluation
Dependence Analysis
scalar dependence
transformation of induction variables
scalar expansion
simple array dependence with equal index expressions
generation of data parallel sections
Alignment Analysis
determinate all access relations between arrays
produce local optimal partitioning
Parallelization
usage of an evolution strategy
usage of a cost model
produce global optimal partitioning
Code generation
data distribution at compile or run time
GNU–C Compiler

Figure 7.1 The prototype system of the SNAP! compiler

comments to guide parallelization. First of all, loops and array bounds are normalized. In addition, `while` and `repeat-until` loops, written in a Fortran manner, are transformed into explicit higher control loops. Then, expression ordering is done and integer expressions are evaluated as far as possible. Subsequently, dead code elimination is performed. To avoid inter–procedural dependence analysis, procedures can be expanded in–line. In the current version this will be user–guided, but it may also be done automatically. It shall be noted that we analyze the whole program.

For instance, see the Fortran–program in Fig. 7.2. It is translated into a C–program, as shown in Fig. 7.3.

7.2.2 Dependence Analysis

We plan to perform a very sophisticated dependence analysis in the extended compiler system, yet in the prototype system only a simple scalar analysis is done for detecting parallel loops. This is broadened to arrays by allowing only identical index expression in the dimension where the loop variable occurs ([3]). The SNAP! compiler uses computations of symbolic expressions. For propagating usages and definitions we use a technique similar to regular sections ([7]). Several patterns of index expressions are forward or backward references and can also easily be detected.

The result is a program where parallelizable loops are marked and loops that could not be parallelized are annotated with the reason why. Forward dependences can be solved by copies, recurrences are replaced by appropriate reduction operations, and the remaining backward dependences stay as they are. The lowest–order loops in this intermediate form are like the six primitives mentioned in [24] and are called *data parallel sections (DPS)*. These are *element_wise* array operations, *shifts* along array axes, *reduce* operations, *extract*ion of array sections, *insert*ion of array sections, and *distribute* operations (replications along new array axes).

Restructuring like loop distribution, loop fusion, and loop interchange will be considered in the extended version.

7.2.3 Alignment analysis

Alignment analysis is done in a straightforward manner [14, 24]. We assume that all data that is used in a DPS is global (possibly replicated) and all data defined in a DPS is local. This is also known as *owner–computes rule*. All DPS will be attributed with this alignment information. With this knowledge we start in the deepest loop nest level and group different DPS in a loop nest level together if they do not conflict.

Each group of DBS implies a partitioning and so possible distributions. This information is also an attribute of the DPS groups. We call this *local* optimization.

With partitioning we mean *block*, *cyclic*, or *no* partitioning of any array dimension. If a dimension is partitioned, this might be done in any granularity and is determined by the parallelization part.

7.2.4 Parallelizer

If we can build different groups of DPS, we will choose the best of them using a cost model. The same holds if groups of DPS must be connected. In addition we weight the groups using an approximation of the computation length. For this we need a machine model which is an approximation of the real architecture and not analytically based. We approximate computation length and the amount of communication. Communication latency may be hidden by computations, and communication cost may depend on the data volume rather than on the distances.

With this pre–partitioning, we use a genetic algorithm (GA) to optimize the partitioning [4, 15]. This means that we need a *population* of *individuals* also called *chromosomes*. Successive populations are called *generations*. The process of creating generations is repeated until a solution is found. This process can be parallelized and is called the *parallel genetic algorithms (PGA)* [18, 16, 17, 2].

A new generation is created in three steps. First the generation is reproduced using a *fitness* value of the individuals. If this value is high, this individual has a good chance to be in the next generation. In the second step, the individuals are recombined to create the offspring. This operation — also called *crossover* — is done over the syntactical structure of the chromosomes and does not use any information about the "meaning" of the chromosome. The last step is called mutation. In this step the individuals can be altered randomly. But this is done with a very low probability. Note: GAs are randomized — but not random — search algorithms.

For each DO loop, a bit represents whether this loop shall be distributed or not. If a DO loop is a DPS, this loop can be parallelized and the alignment information is used to generate data distributions. Otherwise the loop can only be distributed, and synchronization has to take place.

Alignment information are also stored in a chromosome. But they are not represented by a bit vector but by a list of all relevant relations between array definitions. This list is recombined by permutation instead of partial exchange. To evaluate the array distribution, one relation after another is taken from this list. If the next relation is in conflict with any of the chosen relations, it will not be used.

With the given loop distribution and the alignment information, a local optimization will be done to generate the "best" program. This is called *local hill climbing*. Then, the machine model and the optimized program is used to determinate the fitness value of this individual.

7.2.5 Code generation

The actual distribution is done at run time if array sizes and loop bounds are not known at compile time; otherwise, it can be done at compile time.

The GNU C Compiler[23] is used as back-end. It generates code for the i860 superscalar microprocessor. Future steps will make use of pipelining, dual instruction and dual operation mode.

```
       *** GLOBAL ***
      PARAMETER (ISLANDS=10,SUBSIZE=10,CHROMSIZE=20,
     + MAXVAL=8)
      COMMON /GLOB/
     + POPULATION (CHROMSIZE, SUBSIZE, ISLANDS),
     + FITVAL (SUBSIZE,ISLANDS)
      INTEGER POPULATION
      REAL FITVAL

       *** PROGRAM ***

      REAL DELTA, EPSILON
      INTEGER ITER
      EXTERNAL NEXTGEN
      READ *, EPSILON, ITER, SIZE
```

```
04      DELTA = 2*EPSILON
05 1    IF (DELTA .GT. EPSILON) THEN
06        DO 3 I=1,ISLANDS
07          DO 2, J=1,ITER
08            CALL NEXTGEN(I)
09 2        CONTINUE
10 3      CONTINUE
11        DELTA = ...
12        GOTO 1
13      ENDIF
        END

        SUBROUTINE NEXTGEN (ILAND)
        INCLUDE GLOBAL
20      INTEGER ILAND
21      CALL REPRO (ILAND)
22      DO 1,I=1,SUBSIZE,2
23        CALL CROSSOVER (I, I+1, ILAND)
24 1    CONTINUE
25      CALL MUTATION (ILAND)
26      CALL NEWFIT (ILAND)
        END

        SUBROUTINE REPRO (ILAND)
        INCLUDE GLOBAL
30      INTEGER TEMP (CHROMSIZE, SUBSIZE), CHOICE, ILAND
31      EXTERNAL SELECT
32      DO 2, I=1,SUBSIZE
33        CALL SELECT (ILAND, CHOICE)
34        DO 1, J=1,CHROMSIZE
35          TEMP (J, I) = POPULATION (J, CHOICE, ILAND)
36 1      CONTINUE
37 2    CONTINUE
38      DO 4, I=1,SUBSIZE
39        DO 3, J=1,CHROMSIZE
40          POPULATION (J, I, ILAND) = TEMP (J, I)
41 3      CONTINUE
42 4    CONTINUE
        END

        SUBROUTINE CROSSOVER (A, B, ILAND)
        INCLUDE GLOBAL
50      INTEGER CUT, A, B, ILAND
51      REAL RAND
52      EXTERNAL RAND
53      CUT = RAND ()*CHROMSIZE
54      TEMP = 0
55      DO 1, I=1,CUT
```

```
       TEMP = POPULATION(I, A, ILAND)
       POPULATION(I,A,ILAND) = POPULATION(I,B,ILAND)
       POPULATION(I, B, ILAND) = TEMP
1    CONTINUE
     END

     SUBROUTINE MUTATION (ILAND)
     INCLUDE GLOBAL
     INTEGER I, J, ILAND
     REAL RAND
     EXTERNAL RAND
     DO 2, I=1,SUBSIZE
       DO 1, J=1,CHROMSIZE
         IF (RAND() .LT. PMUT) THEN
           POPULATION (J,I, ILAND) = RAND()*MAXVAL
         ENDIF
1      CONTINUE
2    CONTINUE
     END

     SUBROUTINE SELECT (ILAND, INDX)
     INCLUDE GLOBAL
     REAL SUM, CHOICE, RAND
     INTEGER I, INDX, ILAND
     EXTERNAL RAND
     SUM = 0.0
     DO 1, I=1,SUBSIZE
       SUM = SUM + FITVAL (I, ILAND)
1    CONTINUE
     CHOICE = RAND() * SUM
     SUM = 0.0
     INDX = 0
2    INDX = INDX + 1
     SUM = SUM + FITVAL (INDX, ILAND)
     IF (SUM .LT. CHOICE) GOTO 2
     END

     SUBROUTINE NEWFIT (ILAND)
     INCLUDE GLOBAL
     INTEGER I, ILAND
     REAL FITNESS
     EXTERNAL FITNESS
     DO 1, I=1,SUBSIZE
       FITVAL (I, ILAND) = FITNESS ()
1    CONTINUE
     END
```

Figure 7.2: Example Fortran program: Genetic Algorithm

The next figure shows the analysed genetic algorithm of the previous figure. DPS are marked with a "parallel" comment (/*//*/). All other loops are not parallel. The sets with the label CONFLICT contains all usages of objects that cause the loop carried dependence. This analyzed program is the base for the PGA which is now under investigation.

```
      *** C-PROGRAM ***

float glob_fitval [10][10];
float glob_population [10][10][20];

         int j, i, iter;
         float size, epsilon, delta;
/*#03 */ read ("%e%d%e\n", &epsilon , &iter , &size);
/*#04 */ delta =2*epsilon;
/*#05 */ while (delta >epsilon)
          /* CONFLICT = glob_fitval [:][:],
                     glob_population [:][:][:]*/ {
/*#06 */  for /*//*/ (i = 0; i < 10; i++) {
           /* CONFLICT = glob_fitval [i][:],
                      glob_population [i][:][:]*/ {
/*#07 */   for (j = 0; j < iter ; j++)
/*=nextgen * * CONFLICT = glob_fitval [i][:],
                       glob_population [i ][:][:]*/
            { int i_1;
/*=repro */  /* CONFLICT = glob_population [i ][:][:]*/
             { int j, i_2, choice, temp [10][20];
/*#32 */      for /*//*/ (i_2 = 0; i_2 < 10; i_2++) {
/*=select */   { int i_3 ; float choice_4, sum ;
/*#73 */        sum = 0.;
                /* CONFLICT = sum */ {
/*#74 */         for (i_3 = 0; i_3 < 10; i_3++)
                 /* CONFLICT = sum */ {
/*#75 */          sum = sum + glob_fitval [i][i_3];
                 }
                }
/*#77 */        choice_4 = rand () * sum;
/*#78 */        sum = 0.;
/*#79 */        choice =0;
/*#80 */        do {
                 /* CONFLICT = sum ,choice */ {
/*#80 */          choice = choice + 1;
/*#81 */          sum = sum + glob_fitval [i][choice-1];
                 }
                } while (sum < choice_4);
               }
/*=repro */
/*#34 */       for /*//*/ (j = 0; j < 20; j++)
```

```
/*#35 */         temp [i_2][j] =
                       glob_population [i][choice-1][j];
                 }
/*#38 */         for /*//*/ (i_2 = 0; i_2 < 10; i_2++)
/*#39 */          for /*//*/ (j = 0; j < 20; j++)
/*#40 */           glob_population [i][i_2][j] =
                                             temp [i_2][j];
/*=nextgen */}
                /* CONFLICT = glob_population [i][*][*],
                              glob_population [i ][*][*]*/
                { int i_5 ;
/*#22 */         i_5 =5;
/*#22 */         for (i_1 = 0; i_1 < i_5 ; i_1++)
                  /* CONFLICT =
                          glob_population [i][i_1*2+1][*],
                          glob_population [i][i_1*2][*]*/
/*=crossover */{ int i_6, cut; float temp;
/*#53 */           cut = rand ()*20;
/*#54 */           temp =0;
/*#55 */           for /*//*/ (i_6 = 0; i_6 < cut ; i_6++) {
/*#56 */            temp = glob_population [i][i_1*2][i_6];
/*#57 */            glob_population [i][i_1*2][i_6]=
                     glob_population [i][i_1*2+1][i_6];
/*#58 */            glob_population [i][i_1*2+1][i_6] = temp;
                   }
/*=nextgen */  }
                }
/*=mutation*/{ float pmut; int j, i_7;
/*#63 */         for /*//*/ (i_7 = 0; i_7 < 10; i_7++)
/*#64 */          for /*//*/ (j = 0; j < 20; j++)
/*#65 */           if (rand ()<pmut)
/*#66 */            glob_population [i][i_7][j] = rand ()*8;
/*=nextgen */}
/*=newfit */ { int i_8 ;
/*#93 */         for /*//*/ (i_8 = 0; i_8 < 10; i_8++)
/*#94 */          glob_fitval [i ][i_8 ]=fitness ();
/*=nextgen*/ }
               }
              }
             }
/*#11 */ delta = ...
             }

}
```

Figure 7.3: The transformed program of Fig. 7.2

7.3 Conclusions

In this paper we introduced our concepts for automatic parallelizing and distributing sequential FORTRAN programs over the processors of a MIMD machine. We applied a variety of known concepts and described our concept for automatic data distribution.

Since this approach is now under investigation, we cannot generally state whether this approach has advantages over others or if it is manageable in a convenient way and leads to the expected results.

Automatic parallelization reaches its limits if some values cannot be determined at compile time. For such situations, annotations provided by the user give information about ranges of index variables and so on. With the combination of extensive automatic parallelization and user–specified constraints, the potential parallelism of a given program can, for the most part, be detected.

References

[1] Barbara M. Chapman, Piyush Mehrotra, and Hans Zima, "Programming in Vienna Fortran", *Scientific Programming*, vol. 1, Oct. 1992.

[2] M. Georges-Schleuter, "Genetic algorithms and population structures — a massively parallel algorithm", Technical report, University of Dortmund, 1990.

[3] Gina Goff, Ken Kennedy, and Chau-Wen Tseng, "Practical dependence testing", *in ACM SIGPLAN '91 Conference on Programming Language Design and Implementation*, Rice University, Houston, Texas, June 1991.

[4] David E. Goldberg, *Genetic Algorithm in Search, Optimization, and Machine Learning*, Addison–Wesley, 1989.

[5] Manish Gupta and Prithviraj Banerjee, "Automatic data partitioning on distributed memory multiprocessors", Technical Report UILU-ENG-90-2248, University of Illinos, Oct. 1990.

[6] Manish Gupta and Prithviraj Banerjee, "Demonstration of automatic data partitioning techniques for parallelizing compilers on multicomputers", *IEEE Transactions on Parallel and Distributed Sytems*, vol. 3, Mar. 1992.

[7] Paul Havlak and Ken Kennedy, "An implementation on interprocedural bounded regular section analysis", *IEEE Transactions on Parallel and Distributed Sytems*, vol. 2, July 1991.

[8] Seema Hiranandani, Ken Kennedy, and Chau-Wen Tseng, "Compiler support for machine–independent parallel programming in Fortran D", Technical Report COMP TR91–149, Department of Computer Science, Rice University, Jan. 1991.

[9] Seema Hiranandani, Ken Kennedy, and Chau-Wen Tseng, "Compiler optimization for Fortran D on MIMD distributed–memory machines", Technical report, Department of Computer Science, Rice University.

[10] Kathleen Knobe, Joan D. Lukas, and Guy L. Steele, "Data optimization: Allocation of arrays to reduce communication on SIMD machines", *Journal of Parallel and Distributed Computing*, 1990.

[11] Kathleen Knobe, Joan D. Lukas, and Guy L. Steele, "Massively parallel data optimization", *in The 2nd Symposium on the Frontiers of Massively Parallel Computation*, Fairfax, Virginia, Oct. 1988.

[12] Kathleen Knobe and Venkataraman Natarajan, "Data optimization: Minimizing residual interprocessor data motion on SIMD machines", *in The 3rd Symposium on the Frontiers of Massively Parallel Computation*, College Park, Maryland, Oct. 1990.

[13] Kathleen Knobe and Venkataraman Natarajan, "Data allocation to minimize data motion on SIMD machines", *in The 3rd Symposium of the Frontiers of Massively Parallel Computation*, College Park, Maryland, Oct. 1990.

[14] Jingke Li and Marina Chen, "Index domain alignment: Minimizing cost of cross-referencing between distributed arrays", Technical Report YALEU/DCS/TR-725, Department of Computer Science, Yale University, Nov. 1989.

[15] Nashat Mansour and Geoffrey C. Fox, "Parallel physical optimization algorithms for allocating data to multicomputer nodes", Technical report, School of Computer and Information Science, and Syracuse Center for Computational Science, Syracuse University, 1992.

[16] Mühlenbein, "Evolution in time and space – the parallel genetic algorithm", in G. Rawlins, editor, *Foundations of Genetic Algorithms*. Morgan–Kaufman, 1991.

[17] Mühlenbein, "Parallel genetic algorithms in combinatorial optimization", in Osman Balci, editor, *Computer Science and Operation Research*. Pergamon Press, 1992.

[18] Heinz Mühlenbein, M. Schomisch, and J. Born, "The parallel genetic algorithm as function optimizer", *Parallel Computing*, vol. 17, 1991.

[19] Cherri M. Pancake and Donna Bergmark, "Do parallel languages respond to the needs of scientific programmers?", *IEEE Computer*, vol. 23, Dec. 1990.

[20] SNAP, *The Power*, Logic Records, 1990.

[21] Friedrich-Wilhelm Schröer, "Gentle", Technical Report 166, GMD, Birlinghoven, Germany, Aug. 1989, in: W.M.Waite, J. Grosch, F.–W. Schröer, Three Compiler Specifications.

[22] Friedrich-Wilhelm Schröer, "Gentle language specification", Technical Report to appear, GMD, Birlinghoven, Germany, 1993.

[23] R.M.Stallmann, "Using and porting GNU CC", Technical report, Free Software Foundation, June 1989.

[24] Skef Wholey, "Automatic data mapping for distributed-memory parallel computers", Technical Report CMU-91-121, Carnegie Mellon University, 1991.

8 Knowledge–Based Automatic Parallelization by Pattern Recognition

Christoph W. Keßler
GRADUIERTENKOLLEG INFORMATIK
SAARBRÜCKEN UNIVERSITY, GERMANY
email: kessler@cs.uni-sb.de

Abstract: We present the top–down design of a new system which performs automatic parallelization of numerical Fortran77, Fortran90 or C source programs for execution on distributed–memory message–passing multiprocessors such as e.g. the INTEL iPSC/860 or the TMC CM–5.

The key idea is a high–level pattern matching approach which in some useful way permits partial reverse–engineering of a wide class of numerical programs. With only a few hundred patterns, we will be able to completely match many important numerical algorithms. This is also applicable to so-called dusty deck sources that may be 'encrypted' by various former machine-specific optimizations.

We show how successful pattern matching enables safe algorithm replacement and allows more exact prediction of the performance of the parallelized target code than usually possible. Together with mathematical background knowledge and parallel compiler engineering, this opens access to a new potential for automatic parallelization that has never been exploited before.

8.1 Introduction and Overview

Current distributed memory multiprocessers are hard to program. Predicting the performance of a nontrivial parallel program is not easy either. Thus it is a natural consequence to leave as much as possible of this – often tedious – work to an optimizing parallelizing compiler. The programmer just wants to feed in the sequential program and get out optimized parallel code.

Today, truly automatic parallelization is yet a dream (and some people believe it will remain so forever). Currently, research on automatic methods appears rather at the border of compilers for parallel programming languages for distributed memory systems, e.g. [7] for Fortran D ([20]) or [10, 11] for Vienna Fortran 90 ([9]).

The state of the art in both parallelizing compilers and compilers for parallel programming languages for distributed memory multiprocessors is semiautomatic parallelization: The programmer supplies the compiler with array distribution specifications (e.g. interactively, as in SUPERB ([15]) or in the form of compiler directives, as in Fortran D), and, generally, transforms the program himself in order to efficiently make use of machine–specific properties (e.g., buffer sizes, message protocols, processor distances and so on). The job of the compiler is to insert masks and communication statements according to the distribution specifications. Automatic optimization of masks and communication is possible in a limited way (see [15]).

The semi-automatic approach enables the programmer to write his code in the single–program–multiple–data programming paradigm which is well suited for scientific (numeric) applications. However, the efficiency of the generated parallel code is heavily dependent on the chosen data distribution.

This user interaction seems inevitable since the problem of determining optimal array distributions is a hard one, and only the user seems to possess sufficient knowledge about his program in order to decide which distributions to choose and how to transform his code to maintain parallel program efficiency.

However, for large application programs with lots of arrays and complex distribution relations between them, this becomes impracticable because the user cannot solve this optimization problem either. Moreover, detailed knowledge of the target machine must be available at this step, and different parts of the application program may require different data partitioning schemes to perform efficiently. Where may redistribution be useful, and where not? Furthermore, the quality of a given data distribution is also dependent on the underlying hardware. There is no automatic guidance in choosing suitable code transformations for better utilization of hardware properties. Changing the hardware platform means also repeating the whole parallelization procedure. Should an average user — who is, in general, not an expert in parallel computing — really care about all this stuff?

Recently some research has been done on automatic derivation of data distribution ([24, 17, 29, 37, 21]), but we are missing a really automatic approach which leaves no partial work to the programmer any more and requires no user interaction.

Some recent research has recommended to apply pattern recognition techniques on a quite low level to facilitate parallelization and optimizations ([17, 33, 10, 11]). We claim that pattern matching can be usefully applied to entire programs as the *core* of an automatic parallelization system. Only high–level pattern recognition will enable knowledge-based program transformations by decrypting the meaning of the program which is often hidden past recognition within the source code by former target–specific transformations and programming styles.

Earlier approaches have suggested to apply program concept recognition to guide vectorization ([5, 4]) and parallelization ([6, 36, 11]) but have not been developed further. The PAT system performs concept recognition for non-numerical codes (see [18, 27]). However, pattern recognition techniques have never been applied on a large scale in a 'fully automatic' parallelization system.

How can pattern recognition techniques be motivated? In order to answer this question, we have examined lots of numerical application algorithms that are typically run on distributed memory multiprocessors, e.g. the algorithms considered in [32] or the algorithms occurring in a parallel numerics course [30]. These algorithms contain basic linear algebra subroutines (see also [28, 12]), direct solvers for linear equation systems (such as Gaussian Elimination, LU, QR or Cholesky decomposition), Simplex, iterative linear equation solvers (such as Jacobi, Gauß–Seidel, JOR, SOR and Conjugate–Gradient solver), fixpoint iterations (e.g. square–rooting a matrix), grid relaxations (used e.g. for numerical solution of differential equations), interpolation problems, numerical integration and differentiation, and multigrid algorithms[1].

We observed that these numerical algorithms are made up of only a few (around 100) characteristic programming schemes (called *patterns*) such as e.g. vector and matrix operations, simple recurrences, relaxation operations or simple reduction operations. We describe these patterns in more detail in section 8.3.

We claim that these few patterns cover a broad range of numerical application codes that are actually run on distributed–memory multiprocessors. We exemplify this in section 8.3 by examining the source codes of actual application programs.

Faced with these real–world codes, the pattern matcher must be robust against semantics preserving code transformations, in order to maintain acceptability. In general, there are several different possibilities (called *templates*) to implement a specific pattern. Thus a pattern is, in some way, a normal form of all its templates. The job of pattern matching is to compare a given piece of the source program with the templates, to choose the corresponding pattern and to replace this program piece by an instance of that pattern. We will describe our pattern matching algorithm in detail in section 8.4.

Once this pattern recognition tool performs well, the rest is quite simple: locally find out what the programmer's intention was, and then select well–suited and highly optimized target code for this piece of the application. If necessary, these code pieces must be connected by appropriate redistribution operations.

The remaining sections describe the other components of our parallelization system called PARAMAT ("PARallelize Automatically by pattern MATching") that use the pattern matcher's output in order to generate efficient parallel code.

8.2 Preprocessing the Source Code

It is very important that the program is rather explicit when it is submitted to automatic parallelization by pattern matching. Beyond a sophisticated dependence analysis, a pass of preparing code transformations[2] should be carried out in order to facilitate pattern recognition. Often, semantics preserving code modifications had been applied to Fortran codes to optimize sequential or pipelined execution. However, this made the code less readable, and for pattern recognition, they impose unnecessary barriers which must be removed[3] by the following transformations:

1. **procedure inlining**[4]

[1]We have focussed in this work on algorithms operating on rectangular dense real matrices. Our approach may easily be extended to other matrix types (e.g., banded, blocked, triangular; complex).

[2]For a detailed description of optimizing transformations, see e.g. [39].

[3]We remind that such optimizations may be re-inserted later on at code generation time – well-tailored to the parallel target machine.

[4]This is only for a prototype version of PARAMAT in order to make the implementation easier. Interprocedural analysis is currently evolving, and we will include interprocedural analysis tools into the final system as soon as they become adequately reliable. Our case studies have shown that for purely numerical programs, procedure inlining will blow up program size by only a small constant factor. Since this only appears at compile time, it can be tolerated.

2. **constant propagation**

   Example: Consider the following situation:

```
N = 1024
.....
NP1 = N + 1
.....
```

   Such constructs are widely used to enforce the compiler to use registers or to avoid recomputation of often–needed common constant subexpressions. Here, `N + 1` should be replaced by its actual value 1025. This propagates information about the constant values into the 'interior' of the program where it is needed at the pattern recognition phase.

3. **induction variable recognition** (substitution, if possible)

   Induction variables are integer variables used to abbreviate array indexing expressions. They often are introduced into program codes to optimize address calculation time and to enforce the compiler to use address registers for these expressions.

   Example: Consider the following code fragment:

```
      DO 20 J=2,NC
       JF=J+J
       DO 10 I=2,NC
        IF1=I+I
        FC(I,J)=2*(FF(IF1,JF)-4.0*UF(IF1,JF)+UF(IF1,JF-1)
     *              + UF(IF1-1,JF)+UF(IF1+1,JF)+UF(IF1,JF+1))
10     CONTINUE
20    CONTINUE
```

   The introduction of the induction variables `JF` and `IF1` saves many integer multiplications by 2 but hides important information from the pattern recognition phase. For this reason, the induction variables must be substituted away by propagating their values `2*J` and `2*I`, respectively.

4. **temporary variable recognition** (substitution if possible)

   Temporary variables have often be inserted into a program only to denote common subexpressions, to enforce use of a data register for that variable or just to make the code more readable. In such a case, the variable may be substituted away.

   Example: Consider the following matrix multiplication code:

```
do i=1,64
 do j=1,64
  temp(i,j) = 0.0
  do k=1,64
   temp = temp + a(i,k) * b(k,j)
```

```
    enddo
    c(i,j) = temp
   enddo
  enddo
```

The variable `temp` can be recognized as temporary and substituted away by `c(i,j)` since the value of `temp` is not used further.

5. **dead code elimination**

   Example: In the example above, the assignment to `c(i,j)` changes into `c(i,j) = c(i,j)` which is redundant and can be removed.

6. **conversion of GOTO's** into if–then–else or while statements, where possible.

   This feature concerning especially old (Fortran77) codes is important since GOTO's cannot be handled by the current version of the pattern recognition tool.

7. **IF-outermosting**

   An IF statement checking a condition not depending on the index of the surrounding loop (after induction variable detection!) should be moved before this loop.

8. **array simplification**

   Each array A containing a dimension d with an extent e_d^A smaller than 16 will be splitted into e_d^A different arrays $A1, \ldots, Ad$ of dimensionality $d-1$ each.[5]

9. **loop distribution**

   If not prevented by data dependency cycles, this transformation supplies the pattern recognition phase with handy, small, mostly perfectly nested loops.

   Example:

```
do i=1,128                       do i=1,128
 do j=1,256                        do j=1,256
  c(i,j)=b(j)*c(i,j)    ---->       c(i,j)=b(j)*c(i,j)
 enddo                             enddo
 a(i)=c(i,1)                     enddo
enddo                            do i=1,128
                                   a(i)=c(i,1)
                                 enddo
```

Furthermore we disallow constructs causing run–time dependencies which cannot be recognized by the prototype version of PARAMAT. This especially concerns index vectors, so programs containing indirect array references will be rejected just at the beginning. For these cases, dynamic techniques must be applied (see e.g. [34]). In this work we restrict ourselves to static parallelization.

[5]Loops stepping through dimension d of A must then be completely unrolled (i.e., replicated $E_d^A - 1$ times) and the Aj must be inserted instead of the $A[j]$. If there arise compile–time–unknown factors in A's indexing, or if loops step through this dimension in an irregular manner, this transformation will not be possible.

8.3 Which Patterns are Supported?

Now, let us describe which patterns should be included into the pattern library of PARAMAT. On the one hand, we want to cover a very high percentage of numerical programs, on the other hand we must not use too many patterns, leading to inacceptable compile times.

The basic algorithms considered in [32] and [30] suggest that a rather small number of patterns will suffice to cover large parts — especially the time–critical ones — of real application programs. In order to exemplify this assumption, we took a closer look to some real–world codes (after being normalized by the transformations described in the last section):

- the Livermore Loops (cf. [31]),
- some kernels from the NAS Benchmark program (cf. [1]),
- a LU decomposition code from the netlib,
- a least–square Conjugate Gradient solver[6] from [30],
- two multigrid programs,
- selected codes from the Perfect Club Benchmarks (especially from the programs FLO52, SPEC77 and DYFESM, see also [3]).
- and others.

Faced with these codes, we created appropriate patterns, subpatterns and templates while carefully making the patterns robust against many possible semantics–preserving code modifications. The result of this research, the current version of the Basic PARAMAT Library, unfortunately cannot presented here for lack of space, but it is listed in [23]. A brief summary of the patterns is given in Tab. 8.1. Some ideas for the efficient distributed–memory parallel implementation of all the patterns occurring in these algorithms are summarized in [32].

As one can see from Tab. 8.1, the number of low–level patterns (expression and statement level) is rather limited; so is the number of medium–level patterns (loop level, e.g. vector instructions). The number of medium–level patterns can additionally be restricted by maintaining loop normal forms generated by loop distribution; we will discuss this following the example of section 8.4.4. The most critical point is how many *high*–level patterns (and which) to include in the library; they are often too specific to include them into the Basic Library. This question will later be alleviated by introducing a modular concept where the pattern library may be individually composed from the basic and other more specific sub–libraries in a hierarchically organized database.

With the current version of the Basic Pattern Library — containing only 120 patterns — we are able to cover *completely* (and thus, to parallelize automatically) a lot of the

[6] E.g. the main patterns generally contained in CG–algorithms are CGINIT$^{(1)}$, MV$^{(2)}$ or VM$^{(2)}$ (vector–matrix multiply), VADD$^{(1)}$, VADDMUL$^{(1)}$ (vector instructions), SSP$^{(1)}$(standard scalar product) and SV$^{(1)}$ (scalar–vector multiply).

order	patterns	number
0	scalar arithm. operations, init, max, min, swap, assign, read write	20
	MULTIADD/-MUL, difference stars and substars (first and second order)	5
1	vector instructions, v-init/-assign/-copy/-swap, v-read/write, SV	16
	reductions: v-sum, scalarproducts, vector norms	8
	reductions: vector maximization/minimizations	6
	1D relaxation steps (Jacobi, Gauss–Seidel)	2
	first order linear recurrences	2
	intermediate forms of 1D convolution	2
2	matrix operations, m-init/-assign/-copy, m-read/-write, SM	12
	vector/matrix multiplication patterns	4
	2D-reductions: m-sum, concurrent v-sum, matrix norms	5
	2D-reductions: m-max/min, row/col-max/min	8
	2D relaxation steps (Jacobi, Gauss–Seidel, ...)	4
	global matrix updates (GJstep, GRstep,..., Mreduce)	6
	1D convolution; intermediate forms of 2D convolution	4
3	matrix multiplication	2
	matrix inversion, Gaussian elimination	2
	intermediate forms of 2D convolution	2
4	2D convolution	1

Table 8.1 A brief summary of the patterns included into the current version of the Basic PARAMAT Pattern Library. No pattern has more than four different templates, most patterns have only one or two. All BLAS routines operating on dense real matrices have been entered.

basic numerical codes from [32] and [30], e.g. Gaussian Elimination (with pivoting), LU decomposition, Simplex, Jacobi relaxation, Gauß–Seidel relaxation, JOR, SOR and CG, iteratively square–rooting a matrix, and others. The results for the Livermore Loops are given in Tab. 8.2. We obtained similar results for the other application codes listed above.

8.4 Pattern Recognition: A Detailed View

Pattern Matching is done in a rather intuitive way. It is supported by a suitable hierarchical representation of the input program and the complexity is diminished by a suitable hierarchical ordering of all patterns. For each template of each pattern there exists a small procedure which tests whether a given piece of program matches this pattern (i.e., an *occurrence* of this pattern), and if yes, it returns an *instance* of this pattern where the formal pattern parameters (*slots*) are bound to the corresponding actual parameters (*slot entries*) occurring in the program piece. [7]

[7] A formal definition of patterns, templates, occurrences, and instances is given in [23].

LL	name	recognized patterns	*lp*	*lr*
1	Hydrofragment	GVOP$^{(1)}$	1	1
3	Inner Product	SSP$^{(1)}$	1	1
5	tri-diag. elim., below diag.	FOLRO$^{(1)}$	1	1
8	A.D.I Integration	VHSTAR$^{(1)}$(3x), GVOP$^{(1)}$(3x)	6	6
9	Numerical Integration	GVOP$^{(1)}$	1	1
10	Numerical Differentiation	GVOP$^{(1)}$	19	19
11	First Sum	FOLR$^{(1)}$	1	1
12	First Difference	VHSTAR$^{(1)}$	1	1
13	2D particle in a cell	VCOPY$^{(1)}$(4x),VADD$^{(1)}$(2x),GVOP$^{(1)}$(4x)	17	10
14	1D particle in a cell	GVOP$^{(1)}$(3x),VCOPY$^{(1)}$(1x),VADD$^{(1)}$(2x)	12	6
18	2D explicit hydrodyn. fragm.	MADDMUL$^{(2)}$(2x)	6	2
21	Matrix Product	MMO$^{(3)}$	1	1
22	Planckian Distribution	GVOP$^{(1)}$(2x)	2	2
23	2D implicit hydrodyn. fragm.	MGAUSSSEIDEL$^{(2)}$	1	1
24	1D Minimization	VMINLOC$^{(1)}$	1	1

Table 8.2 Analysis of the Livermore Loops: currently recognizable patterns. *lp* denotes the number of loops (*lp*) (after applying loop distribution) occurring in a kernel. *lr* indicates how many of these can be covered by patterns from the current version of the PARAMAT Library. GVOP$^{(1)}$ denotes a general vector operation, FOLRO$^{(1)}$ and FOLR$^{(1)}$ first order linear recurrences, VHSTAR$^{(1)}$ a 1D difference star; VMINLOC$^{(1)}$ finds in a vector the location with minimal absolute value.

8.4.1 Program Representation

The source program is represented by an attributed syntax tree. The nodes are control statements (`do`, `if`, etc.), assignment statements, or expression operators ($+, -, *, /$ etc.). There is one root node called `main` which represents the highest program control level.

We distinguish between two kinds of directed edges between nodes:

1. *vertical edges:* these are the edges contained in the syntax tree representation of the program, e.g. from all statement nodes corresponding to the body of a `do` statement to the `do` node, from the `then` resp. `else` statement nodes to the corresponding `if` node, from expression tree nodes to their parent nodes and so on.

2. *cross edges:* these edges establish a partial execution order among several child nodes of the same parent node; they are caused by data dependency. If there might

exist a loop–independent[8] data dependence from a statement S_1 to another statement S_2, then a cross edge e must be drawn in the following way: Let v be the lowest common vertical successor of both S_1 and S_2, and let u_1, u_2 be direct vertical predecessors (*'son statements'*) of v such that u_1 is a vertical successor of S_1 (but not of S_2) and u_2 is a vertical successor of S_2 (but not of S_1), see the figure below:

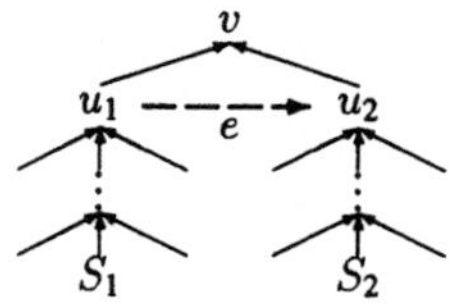

Then the cross edge e must be drawn from u_1 to u_2, implying a partial execution order on the son statements of v. Note that S_1 may be equal to u_1 and S_2 equal to u_2. If $S_1 = S_2$ then there is no edge necessary, of course. If it is not clear at compile time which of several statements is the source of a dependence, then all of them are to be connected with the target node by the way just described. The order among these possible source nodes must be maintained by inserting cross edges following the textual order of the statements in the source program.

Thus the vertical edges form a tree while the cross edges form a directed acyclic graph on each control hierarchy level. For an example, see section 8.4.4.

The cross edges may be extremely useful when trying to recognize patterns from subpatterns which are textually separated by other pieces of code not affecting the relations between these subpatterns. In such "intermixed" computations, statements that belong together (to the same computation thread) are connected by cross edges.

8.4.2 Pattern Hierarchy Graph

The Pattern Hierarchy Graph (PHG) consists of all possible predefined patterns as its nodes. There is a directed edge from one pattern p_1 to another pattern p_2 if p_1 may occur as a subpattern of p_2 (see Fig. 8.1 for an example). Thus the PHG is acyclic.

Each pattern has an *order* number which indicates how many loop nests it contains. Thus an edge from p_1 to p_2 in the PHG implies that $order(p_1) \leq order(p_2)$.

The PHG is called *complete* for a pattern p if it contains p and all possible subpatterns p_i of p and is complete for all p_i.

Usually, a pattern has only a few predecessors and a few successors in the PHG. The pattern matching algorithm only needs to inspect the PHG successor's templates of an already matched pattern p when looking for a possible pattern containing p as a subpattern. That results in a large increase in matching speed compared with simple testing of all predefined templates.

[8] We do not consider loop–carried dependences here because all patterns provided so far allow dependence cycles only from a statement to itself. This is sufficient for most applications if we have applied the restructuring transformations listed in section 8.2 before.

8.4.3 The Matching Algorithm

Starting with *stmtdescend(root)*, the matching algorithm descends the syntax tree as follows:

---

function *stmtdescend(node)*
if *node* is not a leaf **then forall** sons s of *node* (in textual order) **do** *stmtdescend*(s) **od fi**
forall expressions e occurring in *node* **do** *exprdescend*(e) **od**
/⋆ now all vertical predecessors (substatements, subexpressions) of *node* are known ⋆/
/⋆ possible patterns p for *node* are all direct PHG successors (superpatterns)
  of the patterns already computed for the sons s of *node* ⋆/
forall possible patterns p for *node*
do test by *match(p,node)* whether there is an instance q of p that matches *node* **od**
replace *node* by q just computed;
reset pointers to and from *node* correctly;
repeat
  forall direct cross predecessors x of *node* in this block
  do /⋆ x has been visited earlier than *node* ⋆/
    test by *merge*(x,*node*) whether there is an instance y
    of a pattern that consists exactly of x and *node*
  od
  replace x and *node* by y just computed;
  reset edges to or from x and *node* to or from y, respectively;
  rename y by *node*
until there are no mergeable predecessors for *node* left.
end *stmtdescend*()

The function *exprdescend*() traverses the expression trees in a similar way.

Each node of the syntax tree is visited exactly once. For each matched node, there is only a constant number of possibilities for choosing a superpattern, and these are tested deterministically one after another, until one of them matches or all fail. Successful matching along a vertical edge or along a cross edge reduces the number of inner nodes in the syntax tree. Thus, the entire algorithm runs in linear time.

This pattern matcher is similar to other bottom–up pattern matching algorithms such as used in automatically generated code generators, e.g. BURG ([14]), TXL ([8]) or OPTRAN ([38]). These systems automatically[9] generate a tree automaton whose state table – if deterministic – corresponds roughly to our PHG. Unfortunately, all automatic systems work only on (syntax) trees; this disables matching along cross edges as required here. Another advantage of our simple pattern matcher is that it can locally deviate from the general scheme to save patterns and matching time, such as we do e.g. for matching difference stars. The high degree of flexibility required for our purpose cannot be supplied by current tree pattern matching kits.

[9] This would make the pattern specification easier if there were many intermediate patterns which only propagate information upwards and never occur in a final matched program. But this does not really occur in our case.

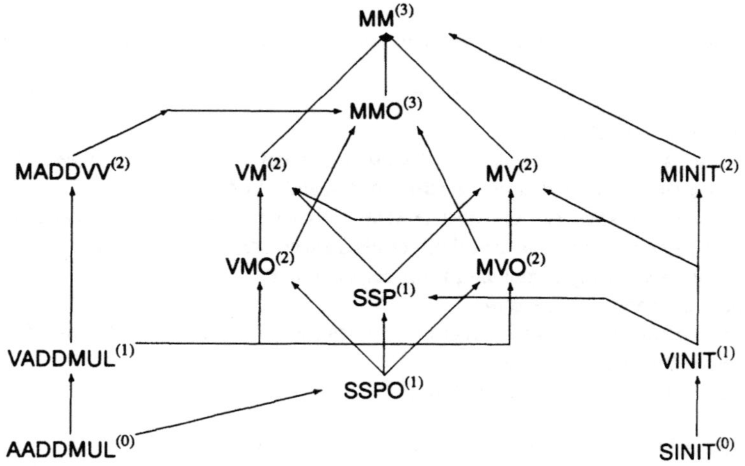

Figure 8.1 The pattern hierarchy graph of Matrix Multiplication. It covers all possible ways how matrix multiplication may be coded without using an auxiliary variable.

8.4.4 Standard Pattern Matching: A simple example

Let us start with a simple example. Matrix multiplication is well suited for this purpose since it is not so trivial but is not made up of too many subpatterns so that its pattern hierarchy graph (Fig. 8.1) remains quite handy.

Suppose the programmer has coded a matrix multiplication in the following way:

```
do i=1,n
  do j=1,m
S1: c(i,j)=0.0
  enddo
  do j=1,m
    do k=1,r
S2:   c(i,j)=c(i,j)+a(i,k)*b(k,j)
    enddo
  enddo
enddo
```

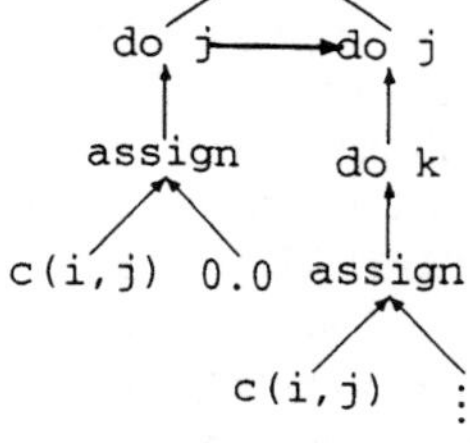

The pattern matcher traverses the syntax tree (see above) by a leftmost depth–first–search. First the assignment node corresponding to S1 will be replaced by the pattern instance `SINIT (c,i,j, 0.0)` since this is the leftmost leaf of the syntax tree (determined by the cross edge caused by the data flow dependence from S1 to S2).

Pursuing this back towards the root, the `do j` loop around S1 will be matched with the SINIT$^{(0)}$ node, resulting in a new pattern instance `VINIT(c(i,*), j,m, 0.0)` (vector initialization).

Then the algorithm descends further towards S2, replaces the assignment statement leaf corresponding to S2 by a pattern instance `AADDMUL(c(i,j),a(i,k),b(k,j))` (accumulatively adding products) and, following the suitable edge in the PHG, merges this with the `do k` loop yielding an SSPO$^{(1)}$ instance (standard scalar product with offset). Now the program corresponding to the modified syntax tree looks as follows:

```
do i=1,n
  VINIT(c(i,*),j,m,0.0)
  do j=1,m
   SSPO(c(i,j),a(i,*),b(*,j),k,r)
  enddo
enddo
```

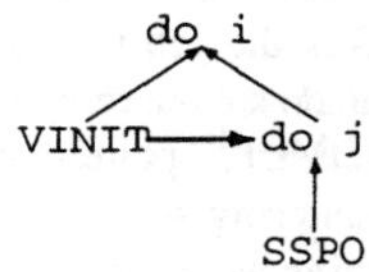

The `do j` loop can be merged with the SSPO$^{(1)}$ instance resulting in an instance `VMO (c(i,*), a(i,*),b, k,r, j,m)` (vector–matrix multiply with offset). Now the VINIT$^{(1)}$ instance is a mergeable cross predecessor of the VMO$^{(2)}$ instance. Merging them yields a new pattern instance `VM (c(i,*), a(i,*),b, k,r, j,m)` (vector–matrix multiply), which, in turn, can be matched with the `do i` loop resulting in an instance `MM(c,a,b, k,r,j,m,i,n)` (matrix multiply) representing this entire piece of code.

We remark that in this small example, no loop distribution had been applied before. This did not matter since the PHG covers all sensible codings of matrix multiplication, with and without loops being distributed, at the expense of a few more patterns and edges in the PHG. In general, we will have to test whether it is more useful to put more intelligence into the PHG (and thus, perhaps, wasting some space and (compile) time), or to rely on non–failing basic transformations such as loop distribution.

It is clearly no problem to include FORTRAN90's array features and intrinsic array manipulation functions. These just occur as additional templates of their corresponding PARAMAT patterns.

The pattern matcher of PARAMAT is able to detect and undo several former machine-specific optimizations that 'encrypt' the meaning of the code, such as redundant IF conditions, loop blocking, loop unrolling, statement reordering and expression reordering. The next subsections give some examples.

8.4.5 Removing redundant IF statements

This example is taken from the MATMUL routine of the Perfect Club Benchmark program DYFESM (see also [3]) and has already been prepared for pattern matching by the techniques of section 8.2:

```
      DO 400 K = 1, N
        DO 100 I = 1, L
          C(I,K) = 0.0
100     CONTINUE
```

```
          DO 300 J = 1, M
            IF (B(J,K) .NE. 0.) THEN
            DO 200 I = 1, L
              C(I,K) = C(I,K) + A(I,J)*B(J,K)
200         CONTINUE
300       CONTINUE
400     CONTINUE
```

The program author has inserted the IF statement during former optimizations. In our case, however, the IF statement - which is obviously redundant regarding semantics - makes the job for pattern recognition unnecessarily harder. But it is no problem to eliminate such a redundant IF statement if we just add a self cycle in the PHG from the VADDMUL$^{(1)}$ pattern to itself which leaves the VADDMUL$^{(1)}$ instance unchanged when encountering such an IF condition on one of the operands. After that, we can proceed matching as in the example above.

8.4.6 Loop Rerolling

Since the BLAS routines ([28, 12]) are widely used, it is very important that they are completely recognized by our tool.

Matching has there additionally been made difficult by loop unrolling. Unrolling can appear

- as **replication at the expression level.**

  For an example, consider the following level-1-BLAS routine (after the preprocessing of section 8.2)[10]:

```
      dtemp = 0.0d0
      do 30 i = 1,mod(n,6)
        dtemp = dtemp + dabs(dx(i))
   30 continue
      do 50 i = mod(n,6) + 1, n, 6
        dtemp = dtemp + dabs(dx(i))   + dabs(dx(i+1))
     *              + dabs(dx(i+2)) + dabs(dx(i+3))
     *              + dabs(dx(i+4)) + dabs(dx(i+5))
   50 continue
```

  The original vector sum has been unrolled 5 times for some reason and written as one single expression. To recognize loop 50 as an occurrence of the VSUM$^{(1)}$ pattern, we must reroll the loop, i.e. undo the former optimization.

[10] At the pattern matching stage, n may be known by constant propagation, and so were `mod(n,6)`. If this expression were zero, then the cleanup loop would disappear. For simplicity let us assume here that n is either unknown at compile–time (symbolic constant), or that n is greater than 6 and `mod(n,6)` is not zero.

Technically, we handle such long right-hand-side expressions by a pattern called MULTIADD$^{(0)}$. MULTIADD($k, s_1, \ldots, s_k$) matches a sum of k expressions whose order in summation does not matter[11]. The operands are ordered lexically in the MULTIADD$^{(0)}$ instance. In the example above, this yields that the `dabs(dx(i))` operands appear in ascending order. MULTIADD$^{(0)}$ may refine (specialize) to several other patterns, e.g. here to an accumulating adding sequence AASUM$^{(0)}$. Matching then proceeds via the `i` loop to the corresponding vector instruction VAASUMO$^{(1)}$, and this finally collapses to VSUMO$^{(1)}$ via a refining PHG edge:

```
VSUM(i,1,mod(n,6),1, dtemp,dx(i), abs)
VSUMO(i,mod(n,6)+1,n,1, dtemp,dx(i), abs)
```

Via new PHG edges from VSUMO$^{(1)}$ and VSUM$^{(1)}$ to VSUM$^{(1)}$, these two instances can easily be merged.

- as **replication at the statement level.**

  Consider e.g. the following level-1-BLAS routine (after the preprocessing of section 8.2)[12]:

```
      do 30 i = 1,mod(n,4)
        dy(i) = dy(i) + da*dx(i)
   30 continue
      do 50 i = mod(n,4)+1,n,4
        dy(i)   = dy(i)   + da*dx(i)
        dy(i+1) = dy(i+1) + da*dx(i+1)
        dy(i+2) = dy(i+2) + da*dx(i+2)
        dy(i+3) = dy(i+3) + da*dx(i+3)
   50 continue
```

The original daxpy loop has been unrolled 3 times for some reason. To recognize this as an occurrence of the VADDMUL$^{(1)}$ pattern, we must reroll the loop. Loop distribution and pattern matching as before generate

```
VADDMUL(1,mod(n,4),1, dy,da,dx)
VADDMUL(mod(n,4)+1,n,4, dy,da,dx)
VADDMUL(mod(n,4)+2,n,4, dy,da,dx)
VADDMUL(mod(n,4)+3,n,4, dy,da,dx)
VADDMUL(mod(n,4)+4,n,4, dy,da,dx)
```

Now we must first merge the last four VADDMUL$^{(1)}$ instances to get

[11] This is sometimes a problem in FORTRAN since addition or multiplication is in general not commutative, sometimes even not associative for FORTRAN reals. We however remind that (1) this is only for easier pattern recognition, and the original operand order may be rearranged at code generation time, and (2) this problem is also ignored for many parallelizing transformations such as summing up the VSUM operands in a tree-like fashion for parallel execution.

[12] For simplicity let us assume again that n is symbolic or greater than 4 and mod(n,4) is not zero.

```
VADDMUL(1,mod(n,4),1, dy,da,dx)
VADDMUL(mod(n,4)+1,n,1, dy,da,dx)
```

this is technically arranged by a self-cycle in the PHG from $\mathsf{VADDMUL}^{(1)}$ to itself[13]. After that, it is no problem to merge these two instances into a single $\mathsf{VADDMUL}^{(1)}$ instance via another PHG-self-cycle for $\mathsf{VADDMUL}^{(1)}$.

- as **blocking at the loop level** (also known as strip mining (one-dimensional) or tiling (more-dimensional)).

  This often occurs in old codes which have been tuned for efficient use of caches or vector registers (see e.g. [22]). For daxpy, this looks as follows:

```
   if( mod(n,k) .ne. 0 ) then
   do 30 i = 1,mod(n,k)
     dy(i) = dy(i) + da*dx(i)
30 continue
   do 50 i = mod(n,k)+1,n,k
    do 40 j=i,i+k-1
     dy(j) = dy(j) + da*dx(j)
40  continue
50 continue
```

  Here matching of the second loop nest is also enabled via a PHG self-cycle of the $\mathsf{VADDMUL}^{(1)}$ pattern[14]:

```
   VADDMUL(i,1,mod(n,k),1, dy,da,dx)
   do 50 i = mod(n,k)+1,n,k
    VADDMUL(j,i,i+k-1,1, dy,da,dx)
50 continue
```

  Via this PHG edge, the second $\mathsf{VADDMUL}^{(1)}$ instance merges with the `i` loop into

```
VADDMUL(i,1,mod(n,k),1, dy,da,dx)
VADDMUL(i,mod(n,k),n,1, dy,da,dx)
```

  which then collapses into a single $\mathsf{VADDMUL}^{(1)}$ as in the previous example.

Using these techniques, we can completely match the Level 1 BLAS routines:

[13] More exactly: there is an auxiliary 'collecting' pattern for $\mathsf{VADDMUL}^{(1)}$ (and, correspondingly, also for other patterns such as $\mathsf{VADD}^{(1)}$, $\mathsf{VSUM}^{(1)}$, ...) which just tries to merge 'similar' $\mathsf{VADDMUL}^{(1)}$ instances and which is also robust against changes in the order of the sequence of $\mathsf{VADDMUL}^{(1)}$ instances within the program representation. It is also possible to have the cleanup loop at the end of the sequence, as in [22].

[14] For simplicity, let us assume again that the value of `mod(n,k)` is unknown at compile time or not zero.

BLAS1 routine	pattern covering this routine
dasum	VSUM$^{(1)}$(with abs flag set)
daxpy	VADDMUL$^{(1)}$
dcopy	VCOPY$^{(1)}$
ddot	VSUM$^{(1)}$
dnrm2	ENORM$^{(1)}$
drot	VROT$^{(1)}$
drotg	(scalar computation)
dscal	SV$^{(1)}$
dswap	VSWAP$^{(1)}$
idamax	VMAXLOC$^{(1)}$(with abs flag set)

8.4.7 Difference Stars

Difference stars appear e.g. at PDE discretization (in the context of grid relaxations (Jacobi, Gauß–Seidel), as coarser-to-finer grid interpolation and so on).

Example: (Jacobi relaxation)

```
   do 10 j=2,n-1
    do 10 i=2,n-1
     uhelp(i,j) = (1-omega)*u(i,j) + omega*0.25*( f(i,j)
*          + u(i-1,j) + u(i+1,j) + u(i,j+1) + u(i,j-1) )
10 continue
```

PARAMAT provides difference star patterns for one (HSTAR$^{(0)}$) and two (STAR$^{(0)}$) dimensions on the expression level. These are both specializations of the MULTIADD$^{(0)}$ pattern mentionned above. The most important *relative grid positions* of a 1D or 2D difference star are numbered from [i-1,j-1] (= pos. 1) to [i+1,j+1] (=pos. 9) in lexicographic order:

```
[i-1]        [i]         [i+1]              ---> HSTAR   4   5   6

[i-1,j-1]    [i-1,j]     [i-1,j+1]                       1   2   3
[i,j-1]      [i,j]       [i,j+1]            ---> STAR    4   5   6
[i+1,j-1]    [i+1,j]     [i+1,j+1]                       7   8   9
```

The i's and j's in these index patterns may be preceded by a constant integer scaling factor (restriction factor); in the example above, this factor is 1, but for coarser-to-finer (or vice versa) grid interpolations occurring e.g. in multigrid programs, a factor of 2 can occur.

The slots of both patterns are:

- C[1],...,C[9]: The immediate coefficient expressions. They may also contain arrays indexed by [i,j]. They are zero if the corresponding star position is not present.
- Cges : common factor for all star positions
- C5 : coefficient of an extra occurrence of the rhs array
- LHS : *lhs* array name, may be equal to RHS

- starvar : rhs array indexed by this star
- F: additional quasiscalar array ($\neq starvar$) access indexed in [i,j]
- CF: factor for F; 1.0 if not present
- RI, RJ: restriction factors (must occur in all rhs accesses)
- dim1, ivar1, dim2, ivar2 : dimensions and names of i and j.

The right–hand–side expression may be permuted in many variants, but in case it should match a HSTAR$^{(0)}$ or STAR$^{(0)}$, there always must be an occurrence of MULTIADD$^{(0)}$. A MULTIADD$^{(0)}$ instance which meets the condition that among its operands there is an array occurring at least 2 times, with different indexing as permitted above, will be refined to HSTAR$^{(0)}$or STAR$^{(0)}$instance by calling an auxiliary routine called *stargazer*. This routine successively tries to fill in more slots while ascending the rhs expression tree; it cycles to itself (while consuming text) as long as it can enter a new operand into the slots, until it reaches the assignment[15].

For the example above (Jacobi), the slots are filled as follows:

- C[1]=0.0, C[2]=1.0, C[3]=0.0, C[4]=1.0, C[5]= 0.0, . . ., C[8]=0.0, C[9]=1.0
- Cges=`0.25*omega`, C5=`1-omega`,
- LHS = `uhelp`, starvar = `u`, F = `f`, CF = 1.0
- RI=1, RJ=1, dim1=1, ivar1=`i`, dim2=2, ivar2=`j`

If successful, *stargazer* returns either a STAR$^{(0)}$ (full star) or a HSTAR$^{(0)}$ (half star, i.e. there are only either positions 2,5,8 or 4,5,6 filled by operands). It is now no problem any more to detect Jacobi, Gauß–Seidel or other relaxation steps when going on matching the indexing loops around the star.

8.4.8 Beyond standard matching: Identification of multigrid hierarchies

Multigrid programs (see e.g. [35]) operate on a grid hierarchy of several grids of different size. For instance, in the figure below, G_1 is the finest grid (64 elements) and G_3 the coarsest one (4 elements):

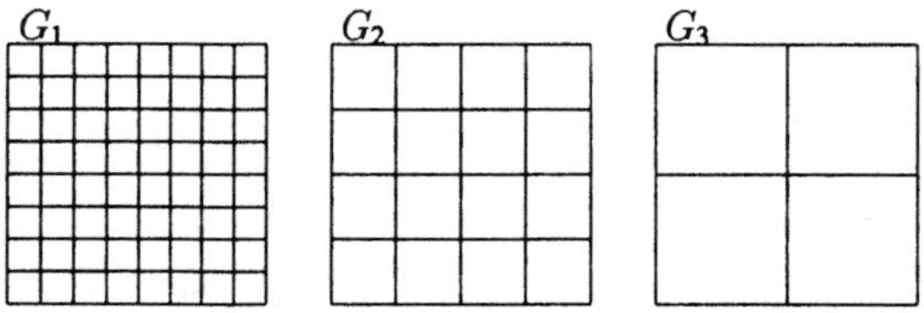

The main components of multigrid programs are:

- a relaxation algorithm,
- a finer-to-coarser-grid restriction operator,
- a coarse grid solution algorithm, and

[15] This procedure deviates locally from the standard pattern matching method we described above. It arises that standard pattern matching can recognize complex stars only with large space and time overhead. By this tricky procedure, we make star recognition handy. One may regard *stargazer* as an 'intelligent pattern' within the PHG.

- a coarser-to-finer-grid interpolation operation.

Continuing the example above, consider the following restriction operation (after preprocessing):

```
do i=1,3
 do j=1,3
  G2(i,j)= f1(2*i,2*j)  - 4.0*G1(2*i,2*j)  + G1(2*i,2*j-1)
         + G1(2*i,2*j+1) + G1(2*i-1,2*j)  + G1(2*i+1,2*j)
```

This code will be recognized by *stargazer*, as discussed above, as a full $\mathsf{STAR}^{(0)}$with restriction factors RI=RJ=2 and finally matches with the surrounding indexing loops to a $\mathsf{RESTR}^{(2)}$ instance. This also establishes further knowledge on the grid hierarchy. This additional knowledge may be used to find out the grid hierarchy. Our current research investigates this direction.

Another difficulty may arise here due to former (space) optimizations of the underlying code. Real multigrid programs are often coded by storing all grid hierarchy levels of the same array into a large linear workarray:

G_1	G_2	G_3	...

Due to procedure inlining in the preprocessing phase, the code submitted to the pattern matcher contains only one-dimensional grid accesses and looks quite awful. For this case, PARAMAT must provide a second set of templates for all grid relaxation patterns which handle the linearized versions[16]. We are currently working on this issue. We are confident that PARAMAT will finally be able to detect the whole underlying work space concept of a multigrid code even in this case. Here, in particular, knowledge about the hidden grid hierarchy is essential for the computation of efficient array distributions (see also [16], there user directives tell the compiler (SUPERB) about the grid hierarchy within the working array) since — if not detected — the linear array will most probably be distributed over the processors as equally sized slices, and that results in suboptimal load balancing and unnecessary communication.

8.5 A Parallel Algorithm for each Pattern

For each predefined pattern there exists a suitable parallel algorithm implementing this pattern, parameterized by the problem size (e.g. matrix extents) and, if necessary, also by the data partitionings for the arrays involved in this pattern.

A major benefit of this technique is that once the pattern is recognized, the best possible algorithm for this pattern will be chosen. For instance, if the programmer has implemented a Gauß–Seidel relaxation in a wave–front manner, the system should choose another implementation which is better suited for efficient parallelization, e.g. a red–black

[16]If the workspace array is accessed indirectly via index vectors, pattern matching is disabled as dependence analysis is unable to cope with index vectors unless constant (array) propagation supplies the values of the index vector elements at compile time.

scheme (which has the same convergence property as the wavefront scheme) or replace it by the double number of Jacobi– or Gauß–Seidel–Jacobi hybrid iterations[17].

Another occasion for algorithm replacement are simple linear recurrences. Consider for instance the following piece of code:

```
      X[1] = A[1]
      DO 1 I=2,1000
         X[I] = A[I] + B[I] * X[I-1]
1     CONTINUE
```

Independent of the data partitioning, this code is doomed to sequential execution due to the loop–carried data dependence on array X. Once recognized as an instance of the FOLR$^{(1)}$ pattern (First Order Linear Recurrence), this piece of code will be replaced by recursive doubling techniques[18] described in [26].

For some patterns, the programming environment may supply highly–optimized parallel implementations, e.g. for VSUM$^{(1)}$ (global summation of vector elements). In such a case the pattern instance is simply converted into a runtime library call.

If the target machine has, for example, pipelined vector units as e.g. the TMC CM5, then there should be done code optimization for vector register allocation. This is particularly worth doing for vector operations, i.e. for instances of the VADD$^{(1)}$, VMUL$^{(1)}$, ..., GVOP$^{(1)}$ patterns. Especially for machines with small register files, the vector register allocation and scheduling techniques from [22] can speed up execution of basic blocks of vector instructions considerably.

Thus, algorithm replacement enables sophisticated target–machine specific code optimizations that are hidden for the non-expert user. As remarked above, it is no problem to re-introduce here optimizations that have been removed before or within the pattern recognition phase. It is also possible to locally deviate here from the strict owner-computes-rule by selecting suitable implementations.

For each parallel implementation of a pattern (located in a large implementation library) there is an assigned cost function which is also parameterized by problem size and array partitionings. This function models the run time behaviour of the algorithm under consideration. Section 8.7 explains how it is determined.

8.6 Alignment and Partitioning

The problem of array partitioning consists of two steps. First, it must be determined how arrays should be *aligned* with each other, i.e. which elements of different arrays should be mapped together to the same (virtual) processor (if possible) to minimize interprocessor communication. The alignment preferences are induced by the array references occurring

[17]The latter replacements should be a priori allowed by the user. We expect that the average user does not want to compare Gauß–Seidel with Jacobi but to get the actually fastest parallel implementation — independent of a particular relaxation coding.

[18]The optimal number of recursive doubling steps depends on the number of iterations and on the message startup time of the target machine. For small problem sizes, sequential execution will be faster.

pattern	algorithm	alignment recomm.	distribution recomm.
MCOPY$^{(2)}(A, B)$	matrix copy	$A \equiv B$	arbitrarily
VCOPY$^{(1)}(V, W)$	vector copy	$V \equiv W$	arbitrarily
MJACOBI$^{(2)}(A, B)$	one Jacobian relax. step	$A \equiv B$	quadratic blocks
MM$^{(3)}(C, A, B)$	matrix multiplication	$A \equiv C \vee B \equiv C$	A by row, B by col
MTRANSP$^{(2)}(A, B)$	matrix transpose	$A \equiv^{-1} B$	arbitrarily
VSUM$^{(1)}(s, V)$	vector summation	arbitrarily	arbitrarily
SSP$^{(1)}(s, V, W)$	standard scalar product	$V \equiv W$	arbitrarily

Table 8.3 Array alignment and distribution recommendations for some patterns

in the source program. Second, the array elements must be *distributed*, i.e. actually mapped to a concrete processing element of the (physical) target machine. At this stage, aligned array sections can be handled as an entity.

For alignment and partitioning issues, we will use well–known techniques introduced by Li and Chen ([29]), Knobe et al. ([24, 25]) or Wholey ([37]). The cost estimate functions in these approaches will be replaced by our own cost functions being described in the next section.

The problem of determining optimal data alignment and distribution is well–known to be NP–complete (cf. [29]), thus automatic partitioning may take exponential time in the worst case. That is why we intend to limit the number of distribution alternatives severely[19]. Furthermore, we limit the number of partitionable array dimensions to 2. Together with the simplification of the source program by pattern matching, these restrictions enable the application of a branch–and–bound search for the optimal distribution, as done in [19].

For each pattern there generally exists one locally optimal data distribution scheme. E.g. for matrix multiplication $C = A \cdot B$, matrix A should be distributed by row and matrix B should be distributed by column, and furthermore, C should be aligned with either A or B. PARAMAT provides a default recommendation for alignment and one for array distribution for each pattern[20]. If these recommendations cause an alignment or distribution conflict throughout the program (and they will usually do), the given recommendations will be the first choices when searching for the optimal data distribution.

Some recommendation examples are summarized in Tab. 8.3.

The points between the pattern instances in the final matched program representation are natural places for possible redistribution of arrays. In [21] an interesting method for (static) redistribution has been presented (see also [7] in this volume). We will include it

[19] In fact we will only allow the following six possibilities (for two-dimensional arrays): row-/column-/block-contiguous and row- or column–cyclic (cf. e.g. [17]). For all the applications considered so far these are enough to supply good distributions.

[20] Note that the alignment recommendation depends only on the pattern itself whereas the distribution recommendation is, in general, also dependent on the target machine and on the problem size (cf. [21]).

into the PARAMAT system with small modifications. The details will be given in a later paper.

8.7 Determining Cost Functions: Estimating and Benchmarking

A simple way to determine the run time of a given parallel algorithm parameterized by problem size and array partitions is to estimate it from the basic computation and communication statements occurring in that algorithm (see e.g. [13]).

In reality, however, it seems that these estimations very rarely meet the actual run time since a parallel computer such as the INTEL iPSC/860 behaves as a chaotic system, its performance heavily depending on the actual network traffic, which, in turn, depends on the algorithm under consideration. This problem has been adressed in [2]. There performance estimation is based on benchmarking of simple communication patterns and propagating this information 'up' through the program's syntax tree.

PARAMAT will be able to inspect precomputed tables of *really measured* run times for *all* pattern implementations (especially, for high–level patterns!), as indicated above. We expect the accuracy of performance prediction being substantially improved by this method.

Problems with performance prediction arise if the target machine has a cache. Then, run time also depends on whether operands (arrays or parts thereof) already reside in the cache or must be reloaded first. This scenario is influenced by all former operations. Here more research has to be done.

8.8 Implementation and Future Extensions

The overall PARAMAT system is outlined in Fig. 8.2. Note that the time–consuming work concerning parallel algorithm development (either optimized SPMD routines or just operating system calls) and benchmarking their run times for all possible array distributions has not to be performed at compile time but at an earlier stage (at compiler generation time). We intend to develop an automatic benchmarking tool that does this tedious job for us.

Furthermore it will be useful to arrange the Pattern Library as a hierarchical collection of modules which may be individually composed for special application areas.

The pattern recognition tool — as described in this paper — has been implemented and tested. The current (July 1993) implementation consists of around 10000 lines of C code and reliably recognizes 68 nontrivial patterns with 117 nontrivial templates[21], including special routines for loop rerolling and identification of difference stars. The high degree of robustness against loop interchange, loop distribution, loop unrolling and statement reordering has been exemplified in practice.

[21]Each template is technically represented by a C routine of around 20 to 50 lines that tests syntactic and semantic conditions and, if successful, generates the pattern instance and fills in the slot entries.

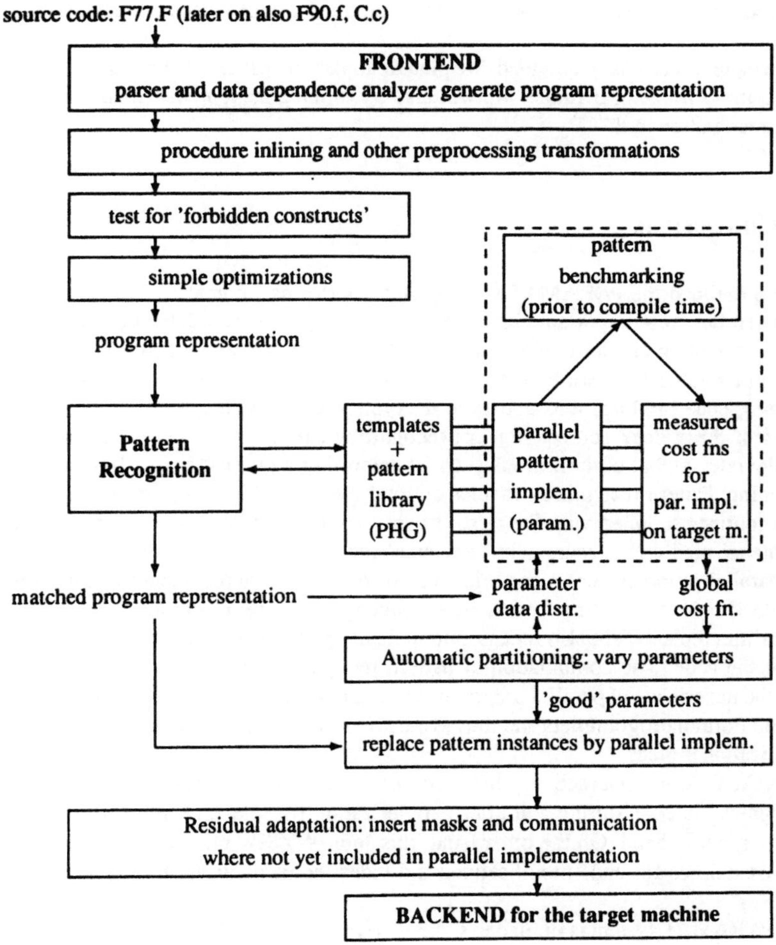

Figure 8.2 Block diagram of the overall PARAMAT system. Only the components enclosed in the dashed rectangle (and the back end, of course) are dependent on the target machine. Parallel algorithms for each pattern and their run–time approximations, parameterized by the data partitionings of the arrays involved in the resp. pattern instance, have to be precomputed once for each hardware constellation (pattern benchmarking) *before* compile time.

In order to determine cross edges properly, we have implemented a simple version of exact array data flow analysis. This (in general very problematic) analysis is here highly simplified by the exact data flow information[22] supplied with the instances of recognized patterns.

More patterns can easily be added. We plan to implement patterns from image processing algorithms in the near future. We will also try to integrate loop distribution into the pattern recognition tool.

8.9 Conclusions

We have outlined the PARAMAT system which performs automatic parallelization of a restricted but quite important class of numerical programs. Parallelization is done by pattern recognition and local algorithm replacement. The pattern recognition algorithm with the hierarchical pattern base described above is robust against common semantics preserving code modifications and even decrypts many former optimization transformations of dusty deck sources. Pattern recognition simplifies the program graph and thus alleviates global optimizations such as determining optimal array alignment and partitioning. Pattern recognition enables optimal use of the highly optimized operating system routines supplied with the target hardware environment. It also supports better performance prediction accuracy by benchmarking higher–level patterns. Beyond automatic parallelization, pattern recognition may be of great use at reengineering sequential dusty–deck codes for porting them to other languages or target machines.

Algorithm replacement also means automatically performing optimizing transformations of the code. The combination of pattern recognition and algorithm replacement makes the experience of parallel programming and optimization experts accessible to all scientific Fortran programmers and thus avoids re-inventing the wheel for each program parallelization project.

PARAMAT is *not* interactive. This is not necessary either because the user has not to recognize his code during and after parallelization for selecting transformations or further tuning by hand. On the other hand, this 'non-WYSIWYG' system offers many more possibilities for code modifications and hides the parallelization details from the user.

The PARAMAT system is limited in some ways. First, it is unable to process *all* source programs. This is taken into account to obtain a really automatic parallelizing compiler *without any* interaction or directives supplied by the user at compile time. Second, the search space for possible array distributions has to be severely restricted to maintain acceptable compile time. In general, heuristics will have to be applied.

A prototype of PARAMAT is currently being implemented at Saarbrücken university. The implementation of the pattern recognition tool has reached the state described in this paper. The first target machine will be the Intel iPSC/860.

The PARAMAT system is open for extensions. The pattern library can be extended by adding more pattern modules according to individual application areas. The computation of run time approximation functions can be automated by a universal benchmarking tool.

[22]For each (array) slot, there is an associated *descriptor* that exactly (symbolically) describes which elements are accessed in the array.

Changing the hardware platform means only to load another base of parallel pattern implementations and their run time functions. Thus the PARAMAT system will always be up to date for the latest hardware environments available.

Acknowledgements

We would like to thank Prof. A. K. Louis, Prof. W. J. Paul, Prof. R. Wilhelm, Prof. H. Zima, Barbara Chapman, Christian Ferdinand and all AP'93 participants for their comments and suggestions to this work.

References

[1] David H. Bailey and John T. Barton. The NAS Kernel Benchmark Program. Numerical Aerodynamic Simulations Systems Division, NASA Ames Research Center, June 1986.

[2] Vasanth Balasundaram, Geoffrey Fox, Ken Kennedy, and Ulrich Kremer. A Static Performance Estimator to Guide Data Partitioning Decisions. In *ACM SIGPLAN Symposium on Principles and Practices of Parallel Programming*, volume 3, pages 213–223, 1991.

[3] Michael Berry (Editor). Scientific Workload Characterization by Loop Based Analyses. *Performance Evaluation Review*, 19, February 1992.

[4] Pradip Bose. Heuristic Rule-Based Program Transformations for Enhanced Vectorization. In *Proc. of Int. Conf. on Parallel Processing*, 1988.

[5] Pradip Bose. Interactive Program Improvement via EAVE: An Expert Adviser for Vectorization. In *Proc. Int. Conf. on Supercomputing*, pages 119–130, July 1988.

[6] Thomas Brandes and Manfred Sommer. A Knowledge-Based Parallelization Tool in a Programming Environment. In *16th Int. Conf. on Parallel Processing*, pages 446–448, 1987.

[7] Alan Carle, Ken Kennedy, Ulrich Kremer, and John Mellor–Crummey. Automatic Data Layout for Distributed Memory Machines in the D Programming Environment. In *Proc. of AP'93 Int. Workshop on Automatic Distributed Memory Parallelization, Automatic Data Distribution and Automatic Parallel Performance Prediction, Saarbrücken, Germany*, March 1993.

[8] Ian A. Carmichael and James R. Cordy. *TXL - Tree Transformational Language Syntax and Informal Semantics*. Dept. of Computing and Information Science, Queen's University at Kingston, Canada, February 1992.

[9] Barbara Chapman, Piyush Mehrotra, and Hans Zima. Programming in Vienna Fortran. In *Third Workshop on Compilers for Parallel Computers*, 1992.

[10] Barbara M. Chapman, Heinz Herbeck, and Hans P. Zima. Automatic Support for Data Distribution. Technical Report ACPC/TR 91-14, Austrian Center for Parallel Computation, July 1991.

[11] Barbara M. Chapman, Heinz Herbeck, and Hans P. Zima. Knowledge-based Parallelization for Distributed Memory Systems. Technical Report ACPC/TR 91-11, Austrian Center for Parallel Computation, April 1991.

[12] J. J. Dongarra, J. DuCroz, S. Hammarling, and R. Hanson. An Extended Set of Fortran Basic Linear Algebra Subprograms. *ACM Trans. on Math. Software*, 14(1):1–32, 1988.

[13] Thomas Fahringer, Roman Blasko, and Hans Zima. Automatic Performance Prediction to Support Parallelization of Fortran Programs for Massively Parallel Systems. In *Int. ACM Conference on Supercomputing*, 1992. Washington DC.

[14] Christopher W. Fraser, Robert R. Henry, and Todd A. Proebsting. BURG — Fast Optimal Instruction Selection and Tree Parsing. *SIGPLAN Notices*, 27(4):68–76, April 1992.

[15] Hans Michael Gerndt. *Automatic Parallelization for Distributed-Memory Multiprocessing Systems*. PhD thesis, Universität Bonn, 1989.

[16] Michael Gerndt. Parallelization of Multigrid Programs in SUPERB. Technical Report ACPC/TR 90-6, Austrian Center for Parallel Computation, October 1990.

[17] Manish Gupta and Prithviraj Banerjee. Automatic Data Partitioning on Distributed Memory Multiprocessors. Technical Report CRHC-90-14, Center for Reliable and High-Performance Computing, University of Illinois at Urbana-Champaign, Oct. 1990.

[18] Mehdi T. Harandi and Jim Q. Ning. Knowledge-based program analysis. *IEEE Software*, pages 74–81, January 1990.

[19] Roman Hayer. Automatische Parallelisierung, Teil 2: Automatische Datenaufteilung für Parallelrechner mit verteiltem Speicher. Master thesis, Universität Saarbrücken, 1993.

[20] Seema Hiranandani, Ken Kennedy, and Chau-Wen Tseng. Compiler–Support for Machine–Independent Parallel Programming in Fortran-D. Technical Report Rice COMP TR91-149, Rice University, March 1991.

[21] Ken Kennedy and Ulrich Kremer. Automatic Data Alignment and Distribution for Loosely Synchronous Problems in an Interactive Programming Environment. Technical Report COMP TR91-155, Rice University, April 1991. See also this volume.

[22] C.W. Keßler, W.J. Paul, and T. Rauber. Scheduling Vector Straight Line Code on Vector Processors. In R. Giegerich and S.L. Graham, editors, *Code Generation – Concepts, Tools, Techniques*, Springer Workshops in Computing Series, pages 77–91, 1992.

[23] Christoph W. Keßler. The Basic PARAMAT Pattern Library, May 1993.

[24] Kathleen Knobe, Joan D. Lukas, and Guy L. Steele. Data Optimization: Allocation of Arrays to Reduce Communication on SIMD Machines. *Journal of Parallel and Distributed Computing*, 8:102–118, 1990.

[25] Kathleen Knobe and Venkataraman Natarajan. Data Optimization: Minimizing Residual Interprocessor Data Motion on SIMD machines. In *Third Symposium on the Frontiers of Massively Parallel Computation*, pages 416–423, 1990.

[26] Peter M. Kogge and Harold S. Stone. A Parallel Algorithm for the Efficient Solution of a General Class of Recurrence Equations. *IEEE Transactions on Computers*, C-22(8), August 1973.

[27] Wojtek Kozaczynski, Jim Ning, and Tom Sarver. Program concept recognition. In *Proc. of KBSE'92 Seventh Knowledge-Based Software Engineering Conference*, pages 216–225, 1992.

[28] C. Lawson, R. Hanson, D. Kincaid, and F. Krogh. Basic Linear Algebra Subprograms for Fortran Usage. *ACM Trans. on Math. Software*, 5:308–325, 1979.

[29] Jingke Li and Marina Chen. Index Domain Alignment: Minimizing Cost of Cross-referencing between Distributed Arrays. In *Third Symposium on the Frontiers of Massively Parallel Computation*, pages 424–433, 1990.

[30] A. K. Louis. Parallele Numerik. Course script and selected programs, unpublished, Universität Saarbrücken, 1992.

[31] Frank McMahon. The Livermore Fortran Kernels: A Test of the Numeric Performance Range. Technical report, Lawrence Livermore National Laboratory, 1986.

[32] Silvia M. Müller. Die Auswirkung der Startup-Zeit auf die Leistung paralleler Rechner bei numerischen Anwendungen. Master thesis, Universität Saarbrücken, 1989.

[33] Shlomit S. Pinter and Ron Y. Pinter. Program Optimization and Parallelization Using Idioms. In *Principles of Programming Languages*, pages 79–92, 1991.

[34] J. Saltz, K. Crowley, R. Mirchandaney, and H. Berryman. Runtime Scheduling and Execution of Loops on Message Passing Machines. *Journal of Parallel and Distributed Computing*, 8:303–312, 1990.

[35] Klaus Stüben and Ulrich Trottenberg. Multigrid methods: Fundamental algorithms, model problem analysis and applications. In *Springer Lecture Notes in Mathematics, Vol. 960*, 1982.

[36] Ko-Yang Wang and Dennis Gannon. Applying AI Techniques to Program Optimization for Parallel Computers. In Kai Hwang and D. DeGroot, editors, *Parallel Processing for Supercomputers and Artificial Intelligence*, pages 441–485, 1989.

[37] Skef Wholey. *Automatic Data Mapping for Distributed-Memory Parallel Computers*. PhD thesis, Carnegie Mellon University, Pittsburgh, PA 15213, 1991.

[38] Reinhard Wilhelm. Computation and Use of Data Flow Information in Optimizing Compilers. *Acta Informatica*, 12:209–225, 1979.

[39] Hans Zima and Barbara Chapman. *Supercompilers for Parallel and Vector Computers*. ACM Press Frontier Series. Addison–Wesley, 1990.

9 Automatic Data Layout for Distributed-Memory Machines in the D Programming Environment

Ulrich Kremer [1] John Mellor-Crummey Ken Kennedy Alan Carle
DEPARTMENT OF COMPUTER SCIENCE
RICE UNIVERSITY, HOUSTON, TEXAS
email: kremer@cs.rice.edu

Abstract: Although distributed-memory message-passing parallel computers are among the most cost-effective high performance machines available, scientists find them extremely difficult to program. Most programmers feel uncomfortable working with a distributed-memory programming model that requires explicit management of local name spaces. To address this problem, researchers have proposed using languages based on a global name space annotated with directives specifying how the data should be mapped onto a distributed memory machine. Using these annotations, a sophisticated compiler can automatically transform a code into a message-passing program suitable for execution on a distributed-memory machine. The Fortran77D and Fortran90D languages support this programming style. Given a Fortran D program, the compiler uses data layout directives to automatically generate a single-program, multiple data (SPMD) node program for a given distributed-memory target machine.

To achieve high performance with such programs, programmers must select a good data layout. Current tools provide little or no support for this selection process. This paper describes an automatic data layout strategy being investigated for use in the D programming tools currently under development at Rice University. The proposed technique considers the profitability of dynamic data remapping as it explores a rich search space of reasonable alignment and distribution schemes.

9.1 Introduction

The goal of the D programming tools project is to develop techniques and tools that aid scientists in the construction of programs in abstract parallel languages such as Fortran D [11] and High Performance Fortran (HPF) [15]. A short introduction to the Fortran D language is given in the appendix. Developing efficient programs in languages such as HPF or Fortran D can be challenging since understanding the performance implications of small perturbations of the program at the source level requires a deep understanding of the compiler technology upon which the language implementation is based. In particular,

[1]Corresponding author; e-mail: kremer@cs.rice.edu. This research was supported by the Center for Research on Parallel Computation (CRPC), a Science and Technology Center funded by NSF through Cooperative Agreement Number CCR-9120008. This work was also sponsored by DARPA under contract #DABT63-92-C-0038, and the IBM corporation. The content of this paper does not necessarily reflect the position or the policy of the U.S. Government and no official endorsement should be inferred.

understanding the impact of data distributions on the data parallelism that will be realized by the compiler is vitally important for users to be able to write efficient programs.

The primary focus of the D project is on developing program analysis infrastructure to support an intelligent editor that will provide users with detailed information about how effectively an underlying compiler implementation can exploit data parallelism in the program. The D editor will bring together a wide range of program analysis technology including program dependence analysis to identify inherently sequential constraints on the order in which values must be computed, static performance estimation to determine the relative merits of particular data distribution alternatives, dynamic performance information to refine the costs associated with particular design alternatives, and automatic data layout.

A proposed automatic data layout tool for the D system will first determine a set of efficient data decomposition schemes for the entire program. Subsequently, the user will be able to select a region of the input program and the system will respond with a set of potential decomposition schemes and their performance characteristics for the selected region. For each scheme, the tool will provide information about the location and type of the communication operations generated by the compiler. This will enable the user to obtain insight into the characteristics of the program when executed on a distributed memory machine, and the capabilities of the underlying compilation system.

In this paper we focus on automatic data layout techniques for regular problems in the context of an advanced compilation system that allows dynamic data decompositions. We describe an initial analysis framework for reasoning about dynamic data layouts at compile time for programs without subroutine calls. The paper is structured as follows. Section 9.2 provides a short introduction to the Fortran D compilation system. Section 9.3 contains examples that motivate the need for dynamic data decomposition in an automatic tool. Section 9.4 discusses an initial framework to solve the dynamic data decomposition problem. The paper concludes with a discussion of related work and our future plans.

9.2 Compilation system

The choice of a good data decomposition scheme for a program depends on the compilation system, the target machine and its size, and the problem size [3, 4, 29, 13, 39]. Advances in compiler technology make it even more difficult for a programmer to predict the performance resulting from a given data decomposition scheme without compiling and running the program on the specific target system. State-of-the-art compilers perform a variety of intra- and inter-procedural optimizations. The applicability and profitability of these optimizations depend on the specified data decomposition schemes.

Compilation of a Fortran D program involves translating it into a Fortran 77 SPMD node program that contains calls to library primitives for interprocessor communication. A vendor-supplied Fortran 77 node compiler is used to generate an executable that will run on each node of the distributed-memory target machine. A Fortran D compiler may support optimizations that reduce or hide communication overhead, exploit parallelism, or reduce memory requirements. Procedure cloning or inlining may be applied under certain conditions to improve context for optimization [17, 18, 14, 37]. Node compilers may perform optimizations to exploit the memory hierarchy and instruction-level parallelism available on the target node processor [6, 40, 5].

At present, the principal target of our prototype Fortran D compilation system [37] is the Intel iPSC/860. Eventually, the compilation system will target a variety of distributed-memory multiprocessors such as Intel's iPSC/860 and Paragon, Ncube's Ncube-1 and Ncube-2, and Thinking Machine Corporation's CM-5. Our proposed strategy for automatic data decomposition is intended for use with our state-of-the-art Fortran D compilation system.

9.3 Dynamic Data Layout: Two Examples

The following program examples illustrate the difficulty of predicting the performance impact of dynamic remapping in the context of an advanced compilation system. For this reason, we believe that an automatic tool is needed to determine when data remapping can be used effectively.

The availability of fast collective communication routines is crucial for the profitability of data realignment and redistribution. In our experiments we used a transpose library routine distributed by Intel in a set of example programs for the iPSC/860.

Two-dimensional Fast Fourier Transform (2D-FFT)

The computation performed by a two-dimensional FFT can be described as a sequence of one-dimensional FFTs (1D-FFTs) along each row of the input array, followed by one-dimensional FFTs along each column. The input array in our example is of type complex. The butterfly version of the 2D-FFT distributes the first dimension of the two-dimensional array. This leads to communication during the computation of the 1D-FFTs along each column. This communication can be avoided if the array is transposed after all 1D-FFTs along each row have been performed. The transpose version uses a row-distribution for the row-wise 1D-FFTs and a column-distribution for the column-wise 1D-FFTs. Both versions were compiled using if77 under -O4 option and executed on the iPSC/860 at Rice (32 processors) and Caltech (64 processors). Both machines have a two-way set associative instruction cache (4Kbytes) and data cache (8Kbytes). The cache lines are 32 bytes long. Table 9.1 lists execution times in seconds for the butterfly and transpose implementation alternatives over a variety of data sizes and processor configurations. For each implementation alternative, the table lists the total execution time and the fraction of the time spent communicating. The last column lists the relative speed-ups of the transpose version over the butterfly version for different problem sizes and processor configurations. In almost all cases redistribution leads to a better performance as compared to a static row partitioning. The most significant improvements occur for small problems and a high number of processors.

If the compiler is not able to detect the FFT (butterfly) communication pattern, we expect the compiler-generated program for the static row partitioning to run slower than the butterfly version, increasing the benefits of the transpose version even more.

#procs	problem size	butterfly			transpose			relative
		total	communic. only	(% of total)	total	communic. only	(% of total)	speed-up
	128 × 128							
2		0.423	0.016	3.8%	0.432	0.019	4.4%	**0.98**
4		0.272	0.061	22.4%	0.217	0.015	6.9%	**1.25**
8		0.207	0.092	44.4%	0.113	0.012	10.6%	**1.83**
16		0.187	0.119	63.6%	0.062	0.011	17.7%	**3.02**
32		0.193	0.147	76.1%	0.042	0.017	40.5%	**4.60**
64		0.160	0.124	77.5%	0.035	0.022	62.8%	**4.57**
	256 × 256							
2		1.731	0.036	2.0%	1.819	0.070	3.8%	**0.95**
4		0.979	0.119	12.1%	0.903	0.050	5.5%	**1.08**
8		0.630	0.181	28.7%	0.459	0.031	6.7%	**1.37**
16		0.485	0.238	49.0%	0.237	0.023	9.7%	**2.05**
32		0.444	0.296	66.6%	0.130	0.023	17.7%	**3.42**
64		0.352	0.250	71.0%	0.081	0.026	32.0%	**4.34**
	512 × 512							
2		7.199	0.057	0.8%	7.822	0.299	3.8%	**0.92**
4		3.812	0.235	6.1%	3.814	0.194	5.0%	**1.00**
8		2.178	0.360	16.5%	1.919	0.108	5.6%	**1.13**
16		1.428	0.474	33.2%	0.969	0.064	6.6%	**1.47**
32		1.127	0.597	53.0%	0.498	0.046	9.2%	**2.26**
64		0.826	0.503	60.9%	0.270	0.040	14.8%	**3.06**
	1024 × 1024							
4		15.640	0.444	2.8%	16.561	0.836	5.0%	**0.94**
8		8.332	0.718	8.6%	8.274	0.432	5.2%	**1.01**
16		4.827	0.939	19.4%	4.156	0.238	5.7%	**1.16**
32		3.324	1.274	48.8%	2.097	0.137	6.5%	**1.59**
64		2.152	1.005	46.7%	1.083	0.090	8.3%	**1.99**
	2048 × 2048							
16		18.323	1.895	10.3%	18.360	0.893	4.9%	**0.99**
32		10.764	2.356	21.9%	9.215	0.487	5.3%	**1.17**
64		6.456	2.007	31.1%	4.687	0.277	5.9%	**1.38**

Table 9.1 Performance of two versions of 2D-FFT on the iPSC/860

Alternating-Direction-Implicit Integration (ADI)

The sequential code is shown in Figure 9.1. Each iteration of the DO-loop in line 2 consists of a forward and backward sweep along the rows of arrays x and b, followed by a forward and backward sweep along the columns. The *pipeline* version of the code uses a static column-wise partitioning of the perfectly aligned arrays x, a, and b. We specified this data layout using Fortran D language annotations and compiled the program using the current Fortran D compiler prototype. The compiler generated a coarse-grain pipelined loop for the forward and backward sweeps along the rows of arrays x and b. The sweeps along columns do not require communication under this data layout, although the row sweeps do. The *transpose* version transposes arrays x and b between the row and column sweeps, i.e. twice per iteration of the outermost DO-loop (line 2). No communication is needed during each sweep.

The execution times for 10 iterations (MAXITER = 10) for the iPSC/860 is shown in Table 9.2. The timings are given in seconds. Since the selected problem sizes are powers of two, cache conflicts lead to a significant increase of the total execution time for the transpose version. To alleviate this problem, we added a single column or row to each local segment of the arrays in the node SPMD program. We expect a sophisticated

```
REAL x(N, N), a(N, N), b(N, N)
DO iter = 1, MAXITER
    // ADI forward & backward sweeps along rows
    DO j = 2, N
        DO i = 1, N
            x(i, j) = x(i, j) − x(i, j−1) ∗ a(i, j) / b(i, j−1)
            b(i, j) = b(i, j) − a(i, j) ∗ a(i, j) / b(i, j−1)
        ENDDO
    ENDDO
    DO i = 1, N
        x(i, N) = x(i, N) / b(i, N)
    ENDDO
    DO j = N−1, 1, −1
        DO i = 1, N
            x(i, j) = ( x(i, j) − a(i, j+1) ∗ x(i, j+1) ) / b(i, j)
        ENDDO
    ENDDO
    // ADI forward & backward sweeps along columns
    DO j = 1, N
        DO i = 2, N
            x(i, j) = x(i, j) − x(i−1, j) ∗ a(i, j) / b(i−1, j)
            b(i, j) = b(i, j) − a(i, j) ∗ a(i, j) / b(i−1, j)
        ENDDO
    ENDDO
    DO j = 1, N
        x(N, j) = x(N, j) / b(N, j)
    ENDDO
    DO j = 1, N
        DO i = N−1, 1, −1
            x(i, j) = ( x(i, j) − a(i+1, j) ∗ x(i+1, j) ) / b(i, j)
        ENDDO
    ENDDO
ENDDO
```

Figure 9.1 Sequential ADI code, REAL

node compiler to perform such an optimization. The performance of the modified node programs are listed under the problem sizes marked with asterisks in Table 9.2. In contrast to the 2D-FFT example, redistribution leads to a decrease in performance in all cases. The extent of improvement of the pipeline version over the transpose version depends on the ability of the compiler to deal with the cache effects on the target machine.

#procs	problem size	pipeline			transpose			relative
		total	communic. only	(% of total)	total	communic. only	(% of total)	speed-up
2	128 × 128	2.305	0.021	0.9%	3.894	0.371	9.5%	**0.59**
4		1.265	0.053	4.2%	1.547	0.298	19.3%	**0.82**
8		0.720	0.077	10.7%	1.371	0.246	17.9%	**0.52**
16		0.485	0.103	21.2%	0.617	0.280	45.4%	**0.78**
32		0.404	0.141	34.9%	1.137	0.444	39.0%	**0.35**
64		0.431	0.235	54.5%	1.130	0.821	72.6%	**0.38**
2	128 × 128*	2.283	0.020	0.9%	2.486	0.365	14.7%	**0.92**
4		1.281	0.053	4.1%	1.381	0.308	22.3%	**0.93**
8		0.715	0.080	11.1%	0.835	0.255	30.5%	**0.85**
16		0.505	0.116	23.0%	0.614	0.348	56.7%	**0.82**
32		0.402	0.143	35.6%	0.596	0.454	76.2%	**0.67**
64		0.430	0.236	54.9%	0.921	0.845	91.7%	**0.47**
2	256 × 256	9.142	0.041	0.4%	21.585	1.351	6.2%	**0.42**
4		4.781	0.106	2.2%	10.261	1.009	9.8%	**0.46**
8		2.598	0.162	6.2%	4.250	0.677	15.9%	**0.61**
16		1.531	0.180	11.7%	3.192	0.532	16.6%	**0.48**
32		1.064	0.215	20.2%	2.050	0.607	29.6%	**0.52**
64		0.838	0.307	36.6%	3.046	0.921	30.2%	**0.27**
2	256 × 256*	9.045	0.042	0.5%	10.116	1.368	13.5%	**0.89**
4		4.758	0.106	2.2%	5.296	1.009	19.0%	**0.90**
8		2.566	0.167	6.5%	2.844	0.678	23.8%	**0.90**
16		1.566	0.204	13.0%	1.709	0.596	34.9%	**0.92**
32		0.986	0.220	22.3%	1.235	0.623	50.4%	**0.80**
64		0.828	0.320	38.6%	1.255	0.958	76.3%	**0.66**
2	512 × 512	39.553	0.084	0.2%	161.896	5.504	3.4%	**0.24**
4		20.270	0.209	1.0%	81.868	3.717	4.5%	**0.25**
8		10.612	0.308	2.9%	39.072	2.289	5.8%	**0.27**
16		5.780	0.352	6.0%	10.980	1.439	13.1%	**0.53**
32		3.406	0.379	11.1%	6.576	1.110	16.9%	**0.52**
64		2.289	0.468	20.4%	5.704	1.257	22.0%	**0.40**
2	512 × 512*	35.913	0.083	0.2%	144.500	5.561	3.8%	**0.25**
4		18.434	0.207	1.1%	21.365	3.768	17.6%	**0.86**
8		9.573	0.313	3.3%	10.795	2.270	21.0%	**0.89**
16		5.302	0.372	7.0%	5.799	1.497	25.8%	**0.91**
32		3.060	0.376	12.2%	3.329	1.132	34.0%	**0.92**
64		2.083	0.467	22.4%	2.402	1.296	54.0%	**0.87**
2	1024 × 1024	168.055	0.175	0.1%	949.241	27.171	2.9%	**0.18**
4		85.106	0.411	0.5%	388.358	15.016	3.9%	**0.22**
8		43.605	0.602	1.4%	237.368	8.449	3.5%	**0.18**
16		22.860	0.678	3.0%	98.511	4.854	4.9%	**0.23**
32		12.509	0.686	5.5%	52.708	2.969	5.6%	**0.24**
64		7.351	0.788	10.7%	13.927	2.283	16.4%	**0.53**
2	1024 × 1024*	147.682	0.177	0.1%	752.135	27.400	3.6%	**0.20**
4		73.467	0.410	0.5%	352.282	15.162	4.3%	**0.21**
8		37.484	0.608	1.6%	43.869	8.534	19.4%	**0.85**
16		19.860	0.714	3.6%	22.066	4.866	22.0%	**0.90**
32		10.820	0.683	6.3%	11.629	2.980	25.6%	**0.93**
64		6.466	0.786	12.1%	6.727	2.325	34.6%	**0.96**
4	2048 × 2048	337.115	0.909	0.3%	*memory*	*memory*		
8		170.599	1.219	0.7%	815.495	34.042	4.2%	**0.21**
16		87.407	1.365	1.6%	602.598	17.979	3.0%	**0.14**
32		45.911	1.353	2.9%	193.612	10.004	5.2%	**0.24**
64		25.098	1.452	5.8%	131.027	6.052	4.6%	**0.19**
4	2048 × 2048*	*memory*	*memory*		*memory*	*memory*		
8		146.694	1.241	0.8%	671.508	34.311	5.1%	**0.22**
16		75.563	1.414	1.9%	89.174	18.161	20.4%	**0.85**
32		39.464	1.353	3.4%	44.293	9.913	22.4%	**0.89**
64		21.691	1.450	6.7%	23.345	6.078	26.0%	**0.93**

Table 9.2 Performance of pipeline and transpose versions of ADI on the iPSC/860

Discussion

The 2D-FFT example shows that dynamic remapping can result in significant performance improvements over a static data layout scheme. A programmer might have expected a similar performance improvement for the ADI example program. However, due to the coarse grain pipelining optimization performed by the Fortran D compiler dynamic data remapping is not profitable even if we ignore cache conflicts.

9.4 Towards Dynamic Data Layout

The first step of our proposed strategy for automatic data layout in the presence of dynamic remapping is to partition the program into code segments, called program *phases*. Phases are intended to represent program segments that perform operations on entire data objects. In the absence of procedure calls we operationally define a phase as follows: A phase is a loop nest such that for each induction variable that occurs in a subscript position of an array reference in the loop body the phase contains the surrounding loop that defines the induction variable. A phase is minimal in the sense that it does not include surrounding loops that do not define induction variables occurring in subscript positions. Data remapping is allowed only between phases. Note that the strategies for identifying program phases is a topic of current research.

Our strategy for investigating data layout with dynamic data remapping explores a rich search space of possible alignment and distribution schemes for each phase. Pruning heuristics will have to be developed to restrict the alignment and distribution search spaces to manageable sizes. A first discussion of possible pruning heuristics and the sizes of their resulting search spaces can be found in [21].

Here we describe an initial analysis framework suitable for programs without procedure calls that contain no control flow other than loops. We assume that the problem size and the number of processors used is known at compile time. Furthermore, we assume that every alignment and distribution scheme specifies the data layout of all arrays in the program that may be partitioned and mapped onto different local memories of the machine.

A data layout for a program is determined in three steps. First, alignment analysis builds a search space of reasonable alignment schemes for each phase. Then, distribution analysis uses the alignment search spaces to build decomposition search spaces of reasonable alignments and distributions for each phase. Finally, a decomposition scheme for each phase is selected, resulting in a data layout for the entire program. Our three step approach to automatic data layout is described in more detail in the following sections. A summary of the basic algorithm is shown in Figure 9.4.

9.4.1 Alignment Analysis

Alignment analysis is used to prune the search space of all possible array alignments by selecting only those alignments that minimize data movement. Alignment analysis is largely machine-independent; it is performed by analyzing the array access patterns of computations in each individual program phase and across the entire program. All alignment schemes are specified relative to the *alignment space* of the program. The alignment space of a program is unique. It is determined by the maximal dimensionalities and maximal dimensional extents of the arrays in the program.

We intend to build on the inter-dimensional and intra-dimensional alignment techniques of Li and Chen [28], Knobe *et al.* [22], and Chatterjee, Gilbert, Schreiber, and Teng [9]. In contrast to previous work, we will not limit ourselves to a single alignment as the result of the alignment analysis. Rather than eliminating one candidate alignment in the presence of an alignment conflict, both schemes may be added to the alignment search space [21]. The candidate alignments computed for each phase, will serve as input to distribution analysis.

9.4.2 Distribution Analysis

Distribution analysis will consider a rich set of distribution schemes for each of the alignment schemes determined in the alignment analysis. Each dimension of a decomposition can have a block, cyclic, or block-cyclic distribution [11]. Block-cyclic distributions can have different block sizes. In addition, distributions with varying numbers of processors in each of the distributed dimensions of a decomposition are part of the distribution search space. We are currently developing strategies to prune the search space by eliminating candidate distributions that are poorly matched to the program being analyzed. The result of distribution analysis will be a set of candidate decomposition schemes for each single phase in the program. For each phase, a static performance estimator will be invoked to predict the performance of each candidate scheme. The resulting performance estimates will be recorded with each decomposition scheme. A performance estimator suitable for our needs is described in detail elsewhere [4, 16].

9.4.3 Inter-Phase Decomposition Analysis

After computing a set of data decomposition schemes and estimates of their performance for each phase, the automatic data partitioner must solve the *inter-phase* decomposition problem to choose the best data decomposition for each phase. It must consider array remapping between computational phases to reduce communication costs within the computational phases or to better exploit available parallelism. Inter-phase analysis is performed on a *phase control flow graph*. A phase control flow graph is a control flow graph [1] in which all nodes in a phase have been collapsed into a single node. Inter-phase analysis first detects the strongly connected components of the phase control flow graph in a hierarchical fashion using, for example, Tarjan intervals [35]. For each innermost loop, the inter-phase decomposition selection problem is formulated as a single-source shortest path problem over the acyclic *decomposition graph* associated with the loop body. The decomposition graph is similar to the phase control flow graph except that each phase node is replaced by the candidate set of decompositions for that phase, and for each cycle in the graph a shadow copy of the first phase in the cycle is added after

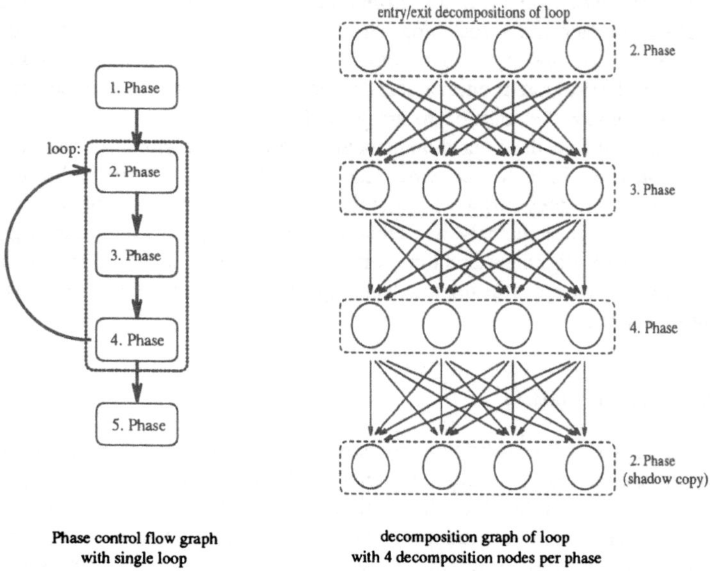

Figure 9.2 Inter-phase decomposition problem with realignment and redistribution

the last phase in the cycle. Each decomposition node is labeled with its estimated overall cost for the phase. The overall cost is determined by computational costs and costs due to synchronization and communication inside the phase. Shadow decomposition nodes are assigned a weight of zero. The flow edges in the phase control flow graph are replaced by the set of all possible edges between decomposition nodes of adjacent phases. The edges are labeled with the realignment and redistribution costs to map between the source and sink decomposition schemes. Edge weights will be determined based on the training set approach [4]. An example phase control flow graph with a single loop and the decomposition graph associated with the loop body is shown in Figure 9.2. For clarity the weights of nodes and edges have been omitted.

The root nodes in the decomposition graph represent entry/exit decomposition schemes for the loop. For each root node a single-source shortest path problem is solved. The length of the shortest path between the root node and its shadow copy multiplied by the number of iterations of the loop gives the cost estimate of the loop for the associated entry/exit decomposition scheme[2]. After determining the costs of each decomposition scheme for an innermost loop, the loop is collapsed into a single *loop summary node* in the phase control flow graph. The algorithm records with the loop summary phase the costs for each entry/exit decomposition scheme and their associated shortest paths. Subsequently, the process of detecting innermost loops, solving the single-source shortest

[2]The length of a path includes the weights on the nodes as well as the weights of the edges along the path.

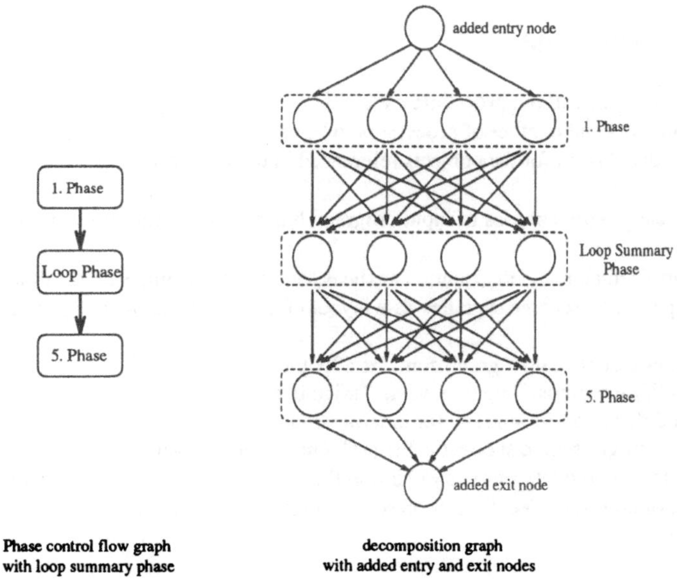

Figure 9.3 Inter-phase decomposition problem with realignment and redistribution (cont.)

paths problem, and collapsing the loops into single nodes continues until the phase control flow graph is acyclic. The final step of the merging algorithm consists of solving a single single-source shortest paths problem on a decomposition graph for the entire program with added entry and exit decomposition nodes. The added nodes and their adjacent edges have zero weight. For our example program in Figure 9.2 the final step is illustrated in Figure 9.3.

Inter-phase analysis selects the decomposition schemes that lie on the shortest path from the added entry decomposition node to the added exit node. Decomposition nodes that represent a loop summary phase are expanded into their associated shortest paths. Following the selected shortest path, dynamic remapping is required if the decomposition at the source of an edge is different from the decomposition at the sink.

A solution to the single-source shortest paths problem in a directed acyclic graph is given in [10]. Let k denote the maximal number of decomposition schemes for each phase and p the number of phases. The resulting time complexity is $\mathcal{O}(pk^3)$. The identification of innermost loops takes time proportional to the number of edges in the phase control flow graph. For our class of control flow graphs $\mathcal{O}(edges) = \mathcal{O}(nodes)$ holds, resulting in $\mathcal{O}(p)$ time for Tarjan's algorithm [35]. Therefore, the entire algorithm for merging decomposition schemes across phases has time complexity $\mathcal{O}(pk^3)$.

It is important to note that the presented solution to the merging problem assumes that each decomposition scheme specifies the data layout of every array in the program that may be partitioned across the machine. If we relax this restriction, for instance by allowing each decomposition scheme for a phase to only specify the layout of arrays

Algorithm DECOMP

Input: program without procedure calls;
problem sizes and number of processors to be used.
Output: data layout for data objects referenced in the input program

Determine program phases of input program; build phase control flow graph.

Perform alignment and distribution analysis for input program; each resulting decompositition scheme specifies data layout of all arrays that may be partitioned.

while phase control flow graph contains a loop *do*
  Identify innermost loop (e.g. using Tarjan intervals).
  Build decomposition graph for innermost loop body.
  Solve single-source shortest paths problem on decomposition graph.
  Replace loop by its summary phase in the phase control flow graph; record cost of entry/exit decomposition schemes together with their shortest paths.
endwhile

Build decomposition graph for collapsed phase control flow graph.
Add entry and exit decomposition nodes.
Solve single-source shortest paths problem on decomposition graph.

Determine data layout for entire program by traversing the lowest cost shortest path from entry node to exit node, expanding loop summary phases by their associated shortest paths.

Figure 9.4 Automatic Data Layout Algorithm

actually referenced in the phase, the dynamic data layout problem becomes NP-complete [27]. A study of real programs will show when the restriction has to be relaxed in order to limit the number of candidate decomposition schemes for each phase. We are currently working on heuristics that will generate efficient, but possibly suboptimal data layouts under the relaxed restriction.

9.5 Related Work

The problem of finding an efficient data layout for a distributed-memory multiprocessor has been addressed by many researchers [28, 30, 22, 24, 23, 12, 38, 9, 2, 7, 32, 31, 19, 33, 34, 20]. The presented solutions differ significantly in the assumptions that are made about the input language, the possible set of data decompositions, the compilation system, and the target distributed-memory machine. A more detailed discussion of some of the related work can be found in [26]. Our work is one of the first to provide a framework for automatic data layout that considers dynamic remapping. However, many researchers have recognized the need for dynamic remapping and are planning to develop solutions.

Knobe, Lukas, and Dally [23], and Chatterjee, Gilbert, Schreiber, and Teng [9] address the problem of dynamic alignment in a framework particularly suitable for SIMD machines. More recently, Anderson and Lam [2] have proposed techniques for automatic data layout for distributed and shared address space machines. Their approach considers dynamic remapping.

9.6 Summary and Future Work

This paper presents an initial framework for automatic data decomposition that allows dynamic remapping between program phases. Our proposed strategy explores a rich search space of alignment and distribution schemes for each program phase. The costs of decomposition schemes for program phases and the data remapping costs between phases will be computed by a static performance estimator. The data layout for the entire program is determined based on solutions to single-source shortest paths problems. These solutions require that each decomposition scheme specifies the layout of all arrays in the program that may be partitioned. For the proposed approach to be feasible, we will need to develop algorithms that will prune the alignment and distribution search spaces.

Relaxing the requirement for decompositions, i.e. allowing decomposition schemes to only specify the layout of a subset of the arrays in the program, makes the inter-phase decomposition problem NP-complete. We will need to explore whether the proposed framework will be practical for real programs or whether heuristics will have to be used to solve the inter-phase decomposition problem. The framework will be extended to handle intra-phase and inter-phase control flow, and to allow programs that consist of a collection of procedures.

We propose using data layout analysis as the basis for a tool that will enable a user to select a region of the input program and have the tool respond with the set of decomposition schemes in its search space and their performance characteristics for the selected region. Such a tool will help the user to understand the impact of data layout schemes on the performance of the program executed on a target distributed-memory machine, and the characteristics of the underlying compilation system. The exact design and functionality of the interface between the user and the automatic data layout tool is currently under development.

References

[1] A. V. Aho, R. Sethi, and J. Ullman. *Compilers: Principles, Techniques, and Tools*. Addison-Wesley, Reading, MA, second edition, 1986.

[2] J. Anderson and M. Lam. Global optimizations for parallelism and locality on scalable parallel machines. In *Proceedings of the SIGPLAN '93 Conference on Program Language Design and Implementation*, Albuquerque, NM, June 1993.

[3] V. Balasundaram, G. Fox, K. Kennedy, and U. Kremer. An interactive environment for data partitioning and distribution. In *Proceedings of the 5th Distributed Memory Computing Conference*, Charleston, SC, April 1990.

[4] V. Balasundaram, G. Fox, K. Kennedy, and U. Kremer. A static performance estimator to guide data partitioning decisions. In *Proceedings of the Third ACM SIGPLAN Symposium on Principles and Practice of Parallel Programming*, Williamsburg, VA, April 1991.

[5] P. Briggs. *Register Allocation via Graph Coloring*. PhD thesis, Rice University, April 1992.

[6] S. Carr. *Memory-Hierarchy Management*. PhD thesis, Rice University, September 1992.

[7] B. Chapman, H. Herbeck, and H. Zima. Automatic support for data distribution. In *Proceedings of the 6th Distributed Memory Computing Conference*, Portland, OR, April 1991.

[8] B. Chapman, P. Mehrotra, and H. Zima. Vienna Fortran - a Fortran language extension for distributed memory multiprocessors. In J. Saltz and P. Mehrotra, editors, *Languages, Compilers, and Run-Time Environments for Distributed Memory Machines*. North-Holland, Amsterdam, The Netherlands, 1992.

[9] S. Chatterjee, J.R. Gilbert, R. Schreiber, and S-H. Teng. Automatic array alignment in data-parallel programs. In *Proceedings of the Twentieth Annual ACM Symposium on the Principles of Programming Languages*, Albuquerque, NM, January 1993.

[10] T. H. Cormen, C. E. Leiserson, and R. L. Rivest. *Introduction to Algorithms*. The MIT Press, 1990.

[11] G. Fox, S. Hiranandani, K. Kennedy, C. Koelbel, U. Kremer, C. Tseng, and M. Wu. Fortran D language specification. Technical Report TR90-141, Dept. of Computer Science, Rice University, December 1990.

[12] M. Gupta. *Automatic Data Partitioning on Distributed Memory Multicomputers*. PhD thesis, University of Illinois at Urbana-Champaign, September 1992.

[13] M. Gupta and P. Banerjee. Demonstration of automatic data partitioning techniques for parallelizing compilers on multicomputers. *IEEE Transactions on Parallel and Distributed Systems*, April 1992.

[14] M. W. Hall, S. Hiranandani, K. Kennedy, and C. Tseng. Interprocedural compilation of Fortran D for MIMD distributed-memory machines. Technical Report TR91-169, Dept. of Computer Science, Rice University, November 1991.

[15] High Performance Fortran Forum. High Performance Fortran language specification, version 1.0. Technical Report CRPC-TR92225, Center for Research on Parallel Computation, Rice University, Houston, TX, May 1993. To appear in *Scientific Programming*, vol. 2, no. 1.

[16] S. Hiranandani, K. Kennedy, C. Koelbel, U. Kremer, and C. Tseng. An overview of the Fortran D programming system. In *Proceedings of the Fourth Workshop on Languages and Compilers for Parallel Computing*, Santa Clara, CA, August 1991.

[17] S. Hiranandani, K. Kennedy, and C. Tseng. Compiler optimizations for Fortran D on MIMD distributed-memory machines. In *Proceedings of Supercomputing '91*, Albuquerque, NM, November 1991.

[18] S. Hiranandani, K. Kennedy, and C. Tseng. Evaluation of compiler optimizations for Fortran D on MIMD distributed-memory machines. In *Proceedings of the 1992 ACM International Conference on Supercomputing*, Washington, DC, July 1992.

[19] D. Hudak and S. Abraham. Compiler techniques for data partitioning of sequentially iterated parallel loops. In *Proceedings of the 1990 ACM International Conference on Supercomputing*, Amsterdam, The Netherlands, June 1990.

[20] K. Ikudome, G. Fox, A. Kolawa, and J. Flower. An automatic and symbolic parallelization system for distributed memory parallel computers. In *Proceedings of the 5th Distributed Memory Computing Conference*, Charleston, SC, April 1990.

[21] K. Kennedy and U. Kremer. Initial framework for automatic data layout in Fortran D: A short update on a case study. Technical Report CRPC-TR93-324-S, Center for Research on Parallel Computation, Rice University, July 1993.

[22] K. Knobe, J. Lukas, and G. Steele, Jr. Data optimization: Allocation of arrays to reduce communication on SIMD machines. *Journal of Parallel and Distributed Computing*, 8(2):102–118, February 1990.

[23] K. Knobe, J.D. Lukas, and W.J. Dally. Dynamic alignment on distributed memory systems. In *Proceedings of the Third Workshop on Compilers for Parallel Computers*, Vienna, Austria, July 1992.

[24] K. Knobe and V. Natarajan. Data optimization: Minimizing residual interprocessor data motion on SIMD machines. In *Frontiers90: The 3rd Symposium on the Frontiers of Massively Parallel Computation*, College Park, MD, October 1990.

[25] C. Koelbel and P. Mehrotra. Compiling global name-space parallel loops for distributed execution. *IEEE Transactions on Parallel and Distributed Systems*, 2(4):440–451, October 1991.

[26] U. Kremer. Automatic data layout for distributed-memory machines. Technical Report CRPC-TR93-299-S, Center for Research on Parallel Computation, Rice University, February 1993. (thesis proposal).

[27] U. Kremer. NP-completeness of dynamic remapping. Technical Report CRPC-TR93-330-S, Center for Research on Parallel Computation, Rice University, August 1993. (also available as D Newsletter #8).

[28] J. Li and M. Chen. Index domain alignment: Minimizing cost of cross-referencing between distributed arrays. In *Frontiers90: The 3rd Symposium on the Frontiers of Massively Parallel Computation*, College Park, MD, October 1990.

[29] J. Li and M. Chen. Synthesis of explicit communication from shared-memory program references. Technical Report YALEU/DCS/TR-755, Dept. of Computer Science, Yale University, New Haven, CT, May 1990.

[30] J. Li and M. Chen. The data alignment phase in compiling programs for distributed-memory machines. *Journal of Parallel and Distributed Computing*, 13(4):213–221, August 1991.

[31] J. Ramanujam. *Compile-time Techniques for Parallel Execution of Loops on Distributed Memory Multiprocessors*. PhD thesis, Department of Computer and Information Science, Ohio State University, Columbus, OH, 1990.

[32] J. Ramanujam and P. Sadayappan. A methodology for parallelizing programs for multi-computers and complex memory multiprocessors. In *Proceedings of Supercomputing '89*, Reno, NV, November 1989.

[33] L. Snyder and D. Socha. An algorithm producing balanced partitionings of data arrays. In *Proceedings of the 5th Distributed Memory Computing Conference*, Charleston, SC, April 1990.

[34] A. Sussman. *Model-Driven Mapping onto Distributed Memory Parallel Computers*. PhD thesis, School of Computer Science, Carnegie Mellon University, September 1991.

[35] R. E. Tarjan. Testing flow graph reducibility. *Journal of Computer and System Sciences*, 9:355–365, 1974.

[36] Thinking Machines Corporation, Cambridge, MA. *CM Fortran Reference Manual*, version 5.2-0.6 edition, September 1989.

[37] C. Tseng. *An Optimizing Fortran D Compiler for MIMD Distributed-Memory Machines*. PhD thesis, Rice University, Houston, TX, January 1993. Rice COMP TR93-199.

[38] S. Wholey. *Automatic Data Mapping for Distributed-Memory Parallel Computers*. PhD thesis, School of Computer Science, Carnegie Mellon University, May 1991.

[39] S. Wholey. Automatic data mapping for distributed-memory parallel computers. In *Proceedings of the 1992 ACM International Conference on Supercomputing*, Washington, DC, July 1992.

[40] M.E. Wolf. *Improving Locality and Parallelism in Nested Loops*. PhD thesis, Stanford University, August 1992.

Appendix: Fortran D Language

The task of distributing data across processors can be approached by considering the two levels of parallelism in data-parallel applications. First, there is the question of how arrays should be *aligned* with respect to one another, both within and across array dimensions. We call this the *problem mapping* induced by the structure of the underlying computation. It represents the minimal requirements for reducing data movement for the program, and is largely independent of any machine considerations. The alignment of arrays in the program depends on the natural fine-grain parallelism defined by individual members of data arrays.

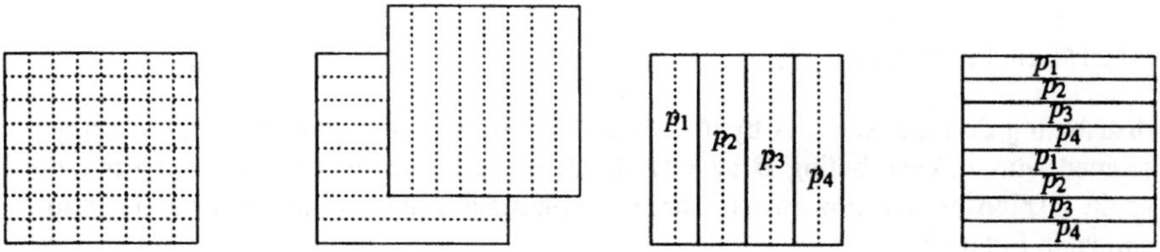


```
DECOMPOSITION     REAL X(N,N)          DISTRIBUTE      DISTRIBUTE
  A(N,N)          ALIGN X(I,J)          A(:,BLOCK)      A(CYCLIC,:)
                   with A(J-2,I+3)
```

Figure 9.5 Fortran D Data Decomposition Specifications

Second, there is the question of how arrays should be *distributed* onto the actual parallel machine. We call this the *machine mapping* caused by translating the problem onto the finite resources of the machine. It is affected by the topology, communication mechanisms, size of local memory, and number of processors of the underlying machine. The distribution of arrays in the program depends on the coarse-grain parallelism defined by the physical parallel machine.

Fortran D is a version of Fortran that provides data decomposition specifications for these two levels of parallelism using `DECOMPOSITION`, `ALIGN`, and `DISTRIBUTE` statements. A decomposition is an abstract problem or index domain; it does not require any storage. Each element of a decomposition represents a unit of computation. The `DECOMPOSITION` statement declares the name, dimensionality, and size of a decomposition.

The `ALIGN` statement maps arrays onto decompositions. Arrays mapped to the same decomposition are automatically aligned with each other. Alignment can take place either within or across dimensions. The alignment of arrays to decompositions is specified by placeholders `I, J, K, ...` in the subscript expressions of both the array and decomposition. In the example below,

```
REAL X(N,N)
DECOMPOSITION A(N,N)
ALIGN X(I,J) with A(J-2,I+3)
```

A is declared to be a two dimensional decomposition of size $N \times N$. Array X is then aligned with respect to A with the dimensions permuted and offsets within each dimension.

After arrays have been aligned with a decomposition, the `DISTRIBUTE` statement maps the decomposition to the finite resources of the physical machine. Distributions are specified by assigning an independent *attribute* to each dimension of a decomposition. Predefined attributes are `BLOCK`, `CYCLIC`, and `BLOCK_CYCLIC`. The symbol ":" marks dimensions that are not distributed. Choosing the distribution for a decomposition maps all arrays aligned with the decomposition to the machine. In the following example,

```
DECOMPOSITION A(N,N), B(N,N)
```

```
DISTRIBUTE A(:, BLOCK)
DISTRIBUTE B(CYCLIC,:)
```

distributing decomposition A by `(:,BLOCK)` results in a column partition of arrays aligned with A. Distributing B by `(CYCLIC,:)` partitions the rows of B in a round-robin fashion among processors. These sample data alignment and distributions are shown in Figure 9.5.

We should note that the goal in designing Fortran D is not to support the most general data decompositions possible. Instead, the intent is to provide decompositions that are both powerful enough to express data parallelism in scientific programs, and simple enough to permit the compiler to produce efficient programs. Fortran D is a language with semantics very similar to sequential Fortran. As a result, it should be easy to use by computational scientists. In addition, we believe that the two-phase strategy for specifying data decomposition is natural and conducive to writing modular and portable code. Fortran D bears similarities to CM Fortran [36], KALI [25], and Vienna Fortran [8]. The complete language is described in detail elsewhere [11].

10 Subspace Optimizations

Kathleen Knobe[1] William J. Dally [1]
ARTIFICIAL INTELLIGENCE LAB
MASSACHUSETTS INSTITUTE OF TECHNOLOGY, CAMBRIDGE, MA
email: {kathyk billd}@ai.mit.edu

Abstract: We distinguish between two different types of communication; we will ignore communication required to align two objects of the same shape. Such communication occurs, for example, when two 2-dimensional arrays must align for an operation to be performed on corresponding elements. Since all the communication can occur concurrently this is less of an efficiency issue than shape changing.

Shape changing arises when an object of some dimensionality must align with multiple parts of a higher dimensioned object. A shape change occurs, for example, when a vector is required to align with each row of a matrix as in the code, `a(i) + b(j,i)`. Since, after alignment, each (virtual) processor holding an element of `b` will also contain the associated element of `a`, `a` has become 2-dimensional (changing its shape).

A shape change that adds a dimension of extent `n` may require a number of communications proportional to O(1), O(lg n), or O(n) communication, depending on related code within the program. For example, it may be replicated or privatized along that dimension. Since optimizing among O(1), O(lg n), and O(n) communication is much more significant than optimizing the alignment of objects of the same shape, we have developed an abstraction that exposes shape changes but ignores alignment. We show a number of optimization based on this abstraction.

10.1 Introduction

Achieving the potential computing power of massively parallel MIMD systems has been difficult. One of the major issues is the cost of communication. In order to address the communication problem, there has been a significant focus in the research community both on techniques for automatically determining good layout strategies and on language extensions for specifying data layout [2, 12, 5, 1, 11].

Some communication arises simply because a value is needed by a processor other than the one on which it resides. Other communications are more complex. They arise because an element at some point in an object is computed based on the value in some

[1] Massachusetts Institute of Technology, Artificial Intelligence Lab, 545 Technology Square, Cambridge, MA 02139. The research described in this paper was supported in part by the Defense Advanced Research Projects Agency under contracts N00014-88K-0738 and N00014-91J-1698, by Air Force Systems under contract F19628-92-C-0045 and by a National Science Foundation Presidential Young Investigator Award, grant MIP-8657531, with matching funds from General Electric Corporation, IBM Corporation, and AT&T.

previously computed point in that object. For example, a row in a 2-dimensional object might be computed from values in the previous row. In this case, a 1-dimensional object, the first row, is becoming a 2-dimensional object as values propagate along the second dimension. This is referred to as *shape changing*.

This paper distinguishes between communication that involves shape changing and communication that does not. We present a categorization of shape changing operations and show some optimizations facilitated by this view.

10.1.1 Data Optimization

Data optimization techniques [8, 9, 10] automatically determine good layout strategies. They are designed to create locality and therefore minimize communication by analysis of the source code. The approach is driven by *preferences* among array occurrences, references to the array in the source. A preference between two array occurrences indicates that if the two occurrences are not aligned, communication will be required. Three types of preferences occur in MIMD programs

- *Conformance Preference*

  The conformance preference occurs between two operands of an operation. For example, in

  ```
  do i = ...
    ... = a(i) + b(i+3)
  enddo
  ```

  if `a(i)` does not align with `b(i+3)` for each `i` within the specified range, communication is required to perform the +.

- *Identity Preference*

  The identity preference occurs between a definition and a use of the same array if dependence analysis cannot prove independence. For example, in

  ```
  do i = ...
   a(i) = ...
        = a(j)
  enddo
  ```

  if an element of the array a might be both defined by the definition and used by the use, then a dependence exists. Such a dependence implies that communication is required to make the defined value available at the use if the definition and the use of that element are not performed on the same processor.

- *Control Preference*

  The control preference occurs between a control expression and operations it controls. For example, in

```
if a then
 do i = 1,20
  ... = b(i) + c(i)
 enddo
endif
```

the processors that might be executing the + require access to a. If the value of a is not available at these processors, communication will be required.

The *preference graph* is the graph consisting of nodes in internal representation of the program and the preferences among those nodes. The preference graph is processed by honoring preferences in order to minimize communication.

One interesting aspect of this process is the creation of *dynamic alignment* [7] which provides the ability to align objects of different dimensionality according to use. For example, the conformance preference created by the code segment

```
a(i) + b(k,i)
```

requires alignment of a 1-dimensional vector with the kth row of a 2-dimensional array. The vector a is said to be dynamically aligned *with respect to* the variable k since the function representing the alignment for a is a function of k. Notice that the same alignment is created by the control preference between a and b in the code segment

```
do i = ...
  do k = ...
    if a(i) then
      ... = ... b(k,i)
    endif
  enddo
enddo
```

Previously we viewed dynamic alignment as alignment of two conforming objects, a 1-dimensional vector and a row of a 2-dimensional array. However here we will view this as a shape changing operation. The vector is *promoted* to a 2-dimensional array since over time it will align with each row. [2]

10.1.2 Shapes

One of the significant challenges in compiling for parallel systems is transforming the code to change the shape of the operations. For vector machines, the goal is to transform operations that are expressed as a sequence of operations of dimensionality zero, e.g., x(i) + y(i) in a loop on i, to fewer operations of dimensionality 1, e.g., x(1:n) + y(1:n), thus changing the shape of the operation. For SIMD machines,

[2] One advantage of the earlier view as conforming 1-dimensional objects is that lifetime analysis more naturally views this situation as a set of smaller objects each with lifetimes within an iteration rather than one larger object with a lifetime that spans all iterations.

the result can include operations on multi-dimensional objects, e.g., `a(1:n,1:k) + b(1:n,1:k)`. In both cases the control flow over these operations remains sequential, that is, this operation can occur in a sequential loop as follows

```
do i = 1, imax
 z(i,1:n) = x(1:n) + y(1:n)
 ...
enddo
```

The shape of the iteration space for a loop nest determines the maximal dimensionality of the shape of the operations within it. The `do` loops below imply a sequence of zero-dimensional operations on this 2-dimensional space. It is up to the compiler to determine the actual shape of the operations, but the maximum dimensionality of that shape is 2.

```
do i = imin, imax, istride
 do j = jmin, jmax, jstride
  a(i,j) = s1*s2 + b(i)
  ...
 enddo
enddo
```

One way of viewing common SPMD compilation rules such as "scalars live on all processors" and "owner computes" is that they are rules that effect the shape of the objects. In the example above these rules imply that both the `+` and the `*` are 2-dimensional. The scalars, `s1` and `s2`, have been replicated since scalars live on all processors. For each `i` and `j` in the appropriate range, `b(i)` is communicated to align with `a(i,j)`. The operations are then performed in each of these locations. This is clearly more communication than is required, and too many processors are performing the operations.

The term *object* as used here refers to an occurrence of an array such as `b(i)` above. The term object also refers to an occurrence of an operation, focusing on the result rather than the operation itself. In the code above `s1*s2` is an object.

One way of viewing a common compiler optimization such as invariant code motion is that it transforms the shape of an object. For example, moving the invariant `s1*s2` out of the loop converts the example above to

```
t = s1*s2
do i = 1, imax
 do j = 1, jmax
  a(i,j) = t + b(i)
  ...
 enddo
enddo
```

changing the shape of `s1*s2` from a 2-dimensional object to a zero-dimensional object. Section 10.2 describes the subspace abstraction which captures the notion of shapes. Section 10.3 categorizes the ways in which objects can be transformed from one subspace to another. Section 10.4 describes optimizing transformations based on the subspace abstraction. Section 10.5 describes how this work relates to alignment.

10.2 Subspaces

[5, 8] distinguish between the virtual machine level and the physical machine level. (Alignment is a virtual machine concept whereas decomposition is a physical machine concept.) The virtual machine is of unbounded size and the specifics of the geometry are abstracted. Improved alignment at the virtual machine level leads to improved efficiency when the code is stripped to the physical machine level. This discussion focuses on compiler optimizations at the subspaces level before the compiler transforms the intermediate representation to the virtual machine level since improvements at this level lead to more significant improvements, as shown in section 10.4.

In this paper, we consider a small language that includes expressions on scalars and subscripted arrays, `do` loops and `if` statements. The abstract machine for this language includes arithmetic operations and communication. `if` statements are handled by an additional boolean argument, a *guard*, based on `if` conditions, which determines if a particular instance of the operation or a sequence of operations should be executed. Guards are also used to limit operations to processors holding elements of the objects specified.

Because the data is totally distributed across the virtual machine, guards and communication maintain the semantics of loops from the source code. Therefore no loops occur at this level. Loops are reintroduced later in the compiler when the machine size is taken into account in order to sequence through multiple elements mapped to a single physical processor.

The virtual machine level considers alignment across the unbounded machine dealing with all the details required to align, for example, `a(i)` with `b(2*i)`, `c(i+3)`, `d(i,j)` or `e(n-i)`.

The subspace abstraction, introduced here, hides these details.

Consider the space $\mathbf{Z}^n$ with basis vector $\{e_1, e_2, ...e_n\}$ where each e_i is an index in the iteration space. This set has 2^n subsets. Each subset spans a subspace of the iteration space.

For example, objects within loops on `i`, `j` and `k` may be in one of the following eight distinct subspaces of the iteration space: {}, {i}, {j}, {k}, {i, j}, {i, k}, {j, k} and {i, j, k}. These correspond geometrically to the origin of the cube ({}), the axes of the cube ({i}, {j}, {k}), the faces of the cube ({i, j}, {i, k}, {j, k}) and the whole cube ({i, j, k}) as seen in Figure 10.1.

Notice that there is a distinction among, for example, the 3 different 2-dimensional planes that have different orientations but there is not a distinction among different positions of parallel planes with the same orientation.

This abstraction focuses on conforming subspaces and on the transformations of objects from one subspace to another. It abstracts away the specifics of alignment within a subspace. In the example

```
do k ...
 do j ...
  do i ...
   ...a(i,j) op b(j*2,i+1,6)
   ...c(i) op d(k-1)
```

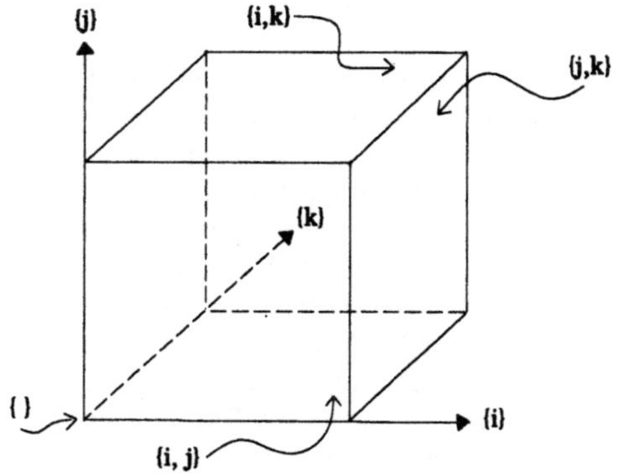

Figure 10.1 Geometric view of the subspaces of the space $\{i, j, k\}$

```
    enddo
  enddo
enddo
```

since a and b reference the same indices and are therefore in the same subspace, we say they *conform*. They both reference a 2-dimensional object (i by j) within a 3-dimensional iteration space $\{i, j, k\}$.[3] In this example, c and d do not conform since they are in different subspaces.

10.3 Subspace Changes

When objects of different subspaces are operated on together, one object must *expand to conform* to a subspace of higher dimensionality. In the invariant code motion example in section 10.1.2, t in subspace $\{\ \}$ must expand to conform to subspace $\{i\}$.

Critical within the subspace level of abstraction is the type of communication required for such an expansion. In the examples above, objects were expanded by replication only. In fact, objects may expand in different ways, called *expansion categories*. Each expansion category has its own semantic restrictions and its own costs. We will begin with a discussion of expansion of scalars and then consider expansion of array sections.

[3] We assume that each subscript refers to 1 or 0 loop indices. It may not be a function of 2 indices. Here we will deal with a(i*h,j,3) for scalar h and loop indices i and j, but not with a(i*j,h,3).

10.3.1 Scalars

Scalars fall into expansion categories based on the characteristics of the communication they require to expand.

- *Replicated:* If the value of the scalar is the same for all iterations, the scalar can be communicated via a fan out tree in O(lg N) time, where N is the extent of the replication. For example,

```
s = ...
  ...
do i = ...
     = ... s ...
enddo
```

- *Privatized:* If, for each iteration, the values of the scalar are computed independently, no communication is required between iterations. For example,

```
do i = ...
 s = ...
     = ... s ...
enddo
```

- *Scanned:* If the scalar is defined by a recurrence that can be computed by a parallel prefix operation, the communication can be performed in O(lg N) time. For example,[4]

```
do i = ...
 s =  s + a(i)
 ... = s  ...
enddo
```

- *Hopping:* If the value of the scalar in one iteration is determined from the value in a previous iteration, the value must be moved from one processor to another. Expansion via hopping requires O(N) time. Hopping results either from a recurrence not computable via a parallel prefix operation or from a conditional assignment to the scalar. For example

[4] There is potentially some confusion of jargon here. The example above is normally termed a reduction since we are reducing all the values stored in `a` to a single value stored in `s`. Here we are using the term expansion to show that if `s` is distributed with respect to `i`, to align with each element of `a`, then the single object `s` will live, although not necessarily at the same time, at all of the locations holding a value of `a`. It has become, in some sense, a 1-dimensional object.

```
do i =
 if
  s = ...
 endif
  ... = s  ...
enddo
```

or

```
do i =
 s = user_func(s)
 ... = s  ...
enddo
```

- *Implicitly distributed:* If the scalar is the index of the loop or computable directly from that index, then it is not necessarily stored on any processor. If the value required can be computed by inverting the alignment function on the processor address. For example, in

  ```
  do i ...
   ... = a(i) + i ...
  enddo
  ```

  since each processor can determine which element of the array a it holds, it can compute the value of the variable i without communication.

Notice that the worst case here is hopping, O(N). However, in the SPMD model, the "scalars are owned by all processors" rule requires O(N*P) messages, where N is the iteration count and P is the number of processors, whenever there is a definition of the scalar within a loop.

10.3.2 Control Expressions

An if statement gives rise to control preferences that treat the condition as an additional operand of the operations it controls. This minimizes the communication of control expressions. The availability of the condition may slow up the operation in exactly the same way that the availability of one of the operands might. Condition values may fall into any of the expansion categories as shown in the following code.

- *Replicated:*

```
do i
 if a then ...
  ... = x(i)
enddo
```

- *Scanned:*

```
do i
 a1 = a1 + b(i)
 if a1 then ...
  ... = x(i)
enddo
```

- *Privatized:*

```
do i
 a2 = ...
 if a2 then ...
  ... = x(i)
enddo
```

- *Hopping:*

```
do i
 a3 = user_func(a3)
  if a3 then ...
   ... = x(i)
enddo
```

- *Implicitly distributed:*

```
do i
 do j
   ...
  if i.gt.j then ...
   ... = y(i,j)
  endif
   ...
enddo
```

10.3.3 Array Sections

Just as the expansion categories above show how a scalar expands to conform to an object of larger dimensionality, an array section of a given dimensionality can expand to conform to an array section of a larger dimensionality.

For example,

```
do i
 do j
  ...
  ... a(i) + b(i,j)
 enddo
enddo
```

Here a(i) is dynamically aligned with respect to j. Expansion of a(i) to conform with subspace {i, j} might be privatized, hopping, replicated or scanned depending on other code within the loop nest. See [13] for discussion of computation of array privatization and [3] for a discussion of its importance.

Array sections may also expand due to control preferences as shown below.

```
do i
 do j
  if a(i) then
   ...
   ... b(i,j)
  endif
 enddo
enddo
```

10.3.4 Explicit Dimensions

Code can be written with the expanded index explicit in the source. For example,

- *Privatized:*

```
do i
 a(i) = ...
  ... = ... a(i)
enddo
```

- *Hopping:*

```
do i
 b(i) = ... b(i-1)
enddo
```

or

```
do i
 if ...
     c(i) =
 endif
  ... = ... c(i)
enddo
```

Notice that these categories are consistent with the expansion categories discussed above but the examples do not really exhibit changes in subspace per se.

Picture this situation not as an object expanding to a subspace that includes an additional index but rather as new values propagating along an existing dimension within a subspace. The communication costs are comparable and the situations are treated identically. For example, an object in {i, j} that expands via hopping to become an object in {i, j, k} incurs a communication cost similar to that of an object in {i, j, k} whose values propagate via hopping along its k axis.

Given this modified view of expansion, we need to modify our view of *conforming* to deal with explicit dimensions of this type. For example, in

```
do i
 do j
  c(i,j) = ... c(i,j-1)
  ... = c(i,j) + d(i)
 enddo
enddo
```

the first statement defines the value of `c(i,j)` from the value of `c(i,j-1)`. Therefore `c` hops along the `j` dimension. So `c` is treated as a 1-dimensional object expanding to a 2-dimensional object via hopping, even though the `j` dimension is explicit in this case. Therefore, `c(i,j) + d(i)` is conforming even though the indices referenced are not identical. Whereas in

```
do i
 do j
  c(i,j) = ... c(i,j-1)
  ... = c(i,j) + e(i,j)
 enddo
enddo
```

because `c` hops with respect to its explicit second dimension, `j`, `c(i,j) + e(i,j)` is non-conforming even though the indices referenced are identical.

10.3.5 Reductions

The sections above have shown how expansions can appear in a variety of forms in the source code and how the communication requirements for expansions depend on other code within the same loops. However, when an object expands from subspace s_1 to subspace s_2 on entry to a loop, then on exit from that loop, it must be *reduced* from subspace s_2 to subspace s_1.

One instance of the object along the promoted axis is taken to be the reduced object. Specifically, if an object in {i, j} is promoted along axis k on loop entry, and k_{last} is the last iteration of the k loop actually executed, then on loop exit, the reduced object is an object in {i, j} at the single point corresponding to k_{last} on the k axis. At the subspace level, this object simply conforms with other objects in subspace {i, j} even though at the virtual machine level it may require communication to actually use it.

Since reductions cost nothing with respect to subspaces they are not addressed further.

10.4 Subspace Optimizations

This section introduces a cost model and shows several transformations on subspaces that are optimizations with respect to this model. These optimizations are performed prior to alignment. In other words, the compiler includes:

- a subspace optimizer that transforms the internal representation (IR) according to the optimizations presented here, generating IR at the subspace level.
- a data optimizer that optimizes the alignment of the subspace IR, generating IR at the virtual machine level.
- a strip miner [14] that maps IR at the virtual machine level to IR at the physical machine level.

We will first consider a simple example that only includes objects that expand via replication.

```
do i = 1, imax
 do j = 1, jmax
  do k = 1, kmax
   x(i,j,k) = a(i,j) +  e(i,j,k) +
        c(i,j) + d(j) + b(j) + f(i)
  enddo
 enddo
enddo
```

Consider the naive approach of performing all the operations in the context of the left hand side implied by the SPMD owner computes rule.

The *subspace tree* in Figure 10.2 shows the computation for the code above using the owner computes rule. The subspace tree is a way of indicating operations within subspaces. (Note that it is possible for a subspace tree to be a directed acyclic graph, DAG, if common subexpressions are detected.)

The interpretation of this subspace tree is that it specifies the computations required to compute the result for any given `i`, `j` and `k`.

Notice that this tree represents the dependences of a single statement through all the loops controlling its execution. Although it represents only a single statement the operations for this statement depend on other code in the loop. For example, the fact that `f(i)` can be replicated across `j` here relies on knowledge about the entire loop nest.

The `do` loop representation in the source specifies the code that will be executed for each iteration. It therefore makes apparent a set of optimizations consistent with this view, i.e., the standard global optimizations. The subspace tree specifies what will be executed for each statement over all the iterations of the loop. Its value is that it makes a different set of optimizations apparent.

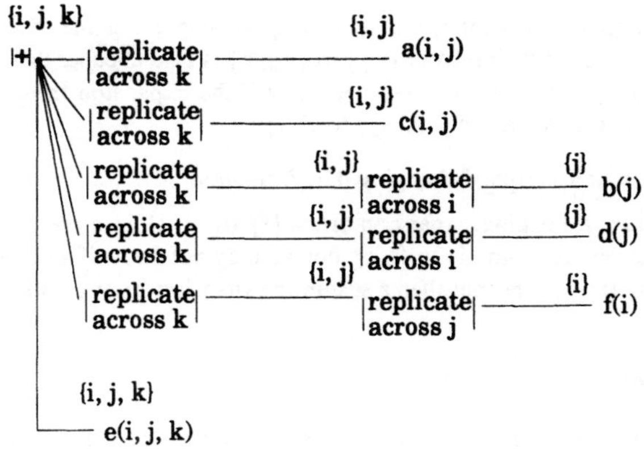

Figure 10.2 Subspace Tree

We see from this subspace tree that the owner computes rule results in the following operations:

- expansions
  - 2 replications from $\{j\}$ to $\{i, j\}$
  - 1 replication from $\{i\}$ to $\{i, j\}$
  - 5 replications from $\{i, j\}$ to $\{i, j, k\}$
- arithmetic operations
  - 5 operations in $\{i, j, k\}$

10.4.1 Relative Costs

For optimizations at the subspace level, we use a simple cost model that provides a partial ordering among the costs of computing various expressions. We only require a relative cost model here since the goal of the model is not to actually determine the costs but to determine what constitutes an optimization.

Each arithmetic operation takes place in a subspace. The relative costs of a single node therefore depends on the following:

- the subspace in which a computation is performed

  For example, an addition performed in the 1-dimensional subspace $\{i\}$ is cheaper than an addition performed in the 2-dimensional subspace $\{i, j\}$. We may not know if an addition in $\{i\}$ is cheaper than an addition in $\{j\}$ or $\{j, k\}$.

- the subspace of the source and of the target of an expansion

  For example, the expansion from {i} to {i, j} is cheaper than the expansion from {i} to {i, j, k}. The expansion from {i, j} to {i, j, k} is also cheaper than the expansion form {i} to {i, j, k}, but we may not know if the expansion from {i} to {i, j} is cheaper than the expansion from {j} to {i, j}.

- the category of a subspace changing transformation

  For example, a hopping expansion from {i} to {i, j} is more expensive than a scanned expansion from {i} to {i, j}, but we may not know if a hopping expansion from {i} to {i, j} is cheaper than a scanning expansion from {j} to {i, j}.

10.4.2 Subspace Minimization

Let us reexamine the example introduced at the beginning of this section. Considering the fixed expression tree without reordering as produced by a possible parse of the source expression (indicated below by the parentheses)

```
x(i,j,k) = (a(i,j) + (e(i,j,k) + (c(i,j) + (d(j)
           + ((b(j) + f(i)))))))
```

we can minimize the shape of the objects generated, the intermediate results, to their *natural shape* by performing each operation in the smallest subspace appropriate for the operands. For example, the smallest subspace for `b(j) + f(i)` is {i, j}. In fact, we can compute `(c(i,j) + (d(j) + ((b(j) + f(i)))))` in subspace {i, j}. The remainder of the expression must be performed in {i, j, k}. The result is

- expansions
  - 2 replications from {j} to {i, j}
  - 1 replication from {i} to {i, j}
  - 2 replications from {i, j} to {i, j, k}
- arithmetic operations
  - 3 operations in {i, j}
  - 2 operations in {i, j, k}

This optimization is similar in flavor to transformations performed in APL compilers to limit the computations required in the presence of shape changes [4].

We can uncover further improvements if we allow the code to be reordered:

```
x(i,j,k) = e(i,j,k) + ((d(j) + b(j))
           + f(i) + c(i,j) + a(i,j))
```

For the reordered version the result is

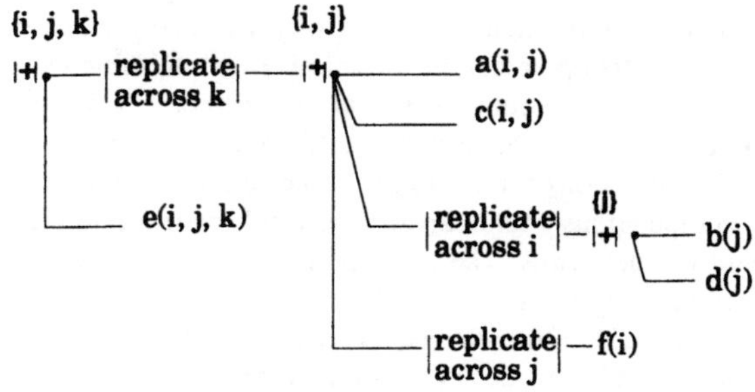

Figure 10.3 Improved Subspace Tree

- expansions
  - 1 replication from {i} to {i, j}
  - 1 replication from {j} to {i, j}
  - 1 replication from {i, j} to {i, j, k}
- arithmetic operations
  - 1 operation in {j}
  - 3 operations in {i, j}
  - 1 operation in {i, j, k}

To assess this optimization, we need a model for the relative cost of the tree based on the relative costs of the nodes. The dilemma in determining the cost of the tree is that its actual cost depends on the mapping. Therefore, we consider both the sum of the nodes on any path and the total sum of the nodes. The most expensive path is a more accurate measure if the mapping is such that siblings in the subspace tree are processed in parallel, that is, if the virtual machine is a good approximation to the actual machine, whereas the total cost of all operations is more accurate when the mapping is such that siblings share processors and must be performed sequentially.

Notice that at the subspace level, the cost of communication due to misalignments between two operands in the same subspace, for example, the cost of aligning a and c within subspace {i, j} in Figure 10.3, does not appear in the cost model. The only communication costs considered are those due to expansions. This is because, for replications, scans and hops, a given processor may have to wait for a series of other communications to occur before the communication it must perform is enabled. This constitutes an inherent delay. Whereas all the messages due to a misalignment between two conforming objects can occur immediately and in parallel. At this level we will then assume an O(1) cost for misalignments. Misalignments can, of course, be costly. In fact, it is possible for a misalignment to result in a longer delay than an expansion if it involves more messages and is limited by throughput. This is why, following subspace optimizations, the compiler performs data optimization to minimize such misalignments.

One additional observation about our use of relative costs: One statement in a loop may produce values used by another statement. Although the analysis of the statement is with respect to all its iterations and the expansion categories for the statement operands are based on all computations within the loop nest, subspace minimization is performed on each statement independently. The assumption is that improvements in the relative costs of each statement improves the over all relative cost.

We now examine the cost of the statement above for both the owner computes version and the version optimized by reordering. Assume that the extent of each dimension in {i, j, k} is 128. Using the longest path cost model, the owner computes version will require 2 * lg 128 or 14 for communication time and 5 + operations for arithmetic. The optimized version has the same longest path cost. This optimization reduces the total time, not the time for the longest path.

Now consider the cost model that compares the sum of all operations. The cost of a replication will be counted as the number of messages sent. This is the size of the target shape minus the size of the source shape.

For owner computes:

- expansions
  - 2 replications from {j} to {i, j}
    2 * ((128 * 128) - 128) = 32,512 messages
  - 1 replication from {i} to {i, j}
    1 * (128 * 128 - 128) = 16,256 messages
  - 5 replications from {i, j} to {i, j, k}
    5 * ((128 * 128 * 128) - (128 * 128)) = 10,403,840 messages
  - total
    10,452,608
- arithmetic operations
  - 5 operations in {i, j, k}
    5 * 128 * 128 * 128 = 10,485,760
  - total
    10,485,760

For the reordered version:

- expansions
  - 1 replication from {i} to {i, j}
    1 * (128 * 128) - 128 = 16,256 messages

- 1 replication from {j} to {i, j}
  1 * (128 * 128) - 128 = 16,256 messages
- 1 replication from{i, j} to {i, j, k}
  1 * ((128 * 128 * 128) - (128 * 128)) = 2,080,768 messages
- total
  2,113,280

• arithmetic operations

- 1 operation in {j}
  128
- 3 operations in {i, j}
  16,384
- 1 operation in {i, j, k}
  2,097,152
- total
  2,113,664

In conclusion, subspace minimization reduced the number of messages from 10,452,608 to 2,113,280 and the number of arithmetic operations from 10,485,760 to 2,113,664 for this statement.

10.4.3 Subspace Minimization with other Types of Expansion

In the example above all the objects that require expansion are expandable via replication. This is not always the case. Consider the following example.

```
do i = 1, imax
 s = a(i) + b(i)
 do j = 1, jmax
   s = user_func(s)
   do k = 1, kmax
    s = s + c(i,j,k)
   enddo
 enddo
enddo
```

Here, s is privatized with respect to i, hopping with respect to j and scanned with respect to k. Therefore, any particular use of s must be preceded by nodes for the scan, the hop and the privatize in the subspace tree representation.

Consider the code:

```
    a(i,j,k) = b(i) + c(i) + d(i,j)
```

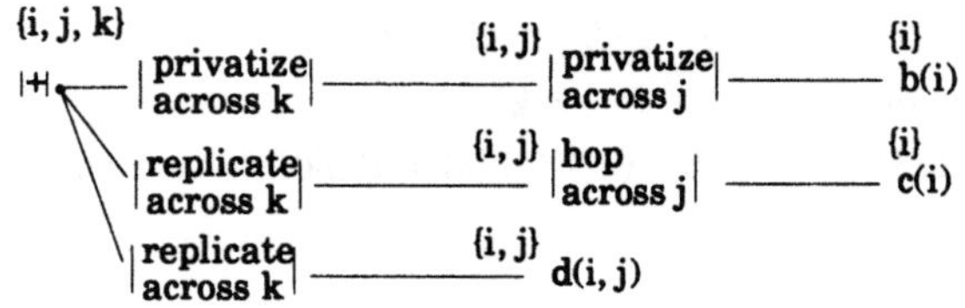

Figure 10.4 Computations at owner with expansions other than replication

We might assume from the subspace minimization discussion that the optimal organization for this code would be:

```
a(i,j,k) = (b(i) + c(i)) + d(i,j)
```

so that `b(i) + c(i)` could be performed in the minimal subspace, {i}, prior to expansion. In fact, this is true if all the expansions to {i, j, k} are replications. However, if other expansion categories are involved, they may restrict the application of subspace minimization causing unexpected results.

Suppose the expansion categories are as shown in Figure 10.4. Then `b(i) + c(i)` cannot be performed in subspace {i} and replicated to {i, j, k} since the result has different values along both the `j` and the `k` axes for any given value of `i`. Thus, this organization simply fixes the ordering of additions within the multi-operand addition in Figure 10.4. It does not result in any reduction of either communications or arithmetic operations. However `c(i) + d(i,j)` can be computed in space {i, j} since, given `i` and `j`, the value of `c(i) + d(i,j)` is identical for any `k`. This result can then be expanded to subspace {i, j, k} via replication as shown in Figure 10.5. Therefore given the expansion categories for this example, the best performance is achieved by:

```
a(i,j,k) = b(i) + (c(i) + d(i,j))
```

The number of messages saved by this approach is $extent(i) * extent(j) * extent(k) - extent(i) * extent(j)$. If each extent is 128, as in the previous example, 2,080,768 messages are saved. The number of additions saved is also 2,080,768.

10.4.4 Combining Multiple Expansions

Notice, in section 10.4.2, we were able to interchange the order of replications and local operations to improve efficiency. This is not always semantically valid with other forms of expansion. However, some optimizations are possible. Recall that we were able to transform multiple replicates to a single replicate as shown in Figure 10.6.

We might be able to perform similar transformations as shown for the example in Figure 10.7. Since both operands of the + are scanned across `i` prior to the addition, it is be possible to perform the addition prior to expansion if the values at intermediate iterations are only used in computing the final result.

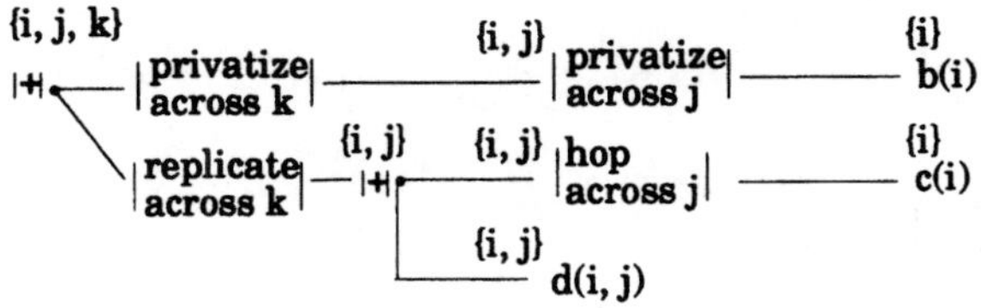

Figure 10.5 Subspace minimization with expansions other than replication

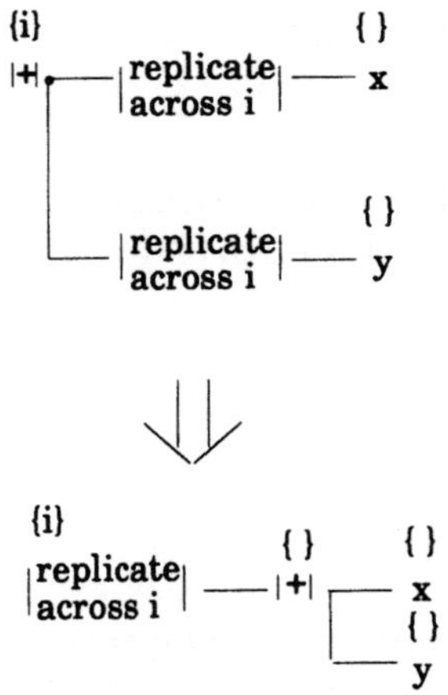

Figure 10.6 Interchange of replicates with a local computation

10.4.5 Expansion Strength Reduction

Transforming an expansion from a communication category of higher cost to one of lower cost is called *expansion strength reduction.*

For example, in the following code

```
do i ...
 if a(i) then
  b = b + c(i)
 endif
enddo
```

the assignment could be computed via a O(lg N) scan operation, but since the value of `c(i)` is conditionally added to the running sum we might naively generate expansion

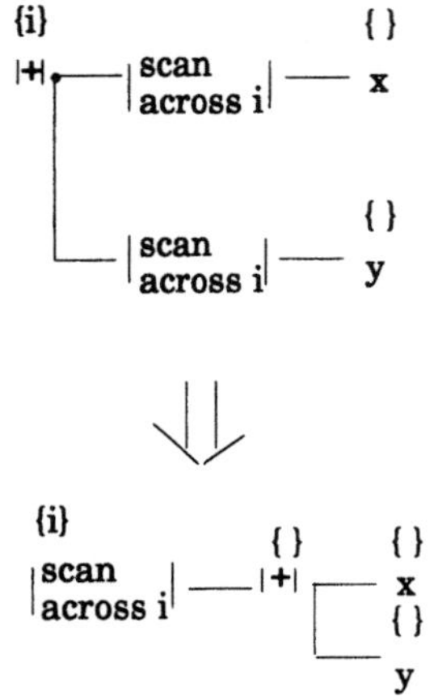

Figure 10.7 Interchange of scans with a local computation

via hopping, which takes O(N) time. However, the effect of the condition can be handled by generating a scan with a mask in O(lg N) time.

Similarly, in the following code

```
do i =
  b = b + 1
  ... = b + a(i)
  ...
enddo
```

the increment of b appears to be a scanned expansion, O(lg N), however, since each processor holding a value of a can determine locally the corresponding value of i and since b can be computed locally from i, we are able to reduce the O(lg N) scan to an O(1) privatization.

10.4.6 Expansion Costs

Section 10.4.2 addressed subspace minimization. Before considering more complex optimizations we must discuss the cost of expansions that are more interesting than simple replication.

We consider the cost of an expansion via hopping in somewhat more detail. The reason the object must hop, as opposed to replicate, is that some local operation may be required on the object in each iteration, at each processor, prior to sending the object on to the next processor for the next iteration. The actual cost of the expansion is then

(the cost of the hops * the cost of the computation within each hop)

We can typically ignore the cost of the computation (as we do for the replicate) when the cost is a small constant and just consider the cost of the communication only. However, if the cost of computing the next value is O(N) or O(lg N), this cost cannot be ignored. Similarly, a sum scan is considered O(lg N) since communication takes O(lg N)

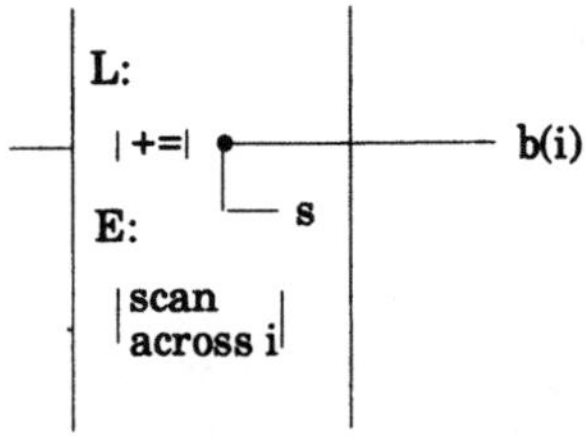

Figure 10.8 Computation within a hopping expansion

time and the sum itself on each processor takes O(1) time. However, if the computation required by the scan is not O(1) then it must also be taken into account.

A node in the subspace tree for a replication simply contains the replication itself. The cost of such a node is simply the cost of the communication. A node for a hop or a scan, on the other hand, will include both the communication and an indication of what part of the subtree below (to the right) is to be performed locally at each node. The rest is considered input required to be available at a node when the hop or scan arrives there.

For example,

```
do i ...
 s = s + b(i)
enddo
```

will appear as shown in Figure 10.8.

Just as the + appeared within vertical bars to indicate the operation at a node in earlier subspace trees, the larger vertical bars indicate the operation at the node here. "`L:`" indicates the local computation required with each communication. The code to the right of the vertical bars can be computed prior to arrival of the hop or scan. "`E:`" indicates the expansion category. To compute the cost of a hop or a scan node such as that above, compute the cost of the computation at the node (within brackets) times the cost of the communication type. For this example the cost is O(lg N) * O(1) or O(lg N).

10.4.7 Reducing the Computation within Expansions

The formula for the cost of expansions leads us to consider reducing the cost of an expansion by reducing the code that is required at each location prior to sending the value on to the next location. One approach is to speculatively execute as much of that code as possible on all processors concurrently instead of waiting for the serial control to arrive at the processor before beginning execution. Consider the following

```
do i = 1, imax
```

```
    if s.gt.a(i) then
     do j = 1, jmax
      s = s + b(i,j)
     enddo
    endif
   enddo
```

Naively, s hops across i since the execution of the j loop that updates s depends on the value of s in the current iteration. Therefore each of O(imax) instances of the j loop takes O(lg jmax) time so the total cost is O(imax * lg jmax).

However if we execute the j loops for all iterations of the i loop saving the results in temporaries, they can all take place in parallel summing b along all the columns in O(lg (jmax)) time. The result, an object of subspace {i}, is then conditionally added up. This addition requires hopping (O(imax) time) to ensure availability of the condition. So the total time is now O(imax + lg(jmax)) instead of O(imax * lg (jmax)).[5]

This is an optimization based on the shortest path cost model only. Although the number of computations performed increases, the total time is reduced by shortening the critical path.

10.5 Subspaces Optimization Compared to Alignment

An expansion implies a delay of O(N) if the expansion is via hopping, O(lg N) if the expansion is via replication or scanning or O(1) if the expansion is via privatization. Reducing the number of subspace changes in the subspace tree, reducing the rank of the subspace of the source and target of a subspace change or reducing the strength (hopping to scanned, for example) are significant optimizations since they can affect the availability of the result by O(N) or O(lg N).

Not all communication arises from subspace transformations. Some communication results from unhonored conformance, identity and control preferences that did not involve changes in subspace. If the operands of the + operations performed in subspace {i, j} in the subspace tree in Figure 10.3 are unaligned, the communication to align them is conformance communication and can take place in parallel in O(1) time. If the reference to c(i,j) is needed in one set of processors for this computation but is defined in another set of processors, the communication to realign c is identity communication and can take place in parallel in O(1) time.

In aligning two objects within the same subspace, a value in one location must move to one other location whereas an expansion which adds an index of extent N to the subspace, a value in one location may have to move to N other locations. Therefore, we first perform transformations that optimize the distinction between communication that takes O(N), O(lg N), or O(1) at the subspace level. Then, given the transformed code, we optimize the alignments at the virtual machine level.

[5] This particular example is analogous to a carry-select adder [6].

The notion of two objects conforming at the subspace level is analogous to the notion of two objects aligning at the virtual machine level. The notion of expanding one object to conform with another at the subspace level is analogous to moving an object to align at the virtual machine level.

10.6 Summary

This paper introduces the subspace abstraction and provides evidence of its value. This abstraction distinguishes between two types of communication, that required to align objects within the same subspace of the iteration space and that required to expand an object from one subspace to another. Since expansions are significantly more expensive than alignments within a subspace, the subspace abstraction makes the first visible while suppressing the second. This enables us to focus on optimizations at this level before analyzing alignment on the transformed code. Several such optimizations presented above include

- limiting the cost of expanding objects according to that required by their expansion category (replicating, privatizing, hopping, scanning or implicitly distributing)
- minimizing the subspace for local operations and for expansions
- reducing the strength of expansion
- reducing the computations within expansions

This constitutes a preliminary investigation of the subspace abstraction. Current work includes investigating the use of the subspace abstraction in

- predicting program performance
- driving automatic alignment and automatic decomposition
- generating non-SPMD code.

10.7 Acknowledgments

Thanks to Joan Lukas, Norm Rubin and Carl Offner for productive discussions and to Ellen Spertus for several careful readings of the paper.

References

[1] Barbara Chapman, Piyush Mehrotra, and Hans Zima. Vienna Fortran - a Fortran language extension for distributed memory multiprocessors. Technical report, Institute for Computer Applications in Science and Engineering, Hampton, Virginia, Sept 1991.

[2] Siddhartha Chatterjee, John R. Gilbert, Robert Schreiber, and Shuang-Hua Teng. Automatic array alignment in data-parallel programs. In *Proceedings of the Twentieth Annual Symposium on Principles of Programming Languages*, Charleston, SC, January 1993. Association for Computing Machinery.

[3] R. Eigenmann, J. Hoefinger, Z. Li, and D. Padua. Experience in the automatic parallelization of four Perfect-Benchmark programs. In *Proceedings of the 4th workshop on Programming Languages and Compilers for Parallel Computing*. Pitman/MIT Press, AUG 1991.

[4] L. Guibas and D. Wyatt. Compilation and delayed evaluation in APL. In *Proceedings of the Fifth Annual Symposium on Principles of Programming Languages*. Association for Computing Machinery, January 1978.

[5] HPF language specification, version 1.0. Technical Report CRPC-TR 92225, Rice University, Houston, Texas, January 1993.

[6] Kai Hwang. *Computer Arithmetic*. Wiley, 1979.

[7] Kathleen Knobe, Joan D. Lukas, and William J. Dally. Dynamic alignment on distributed memory systems. In *Proceedings of the Third Workshop on Compilers for Parallel Computers*, Vienna, Austria, July 1992. Austrian Center for Parallel Computation. Published as technical report ACPC/TR 92-8 of the Austrian Center for Parallel Computation.

[8] Kathleen Knobe, Joan D. Lukas, and Guy L. Steele Jr. Data optimization: Allocation of arrays to reduce communication on SIMD machines. *Journal of Parallel and Distributed Computing*, 8:102–118, 1990.

[9] Kathleen Knobe and Venkataraman Natarajan. Data optimization: Minimizing residual interprocessor data motion on SIMD machines. In *Frontiers '90: The Third Symposium on the Frontiers of Massively Parallel Computation*, College Park, Maryland, Oct 1990. University of Maryland.

[10] Kathleen Knobe and Venkataraman Natarajan. Automatic data allocation to mimimize data motion on SIMD machines. *Journal of Supercomputing*, 1993. to appear.

[11] Jingke Li and Marina Chen. Index domain alignment: Minimizing costs of cross-referencing between distributed arrays. In *Frontiers '90: The Third Symposium on the Frontiers of Massively Parallel Computation*, College Park, Maryland, Oct 1990. University of Maryland.

[12] J. Ramanujam and P. Sadayappan. Compile-time techniques for data distribution in distributed memory machines. *IEEE Transactions on Parallel and Distributed Systems*, 2(4), October 1991.

[13] Peng Tu and David Padua. Array privatization for shared and distributed memory machines. *ACM SIGPLAN Notices*, 28(1), January 1993. Proceedings of the Workshop on Languages, Compilers, and Run-Time Environments for Distributed Memory Multiprocessors.

[14] Michael Weiss. Strip mining on SIMD architectures. In *International Conference on Supercomputing*, Cologne, Germany, June 1991. ACM.

11 Data and Process Alignment in Modula-2*

Michael Philippsen Markus U. Mock
DEPARTMENT OF INFORMATICS
UNIVERSITY OF KARLSRUHE, GERMANY
email: (phlipp|mock)@ira.uka.de

Abstract: Exploiting locality is a central goal of translating problem-oriented parallel programming languages for distributed memory parallel machines. Modula-2* places the burden of automatically deriving good data *and* process distribution on the compiler.

In this paper we present a technique implemented in our optimizing compiler that enhances locality in a source-to-source transformation. Analysis of data access patterns and parallel operations leads to an arrangement graph. Processing of this graph reveals conflicting arrangements. Some assumptions and a heuristic based on dynamic programming enables the compiler to find the best alignment in logarithmic time. The technique has improved runtime performance on benchmarks by over 60%.

11.1 Introduction

Straightforward compilation of FORALL statements and allocation of array elements onto massively parallel machines results in a significant amount of interprocessor data motion. Therefore, data and process distribution is an essential problem of numerous compiler projects targeting distributed memory machines.

There is widespread agreement about the two goals of data and process distribution: (1) Data locality. To reduce the amount of communication and achieve minimal run-time, all data elements which are used by a process should be store locally on the same PE. (2) Parallelism. Using just one processor results in perfect data locality and minimal communication cost. In general, however, the run-time can be improved by exploiting the full degree of parallelism provided by the hardware. A trade-off between the conflicting goals of data locality and parallelism must be found.

Whereas the goals are agreed upon, totally different approaches to reach them have been developed. In many programming languages the user must explicitly provide the data layout. Some languages require an explicit mapping of the data onto the topology [1, 14, 11], others are more abstract and offer either sets of directives for the compiler or interactive or knowledge-based environments that help determine the alignment of array dimensions and mapping functions [4, 10, 8, 3, 2]. Recent work [6, 7, 5, 16, 9] focuses on static compile-time analysis to automatically find a data decomposition that achieves both goals for vector and data-parallel operations.

Modula-2* [17] is designed for high-level, problem-oriented, and machine-independent parallel programming. The programmer can focus on the problem he has to solve, abstracting from the available number of processors and the interconnection network. Therefore, the compiler has to determine an appropriate data and process distribution.

Known approaches to automatically derive good data allocations have been targeting pure data-parallel programming languages, i.e. the parallelism has come from vector manipulations. In these approaches it is sufficient to find good data allocations. Locality is achieved by applying the owner-computes rule to distribute the statement execution onto the processors accordingly.

Modula-2*, however, is not a purely data-parallel programming language. When designing Modula-2*, we wanted to preserve the main advantages of data-parallel languages while avoiding the drawbacks [13]. Although data-parallel programming is possible, the notion of *process* is present. Therefore, both data *and* process distribution must be found by the compiler.

In this paper we present our approach to derive both data and process distribution for Modula-2* programs. Our technique is based on the work of Knobe [7] but extends her ideas with the consideration of process distribution and the clear separation of high-level data arrangement and physical data layout.

In section 11.2 we present the basic characteristics of Modula-2*. Section 11.3 explains the general approach of the Modula-2* compiler. In sections 11.4 and 11.5 we give some more details on the alignment graphs, the conflict detection, and the heuristic search mechanism.

11.2 Modula-2*

The programming language Modula-2* was developed to allow for high-level, problem-oriented and machine-independent parallel programming. As described in [17], it provides the following features:

- An arbitrary number of processes operate on data in the same *single address space*. Note that shared memory is not required; a single address space merely permits all memory to be addressed, but not necessarily at uniform speed.
- Synchronous and asynchronous parallel computations as well as arbitrary nestings thereof can be formulated in a totally machine-independent way.
- Procedures may be called in any context (sequential, synchronous, or asynchronous) at any nesting depth. Furthermore, additional parallel processes can be created inside procedures (recursive parallelism).
- All abstraction mechanisms of Modula-2 are available for parallel programming.

Modula-2* extends Modula-2 with just two language constructs:

1. The only way to introduce parallelism into Modula-2* programs is by means of the `FORALL` *statement*, which has a synchronous and an asynchronous version.

2. The distribution of array data is optionally specified by so-called *allocators*. These machine-independent allocators do not have any semantic meaning. They are just hints about data layout for the compiler.

Because of the compactness and simplicity of these extensions, they could easily be incorporated into other imperative programming languages, such as Fortran, C, or Ada.

11.2.1 FORALL statement

In Modula-2*, the syntax of the FORALL statement is:

```
ForallStatement =
FORALL ident ":" SimpleType IN (PARALLEL | SYNC)
       StatementSequence
END.
```

SimpleType is an enumeration or a possibly *non-static* subrange, i.e. the boundary expressions may contain variables. The FORALL creates as many (conceptual) processes as there are elements in *SimpleType*. The identifier introduced by the FORALL statement is local to it and serves as a runtime constant for every process created by the FORALL. The runtime constant of each process is initialized to a unique value of *SimpleType*.

Each process created by a FORALL executes the statements in *StatementSequence*. The END of a FORALL statement imposes a *synchronization barrier* on the participating processes: the termination of the whole FORALL statement is delayed until *all* created processes have finished their execution of *StatementSequence*.

In a synchronous FORALL, the created processes execute *StatementSequence* in lock-step, while in the asynchronous case, they work concurrently.

The behavior of branches and loops inside synchronous FORALLs is defined with a MSIMD (multiple SIMD) machine in mind. This means that Modula-2* does not require any synchronization between different branches of synchronous CASE or IF statements. The exact synchronous semantics of all Modula-2* statements, including nested FORALLs, are defined in [17].

11.2.2 Allocation of array data

Modula-2* provides a simple, machine-independent construct for controlling the allocation of array data. This construct is optional and does not change the meaning of a program. The modified declaration syntax for arrays is:

```
ArrayType =
ARRAY SimpleType [allocator]
      {"," SimpleType [allocator]} OF type.
allocator =
LOCAL | SPREAD | CYCLE | RANDOM | SBLOCK | CBLOCK.
```

Array elements whose indices differ only in dimensions that are marked `LOCAL` are associated with the same processor. This facility is used to avoid distribution of data in a given dimension.

Dimensions with allocator `SPREAD` are divided into segments, one for each of the available processors. A vector with n elements is assigned to P processors by allocating a segment of length $\lceil n/P \rceil$ to each processor. While utilizing all available processors, it minimizes the cost of nearest-neighbor communication.

Dimensions with allocator `CYCLE` are distributed in a round-robin fashion over the available processors. Given P processors, the elements of a vector whose indices are identical modulo P are associated with the same processor. In contrast to `SPREAD`, `CYCLE` maximizes the cost of nearest-neighbor communication: neighboring array elements are always on different processors, leading to better processor utilization if a parallel algorithm operates on subsegments of a vector.

Dimensions with allocator `RANDOM` are distributed randomly over the available processors. In contrast to `CYCLE`, `RANDOM` leads to a better processor utilization if a parallel algorithms accesses the dimension in a random pattern.

If either `SPREAD`, `CYCLE`, or `RANDOM` apply to several successive dimensions, then these dimensions are "unrolled" into one pseudo-vector with a length that is the product of the lengths of the individual dimensions. This scheme idles fewer processors than applying `SPREAD`, `CYCLE`, or `RANDOM` to individual dimensions.

Allocators `SBLOCK` and `CBLOCK` apply `SPREAD` and `CYCLE` resp. to each dimension individually. For two successive dimensions, `SBLOCK` has the effect of creating rectangular subarrays and assigning those to the processors. With this arrangement, nearest-neighbor communication in all dimensions is best supported when the interconnection network can be configured into the same number of dimensions as the arrays.

`CBLOCK` for two dimensions also creates two-dimensional subarrays, but the rows and columns of these subarrays are then distributed in a round-robin fashion over the processor grid. Again, `SBLOCK` minimizes nearest-neighbor communication, while `CBLOCK` allows high processor utilization if smaller subarrays are processed in parallel.

11.3 Alignment in Modula-2*

In this section we present the general ideas of our data and process alignment strategies.

Data *layout* is the decision which element of an array is physically stored on which processor. *Arrangement* is the process of arranging array elements so that the elements of different arrays which are used together will end up in the same processor.

Although arrangement and layout are seen as one step in the literature, we propose to separate these issues into two phases:

$$\text{Alignment} = \text{Arrangement} + \text{Layout}$$

11.3.1 Data Alignment

In terms of Modula-2* we use a source-to-source transformation in the first phase to achieve the arrangement. For the second phase we have developed an adequate layout algorithm [12] that maps arrays onto the machine depending on their declarations. Consider the following example:

```
VAR A: ARRAY [1..90]  SPREAD OF INTEGER;
    B: ARRAY [0..100] SPREAD OF INTEGER;

BEGIN
  FORALL i:[1..90] IN SYNC
    A[i] := B[i-1];
    B[i] := 0
  END
END
```

To arrange arrays A and B, array A is enlarged and shifted to the left. All index expressions involved are transformed accordingly. After this, elements which are used together have the same index. Note that the new array A is larger than the old one. Since the primary goal of our optimization is runtime performance we allow for moderate waste in storage consumption.

```
VAR (* A: ARRAY [1..90] SPREAD OF INTEGER; *)
    A,B : ARRAY [0..100] SPREAD OF INTEGER;

BEGIN
  FORALL i:[1..90] IN SYNC
    A[i-1] := B[i-1];
    B[i]   := 0
  END
END
```

The analysis would not arrange arrays A and B if the programmer had used different allocators. In this case, the compiler issues a performance warning, which suggests to reconsider the used allocators. If the programmer does not use any allocator, the compiler selects an appropriate one.

In the second phase, the layout algorithm maps both arrays to the available processors in the same way. Since both arrays have the same declaration, elements with the same index end up in the same processor. Our layout algorithm, which is described in [12], reaches the following goals: (a) Exploit fast communication patterns if there is special hardware support, e.g. nearest-neighbor networks. (b) Perform simple address calculations. The computation of processor numbers and addresses of data elements are fast shift and mask operations.

11.3.2 Process Alignment

Up to now we have only dealt with the data alignment and its realization. Process alignment is also achieved by means of a source-to-source transformation. For this purpose, we have augmented the FORALL statement as follows:

```
ForallStatement =
FORALL ident ":" SimpleType IN (PARALLEL | SYNC)
[ALIGNED WITH Designator]
  StatementSequence
END.
```

The ALIGNED WITH term is not present in the original Modula-2* program. It is derived by compile-time analysis. In the example the transformation results in:

```
VAR (* A: ARRAY [1..90] SPREAD OF INTEGER; *)
    A,B : ARRAY [0..100] SPREAD OF INTEGER;

BEGIN
  FORALL i:[0..89] IN SYNC ALIGNED WITH B[i]
    A[i] := B[i]
  END;
  FORALL i:[1..90] IN SYNC ALIGNED WITH B[i]
    B[i] := 0
  END
END
```

The code generator then simply considers the range of the FORALL as an array and invokes the layout algorithm to determine which processor has to simulate which of the conceptual processes in a virtualization loop. In the above example the original FORALL has been split into two parts. In both FORALLs the process with index i will be executed where data element B[i] resides, resulting in purely local accesses. This could not be achieved with a single FORALL. Furthermore, providing the code generator with exact alignment information facilitates easy exploitation of nearest-neighbor communication networks.

The arrangement does not always work that smoothly. In general, there are lots of alignment preferences both for data usage and process alignment. Additionally, suitable cost estimation is required. Depending of the overhead cost of splitting up a FORALL, it may be advantageous on particular parallel hardware to accept some non-locality instead.

The following two sections are more specific and show our arrangement algorithm in some detail.

11.4 Arrangement Graphs and Conflicts

During static compile-time analysis we create an arrangement graph. Nodes of this graph are array references of arbitrary type and FORALL-variables. Edges express arrangement preferences and are attributed with the *type* and the *structure* of the detected preference.

11.4.1 Type and Structure

We found four types of arrangement preferences to be necessary. The first two types were introduced by Knobe and provide data arrangement information.

- An *identity preference* is an arrangement request that relates a defining occurrence of an array to a using occurrence of the same array. It indicates a preference to align identical elements of the array on the same processor for the two occurrences. The idea is to avoid redistribution cost.

- A *conformance preference* relates two array occurrences that are operated on together in a parallel expression. The goal is to group elements of different arrays so that all data accesses can be done locally.

Knobe has introduced a third preference for expressing data arrangement information. An *independence anti-preference* is a property of specific array dimensions if these dimensions contain a potentially parallel subscript. For analysis of Modula-2*, this type of preference is not necessary, because of (a) the allocators already indicate distributed storage and (b) the explicitness of parallelism in array subscripts inside of FORALL statements.

The next two types of arrangement preferences are used to gather information for process alignment.

- A *process preference* relates the FORALL-variable to the leftmost occurrence (LMO) of an array reference if the following conditions are fulfilled: (a) The LMO is in a statement inside of the body of that FORALL and (b) the FORALL-variable appears in the subscript expression of the LMO. Any other array occurrence fulfilling (a) and (b) could be chosen as well.

  Arranging the processes with all LMOs in the body of the FORALL will achieve perfect locality of processes and data that is accessed in parallel. The process will run where the data is located. Since conformance preferences already ensure that all data which is operated on together will be arranged, only LMOs are considered.

- An *LMO preference* relates two successive LMOs of the same array in the body of a FORALL if these are subscripted in the same dimension with an expression using the same FORALL-variable. LMO preferences represent the cost of splitting up FORALLs, i.e. the increased virtualization overhead. If all LMO preferences are honored the FORALL will not be split up.

The arrangement graph contains all four types of edges. If only the first or the last two types are considered the graph is called either *data* arrangement graph or *process* arrangement graph.

For affine index expressions, the edges are labeled with the preferred arrangement structure. For two arrays A and B, this becomes ALIGN (A, d_A, s_A, o_A) WITH (B, d_B, s_B, o_B) for all types of preferences except process preferences. d_A and d_B are the numbers of the dimensions that impose the preference, and the subscript expressions $s_A \cdot$ i+o_A and $s_B \cdot$i+o_B denote elements that should be arranged in the specified array dimensions. Normalization results in structure information of the form ALIGN (., ., 1, 0) WITH (., ., c, d). For LMO preferences we have $s_A = 1$ and $o_A = 0$. Analogously, process preferences have the structure ALIGN i WITH (A, d_A, s_A, o_A) since only one node is an array occurrence.

11.4.2 Conflicts

The arrangement graph usually is not free of conflicts. In general, it is impossible to arrange data elements and processes in a way that all accesses are local without any redistribution of data or processes. We distinguish between data arrangement conflicts and process arrangement conflicts.

11.4.2.1 Data Arrangement Conflicts

In the following example the data arrangement graph (see Figure 11.1) is cyclic.

```
A[.] := ...
B[.] := ...
FORALL i : [1..N] IN PARALLEL
  s[i] := A[2*i] + B[i];
  t[i] := A[ i ] + B[i]
END
```

We do not consider the edges to or from occurrences of s and t, since these do not contribute to the cycle. There are two conformance preferences inside of the FORALL. The first one is caused by the first assignment in the FORALL. It relates A[2*i] to B_1[i]. The second one relates the array occurrences A[i] and B_2[i] of the second assignment.

All array occurrences inside of the FORALL are related to their defining occurrences in front of the FORALL with identity preferences. Thus, there are four identity preferences between (A[.], A[2*i]), (A[.], A[i]), (B[.], B_1[i]), and (B[.], B_2[i]).

It is impossible to achieve locality between the elements A[2*i] and B_1[i], demanded by the conformance preference of the first assignment, and at the same time honor the second conformance preference between A[i] and B_2[i].

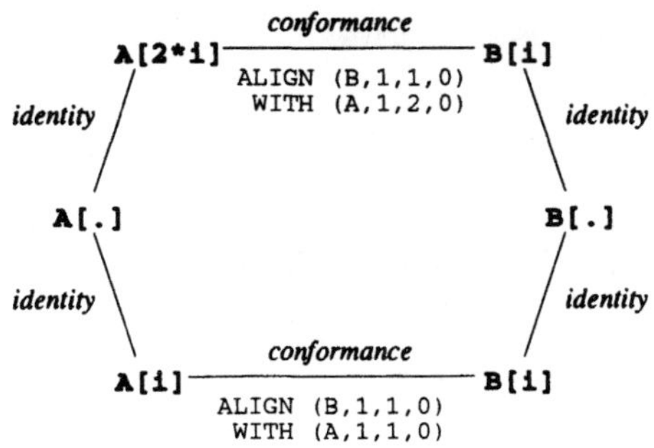

Figure 11.1 Data Arrangement Graph

In our approach, we avoid data redistribution at run-time inside of FORALLs. Therefore, there are two possible data arrangements. In both cases, one conformance preference is honored, the other one is broken.
To determine all possible arrangements, we apply the following algorithm to each cycle in the data arrangement graph:

1. Start with a:=1, b:= 0 at an arbitrary node N of the cycle. D denotes the dimension of the array that is in the cycle.
2. Proceed to the next node in the cycle and change a and b as follows:
   - If the edge is a normalized conformance preference that relates different array occurrences and is attributed with the information `ALIGN (.,.,1,0) WITH (.,.,c,d)` then replace a with $a \cdot c$ and b with $b \cdot c + d$
   - Otherwise, leave a and b unchanged.
3. Repeat step 2, as long as N is not reached again.
4. N is reached at dimension D'. There is
   - an *offset conflict* if $b \neq 0$ and $D = D'$,
   - a *stride conflict* if $a \neq 1$ and $D = D'$, and
   - a *dimension conflict* if $D \neq D'$.

   Otherwise, there is no data arrangement conflict.

The compiler preserves all conflict free data arrangements and all conflicts, i.e. all possible data arrangements that require to break at least one data arrangement preference. The way this information is used is presented in section 11.5.

11.4.2.2 Process Arrangement Conflicts

In the following example the process arrangement graph (see Figure 11.2) is cyclic:

```
FORALL i : [1..N] IN SYNC
  A[ i ] := t[i];
  A[i+1] := A[i+1] + 1
END
```

Only process and LMO preferences are taken into account. In the example there are two process preferences (i, A[i]) and (i, A[i+1]). Additionally, there is an LMO preference between A[i] and A[i+1].

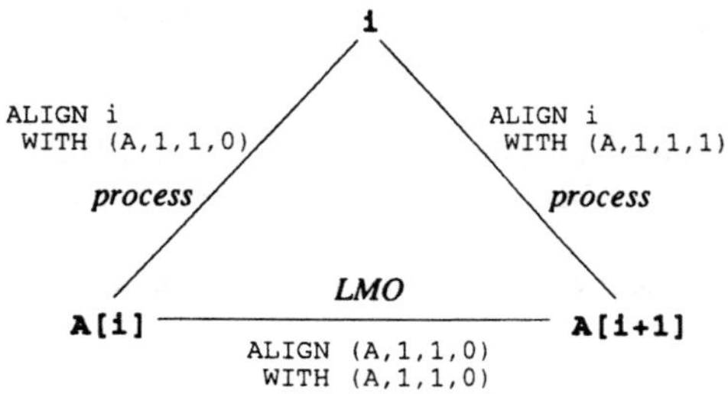

Figure 11.2 Process Arrangement Graph

Although there are no data arrangement conflicts, there are process arrangement conflicts: process preferences to A[i] and A[i+1] contradict.

To determine all possible process arrangements, the process arrangement graph is processed as follows:

1. The process alignment graph is divided into subgraphs that are processed in turn. A subgraph consists of a FORALL-variable, and all LMOs that are related to that FORALL-variable, either directly via process preference edges or indirectly via a chain of LMO preferences..

2. For each cycle in each subgraph that contains the FORALL-variable exactly once, execute steps 3–6:

3. Start with a:=1, b:= 0, and *flag*:=FALSE at the node of the FORALL-variable.

4. Proceed to the next node in the cycle. The edge is attributed with the normalized structure ALIGN . WITH (.,.,*c*,*d*).

   - If the edge is an LMO preference or *flag* =FALSE replace a with $a \cdot c$ and b with $b \cdot c + d$. In case of a process preference, set *flag*:=TRUE.
   - The last edge in the cycle is a process preference with *flag* =TRUE. Replace a with a/c and b with $(b - d)/c$.

5. Repeat step 4, as long as the node of the FORALL-variable is not reached again.

6. There is

   - an *offset conflict* if $b \neq 0$ and

- a *stride conflict* if $a \neq 1$.

7. Consider all edges of a subgraph. There is a *dimension conflict* if among those there is pair of process preference edges with differing dimensions in a single array.

The compiler keeps all conflict free process arrangements and all conflicts, i.e. all possible process arrangements that require to break at least one LMO preference. The way this information is used is presented in the following section.

11.5 Cost Considerations

In the previous section the processing of the data arrangement graph has resulted in a collection of several possible data arrangements for the whole program. For each `FORALL` statement in this program the compiler has derived a collection of possible process distributions.

Finding an optimal process distribution with a brute force algorithm would involve an exponential search space. A `FORALL` with n statements and p possible distributions requires the cost estimation for p^n different combinations.

Unfortunately, the combination of two optimal process distributions for the statement sequences $1 \ldots \lfloor n/2 \rfloor$ and $\lfloor n/2 \rfloor + 1 \ldots n$ does not necessarily result in a global optimum, since redistribution of processes imposes additional costs. With the assumption that the process redistribution cost, i.e., the cost of splitting up a `FORALL` into several `FORALL`s, are small compared to the communication cost due to data access, the probable loss of optimality can be tolerated. Therefore, a dynamic programming approach with a time complexity of $O(n \log n)$ is feasible:

1. For each data arrangement perform steps 2–5.

2. For each process arrangement in each `FORALL` statement perform steps 3–4.

3. Derive the optimal process distribution and thus the appropriate splitting of the `FORALL` by dynamic programming.

4. Select the best alternative for the given data arrangement.

5. Sum up the cost of all `FORALL` statements in the program for the given data arrangement.

6. Select the data arrangement that results in the global optimum.

The above is a high-level description of our technique. In reality the situation is more complex: Loops and nested `FORALL`s require multidimensional cost vectors instead of simple communication costs. The runtime of `IF`- and `CASE`-statements can be improved if different data arrangements are chosen for different branches. To exploit this possibility, the algorithm considers dynamic array redistribution that ensures the unification of different data arrangements after the branching statements. Details can be found in [15].

11.6 Example

Consider the following code fragment:

```
FORALL i : [1..N] IN SYNC
  A[i+1] := T[i] + C[i];
  A[i]   := A[i+1] + T[i];
  A[i+1] := T[i+1] + D[i];
  A[i]   := T[i] + A[i+1];
END
```

The data alignment analysis (see section 11.4.2.1) returns two possible patterns:

```
ALIGN (C,1,1,0) WITH (T,1,1,0)
ALIGN (C,1,1,0) WITH (A,1,1,1)
ALIGN (C,1,1,0) WITH (D,1,1,-1)
```

or

```
ALIGN (C,1,1,0) WITH (T,1,1,0)
ALIGN (C,1,1,0) WITH (A,1,1,0)
ALIGN (C,1,1,0) WITH (D,1,1,-1)
```

The process alignment analysis (see section 11.4.2.2) returns two possible patterns:

```
ALIGN    i    WITH (A,1,1,1)
```

or

```
ALIGN    i    WITH (A,1,1,0)
```

Although the compiler considers both possible data arrangements, in this example we will only consider the second arrangement. Therefore, we will only present steps 2–5 of the search algorithm from section 11.5.

line	(A,1,1,1)	(A,1,1,0)	align	cost
1	2g	1s	0	1s
2	1g+1s	1g	0	1g
3	1g	2g+1s	1	1g
4	1g+1s	1g	0	1g
1-2	3g+1s		0-0	1g+1s
3-4	2g+1s	3g+1s	1-0	2g+1f
1-4	5g+2s	6g+2s+1f	0-0-1-0	3g+1s+2f

In the above table s,g, and f denote the cost of a send operation, a get operation, and the cost of splitting up a FORALL [1]. In the first step, the costs of executing individual lines are computed for all process distributions. Merging lines 1 and 2 is obvious, since in both lines (A,1,1,0) is superior. This is shown by 0—0 in the table. For merging lines 3 and 4 there are three possibilities. All must be considered, since f is not zero. (1) use (A,1,1,1) for both lines at a cost of $2g + 1s$, (2) use (A,1,1,0) for both lines at a cost of $3g + 1s$, or (3) redistribute $1 \rightarrow 0$ at a cost of $2g + 1f$, which is the cheapest. When considering the whole FORALL statement in the last step, there are again three options: (1) select data distribution (A,1,1,1) for all lines at a cost of $3g + 2s$, (2) select (A,1,1,0) for the first two lines and (A,1,1,1) for the last two lines at a cost of $6g + 2s + 1f$, or (3) redistribute again resulting in a cost of $3g + 1s + 2f$. Given the values for g,s, and f, the best process distribution will split up the given FORALL twice, after the second and after the third line.

Assuming the second data arrangement, the code fragment is transformed as follows.

```
FORALL i : [1..N] ALIGNED WITH A[i] IN SYNC
  A[i+1] := T[i] + C[i];
  A[i]   := A[i+1] + T[i];
END;
FORALL i : [1..N] ALIGNED WITH A[i+1] IN SYNC
  A[i+1] := T[i+1] + D[i];
END;
FORALL i : [1..N] ALIGNED WITH A[i] IN SYNC
  A[i]   := T[i] + A[i+1];
END
```

Note that for sake of clarity the transformations related to data arrangement are left out in this example, i.e. all arrays are still presented in their original declaration with the original subscripts.

11.7 Conclusion

In this paper we have presented a technique that enhances locality using a source-to-source transformation. The result of this program transformation is a data and process alignment that results in better performance: first benchmarking yields an improvement of performance by at least 60% on the MasPar MP-1.

We consider this result to be initial evidence that automatic data and process distribution by the compiler is possible and can achieve attractive performance improvements.

[1] In the example we set $s = 128$, $g = 256$, and $f = 20$ time units.

References

[1] Thinking Machines Corporation, Cambridge, Massachusetts. *C* Language Reference Manual*, April 1991.

[2] Barbara M. Chapman, Heinz Herbeck, and Hans P. Zima. Automatic support for data distribution. In *Proc. of the 6th Distributed Memory Computing Conference*, pages 51–58, Portland, Oregon, April 28 – May 1, 1991.

[3] American National Standards Institute, Inc., Washington, D.C. *ANSI, Programming Language Fortran Extended (Fortran 90). ANSI X3.198-1992*, 1992.

[4] Geoffrey Fox, Seema Hiranandani, Ken Kennedy, Charles Koelbel, Uli Kremer, Chau-Wen Tseng, and Min-You Wu. Fortran D language specification. Technical Report CRPC-TR90079, Center for Research on Parallel Computation, Rice University, December 1990.

[5] Manish Gupta and Prithviraj Banerjee. Automatic data partitioning on distributed memory multiprocessors. In *Proc. of the 6th Distributed Memory Computing Conference*, pages 43–50, Portland, Oregon, April 28 – May 1, 1991.

[6] Kathleen Knobe, Joan D. Lukas, and Guy L. Steele. Data optimization: Allocation of arrays to reduce communication on SIMD machines. *Journal of Parallel and Distributed Computing*, 8(2):102–118, February 1990.

[7] Kathleen Knobe and Venkataraman Natarajan. Data optimization: Minimizing residual interprocessor data motion on SIMD machines. In *Frontiers '90:The Third Symposium on the Frontiers of Massively Parallel Computation*, College Park, University of Maryland, October 8–10, 1990.

[8] Charles Koelbel and Piyush Mehrotra. Supporting shared data structures and distributed memory architectures. In *Proc. of the 2nd ACM SIGPLAN Symposium on Principles and Practice of Parallel Programming*, pages 177–186, March 1990.

[9] Jingke Li and Marina Chen. Index domain alignment: Minimizing cost of cross-referencing between distributed arrays. In *Frontiers '90: The Third Symposium on the Frontiers of Massively Parallel Computation*, pages 424–433, College Park, University of Maryland, October 8–10, 1990.

[10] Piyush Mehrotra and John Van Rosendale. The BLAZE language: A parallel language for scientific programming. *Parallel Computing*, 5:339–361, November 1987.

[11] Prentice Hall, Englewood Cliffs, New Jersey. *INMOS Limited: Occam Programming Manual*, 1984.

[12] Michael Philippsen. Automatic data distribution for nearest neighbor networks. In *Frontiers '92:The Fourth Symposium on the Frontiers of Massively Parallel Computation*, pages 178–185, Mc Lean, Virginia, October 19–21, 1992.

[13] Michael Philippsen and Walter F. Tichy. Modula-2* and its compilation. In *First International Conference of the Austrian Center for Parallel Computation, Salzburg, Austria, 1991*, pages 169–183. Springer Verlag, Lecture Notes in Computer Science 591, 1992.

[14] MasPar Computer Corporation. *MasPar Parallel Application Language (MPL) Reference Manual*, September 1990.

[15] Markus U. Mock. Alignment in Modula-2*. Master's thesis, University of Karlsruhe, Department of Informatics, December 1992.

[16] J. Ramanujam and P. Sadayappan. Access based data decomposition for distributed memory machines. In *Proc. of the 6th Distributed Memory Computing Conference*, pages 196–199, Portland, Oregon, April 28 – May 1, 1991.

[17] Walter F. Tichy and Christian G. Herter. Modula-2*: An extension of Modula-2 for highly parallel, portable programs. Technical Report No. 4/90, University of Karlsruhe, Department of Informatics, January 1990.

12 Automatic Parallelization for Distributed Memory Multiprocessors

Anne Dierstein[1] Roman Hayer[1] Thomas Rauber[2]
COMPUTER SCIENCE DEPARTMENT
SAARBRÜCKEN UNIVERSITY, GERMANY
email: `rauber@cs.uni-sb.de`

Abstract: This paper describes a framework for a parallelizing compiler for distributed memory multiprocessor machines (DMMs). The framework provides a compiler and a runtime support library which allows to use the DMMs with a sequential language. The compiler computes a data distribution for the arrays of the source program and parallelizes the inner loops of the program. The data distribution is computed by a branch–and–bound algorithm that uses a performance estimator to evaluate the relative efficiency of different data decomposition schemes for any given program. The performance estimation takes place at compile time and uses several parameters of the used DMM like the startup time and the byte transfer time. The paper also describes a prototype implementation of the framework on an Intel iPSC/860 for the language Pascal and discusses some experimental evaluations.

12.1 Introduction

In current distributed memory computers like the Intel iPSC/860 or the CM-5 from Thinking Machines, each processor has its own address space and inter–processor communication takes place through sending and receiving messages. Typically, passing messages is several orders of magnitude slower than accessing the local memory. For the programmer, this means that it is important to exploit locality of reference when programming distributed memory computers and that the distribution of data plays a central role for the efficiency of the parallel program. The concerns of locality must be balanced against the overall goal of achieving parallel execution and a large speedup.

When using the standard message–passing languages that are provided by the manufacturers of the DMMs, the programmer has to control the distribution of data and code across the processors. Each reference to a non–local data item and each synchronization has to be coded as a call to a runtime library. Unfortunately, this is a very tedious and error–prone process and the resulting parallel programs are extremely machine and operating system specific. Also, debugging a parallel program is much harder than debugging a sequential program. There are several approaches making programming for parallel computers easier:

[1]research supported by the Commission of the European Community, ESPRIT Project #5399 (COMPARE)

[2]Corresponding author, email: `rauber@cs.uni-sb.de`. Research partially supported by DFG, SFB 124 and the International Computer Science Institute, Berkeley, California

1. new or extended languages like Fortran90 [21], Fortran D [15], Vienna Fortran [6], Concurrent C [10], SR [1] or pSather [8] [9]. A good overview of existing parallel languages can be found in [2].

2. intelligent runtime support and libraries like EXPRESS [23], Linda [22] or Jade [27]

3. parallelizing compilers like ASPAR [16], SUPERB [11] [12] or SIMPLE [25].

In this article, we pursue the last approach. By using a parallelizing compiler, the programmer can develop a *sequential* program and can run the program after the automatic parallelization on a parallel machine without dealing with the architectural details of the parallel computer. The programs remain portable and 'old' sequential programs can be transformed to run on the parallel machine. On the other hand, when using a parallelizing compiler, the programmer might not get all possible speedup, because the compiler may be not able to detect all potential parallelism in the sequential program. But the hope is that the degree of parallelization obtained is increasing when the field of automatic parallelization will be better explored.

Most of the parallelization strategies proposed for parallelizing compilers use a single–program-multiple–data (SPMD) programming model: each processor executes the same program on different parts of the program data. Parallelizing a sequential program into a SPMD–style program for distributed memory multiprocessors consists mainly of two steps:

1. distribute the program data among the processors

2. insert the necessary communication statements to access non–local data

Most of the existing parallelizing compilers like SUPERB [11] or MIMDizer [26] require the user to specify a data distribution. The task of the compiler then essentially consists of adapting the program code in such a way that each processor executes all assignments to its local data, inserting communication when necessary. Specifying the data distribution is the most critical step in the parallelization process and the user must have a detailed knowledge of the algorithm and the architecture of the parallel machine. An unsuitable data distribution results in excessive communication and a slow target program.

12.2 Related Work

There are several approaches to determine a data distribution automatically. [4] and [5] give an outline of a knowledge–based software tool that provides automatic support for the data distribution. The tool uses program analysis and knowledge–based techniques, in particular pattern matching facilities in conjunction with the explicit representation and retrieval of knowledge. According to [4], the tool is currently being developed, but the implementation has not yet been finished.

[19] describes a pattern matching approach that uses hierarchically organized patterns and tries to combine the recognized patterns of the source program to larger patterns. For each pattern there exists a suitable parallel algorithm implementing the pattern, parameterized by the data distribution for the involved arrays. The pattern matcher and the corresponding patterns are currently being developed.

[18] proposes an interactive tool that allows the programmer to select regions of the sequential program. The tool responds with a data decomposition scheme and diagnostic information for the selected region. The tool outputs a FORTRAN D program that can be translated by FORTRAN D compiler [15]. This tool is also not yet implemented.

[16] presents the ASPAR system that uses the EXPRESS runtime library and that is able to compute a global data distribution. It uses a symbolic analysis to extract the parallelism from the sequential program by adding suitable calls to the runtime library. The data distribution is found by a knowledge–based approach. The disadvantage of this system lies in the fact that the compiler is not able to arrange a redistribution of the data during program execution. After distributing an array A column wise, it is not possible to redistribute A in a later part of the program, although this might reduce the run time considerably. All these approaches essentially focus on the distribution of arrays.

12.3 Overview

In this article, we present a framework for a parallelizing compiler for DMMs ([14],[7]) that provides a compiler and runtime support which allows to use the DMMs with a sequential language. The compiler determines a data distribution for the arrays of the source program by a branch–and–bound approach and inserts the necessary communication statements to access non–local data according to the computed distribution. The system is able to compute a redistribution of an array, if this results in a better performance. The branch–and–bound algorithm incrementally constructs paths in a decision tree where each node of the path corresponds to the distribution of an array of the source program. For each path, a performance estimator computes the communication costs resulting, when the arrays are distributed in the considered way. The communication costs are computed by determining the number and size of the messages that each processor has to receive during program execution and by also taking sequentializations into account that are caused by data dependences. Based on the communication costs, the data distribution algorithm tries to find the best data distribution by searching the cheapest path from a leaf to the root of the decision tree. By rejecting expensive paths as early as possible, only a few paths, corresponding to a small fraction of the decision tree, are actually built. Therefore, the run time of the data distribution phase remains decent also for larger input programs. Because the costs computed by the performance estimator are quite accurate, the data distribution tool is able to compute very good data distributions that are quite often optimal.

Section 12.4 gives an overview of the transformation steps that are executed to transform a sequential source program into a parallel program. Section 12.5 describes how the system computes the data distribution for a source program, section 12.6 describes the performance estimator that is used to rate the different data distributions. Section

12.7 presents the tests that we made with a prototype implementation of the system on an Intel iPSC/860 for the language Pascal.

12.4 Parallelization Strategy

The proposed compiler uses a similar parallelization strategy as the SUPERB system [11] [4] but includes a module to compute data distributions automatically. The compiler uses a single–program–multiple–data (SPMD) model. Each processor executes the same program on different parts of the data domain. The sequential source program is transformed into an explicitely parallel program that contains calls to a runtime library executing the necessary communication operations. We give here only an overview of the parallelization process. A detailed description is given by Dierstein [7], see also [11]. The parallelization process essentially consists of five steps:

1. Split the sequential input program into a host program and a node program. The host program is executed by the host and performs all I/O–operations. The node program is executed by all node processors and performs all computations.
2. Introduce a mask for each statement that assigns a new value to a distributed variable. The mask ensures that the statement is only executed by a processor to which the distributed variable is local.
3. Compute a data distribution.
4. Introduce communication statements for non–local accesses.
5. Optimize the communication statements.

Splitting the input program into a host and a node program is not a difficult task. The node program is obtained by replacing the I/O–operations by communication statements. The host program contains the I/O–operations of the source program. After each input operation, a `send` to the processor that uses the input data is executed. Before each output operation, a `receive` from the processor that has computed the values to be output is executed.

Programs are parallelized by mapping the data of the sequential program to the processors of the parallel system. Each processor p computes only data mapped to its local memory. This concept is known as the *owner computes rule*. Scalar variables are replicated so that each processor has its own copy of each scalar. An array A of the source program can be *replicated* or *distributed*. Distributing A means that A is partitioned into a number of subsets whose union is A. Each processor p gets one subset of A. This subset is said to be *local* to p. Each processor allocates storage for its *private* variables, i.e. for its local variables and for private copies of non–local variables. Section 12.5 describes how the arrays of the source program are partitioned.

In principle, each array A could be mapped arbitrarily to processors by a partitioning function

$$\gamma_A : \mathbb{N}^{dim_A} \rightarrow P$$

where $P = \{p_1, \ldots, p_m\}$ are the processors and dim_A is the number of dimensions of A. To reduce the number of possible data distributions and the overhead for data accesses, we have limited the distribution of an array A to distributions that can be decribed by *partition vectors* of the form

$$npd = (n_1, \ldots, n_d),$$

where n_i is the number of processors in dimension i. Dimension i is divided up evenly among the processors. If m is the total number of processors, then $m = \prod_{i=1}^{d} n_i$. Thus all regular block partitions like distribution by block, row or column are allowed. Note that this limitation is only for the current implementation. The approach for the array distribution that is presented in the next section, is not limited to these distributions but can easily be extended to other distributions e.g. the cyclic distributions described in [15]. In any case, each processor is able to compute the owner of every element of any distributed array. The distributions computed by the compiler are static and cannot be adapted to input data at run time. Nevertheless, the distributions can be changed at run time according to a redistribution computed at compile time.

A processor may have to access non–local variables to compute a new value for a local variable. These accesses are implemented by calls to message passing routines of the runtime system. The processor q which ownes the accessed data item executes a `send` operation, p executes a `receive` operation.

syntax	semantics
`send(d,p)`	Send data element `d` to processor `p`. If `p` is not ready to receive `d`, `d` is added to `p`'s message queue. (non–blocking send)
`receive(d,p)`	Receive a data element from processor `p`, and store it in the variable `d`. The executing processor waits, if the data element has not yet arrived. (blocking receive).

To store the received non–local array elements, p has to allocate space for private copies of the non–local data items that are updated by the `receive` operation. The additional space is determined by computing an *overlap description* [11] for every access to a distributed array element. Each overlap description determines an *overlap area* which surrounds the local segment of a processor. Elements in the overlap area are used to compute new values for elements in the local area. The union of all overlap areas for a distributed array A determines for each processor the private copies of non–local variables. Each processor allocates space for its local segment of A *and* for its surrounding overlap area. The elements in the surrounding overlap area are received from the neighboring processors. The local elements that are in the overlap area of the neighboring processors are sent to these processors.

The parallelization strategy is outlined in [7, 11]. We illustrate the main ideas by an example.

Example 12.4.1

for i := 1 **to** 99 **do**
    S_1 : $s := a[i+1]$;
    S_2 : $b[i] := s$;
od

According to the *owner computes rule* we have to guarantee that each processor p executes S_2 only for iterations defining values of $b[i]$ that are local to p. Therefore we insert a conditional statement using the runtime function $owned(b,i)$ which compares the bounds of the local area of b with the current value of i in order to determine the owner of $b[i]$. $owned(b,i)$ returns true, if the executing processor p is the owner of $b[i]$. We call the tuple (b,i) the *mask* of S_2 which specifies the execution condition. S_1 defines a scalar variable s that is only used to compute $b[i]$ in S_2. Therefore, we can *propagate* the mask (b,i) to S_1 by enclosing S_1 with the same conditional statement as S_2. That means that S_1 is only executed when S_2 is executed. Usually, a mask is propagated to an assigment statement S for a scalar variable, if there is a data dependence from S to the masked statement and the value computed by S is not used by another statement that has a different mask or no mask at all. Note that mask propagation can cause a statement S to have different masks. These have to be `or`–connected to guarantee that S is executed for each iteration in which the computed value is used for an assignment statement to a distributed variable.

If a processor p executes statement S_1 in example 12.4.1, it may have to communicate with other processors to exchange data elements of array a. Therefore the read access to a is preceded by the procedure call *exch((a,i+1),(b,i))*. This procedure checks first, whether $a[i+1]$ belongs to another processor q than $b[i]$ that is supposed to belong to p. In this case q sends the value of $a[i+1]$ to p. p receives the value of $a[i+1]$ from q. In general, there is a call of *exch()* for each read access to a distributed array in a statement S. These calls are inserted immediately before S. Note that masks can also be propagated to *exch()* statements. Because there is a separate mask for each read access, an *exch()* statement gets exactly *one* mask by propagation. Introducing the masks and inserting the *exch()* statements results in the following parallelized version of the example program 12.4.1:

Example 12.4.2

for i := 1 **to** 99 **do**
    S_0 : $exch((a,i+1),(b,i))$;
    S_1 : **if** $owned(b,i)$ **then** $s := a[i+1]$;
    S_2 : **if** $owned(b,i)$ **then** $b[i] := s$;
od

The communication statements introduced in the fourth step listed above executes the communication element by element. For each data item, a new message is used. Figure 12.1 shows the amount of communication for 4 processors. Because the overhead

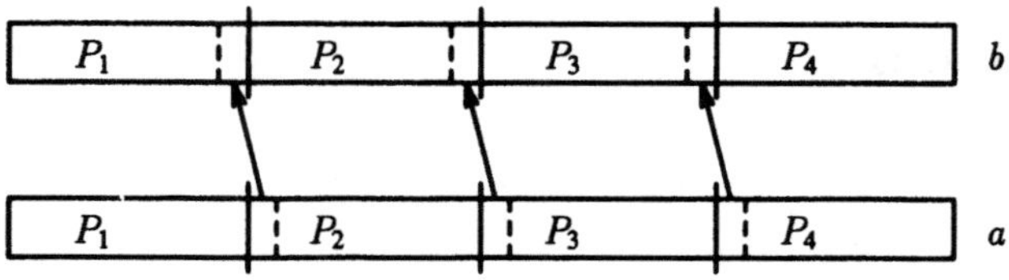

Figure 12.1 Communication amount for example 12.4.2

for sending a message is usually very high, it is important that short messages are combined to larger ones, thus reducing the overhead. This is performed by methods known from vectorizing compilers. The compiler tries to apply the technique of loop distribution to separate the communication statements from the computation statements. If this is successful, the loops containing the communication statements are vectorized, thus combining short messages in the loop body to larger messages that are executed outside the loop.

Another important optimization is the adaption of the loop bounds surrounding the masked computation statements according to the mask. Without this adaption, every processor executes every loop iteration. Most of these iterations are empty, because the masks of the statements of the loop body prohibit the execution of the statement. The empty iterations can be avoided by adapting the loop bounds according to the masks in the loop body. Each processor only has to execute loop iterations that assign new values to its local variables or that execute communication statements with other processors. For each mask, we compute a lower and an upper loop bound by considering the local area and the overlap area of the array in the mask on the executing processor. There may be several masked statements in the loop body. In this case, the lower bound of the loop has to be set to the minimum of the lower bounds that are computed for the different masks to make sure that *all* assignments and communication statements are executed. The upper bound has to be set to the maximum of the upper bounds that are computed for the different masks. For example 12.4.2, vectorizing the communication statement and adjusting the loop bounds results in the following program:

Example 12.4.3

exch_area((a,2,100),(b,1,99));
for i := $lb_b[p]$ **to** $ub_b[p]$ **do**
  S_1 : **if** $owned(b, i)$ **then** s := $a[i + 1]$;
  S_2 : **if** $owned(b, i)$ **then** $b[i]$:= s;
od

$lb_b[p]$ and $ub_b[p]$ are the bounds of the local area of array b belonging to processor p. Because no value of array a is changed inside the loop, we can execute all communication before the loop. This is performed by the procedure call *exch_area((a,2,100),(b,1,99))* which handles the exchange of whole array areas. A processor p executing this call first sends the elements of a in its local array section to the processors q that need these elements to evaluate their local elements of b. Then p receives the elements of a that it uses to compute its local elements of b from other processors.

Other optimizations that are applied to the generated parallel program are the following:

- If several statements in the loop body have the same mask, we can collect them in the body of a single conditional statement with the common mask as condition.
- If all masks in the loop body are identical, we can omit them after having adapted the loop bounds. This is possible, because the adaption of the loop bounds makes sure that each processor executes only assignments to its local array elements. This optimization can be applied to example 12.4.3.
- If there are several masks in the loop body, we can simplify the expressions for the lower or upper bounds of the surrounding loops. These expressions specify a minimum or maximum operation over several expressions that contain the original loop bounds and the bounds of the local areas and the overlap areas of the arrays in the loop body. Because we assume that the loop bounds are constant and because the array distributions are fixed at compile time, we can evaluate the expressions and can determine which one yields the minimal or maximal value.

12.5 Branch–and–Bound Algorithm

The main essential to find a good data distribution for the arrays a_i of the source program is an estimation of the run times of all possible data distributions. In the next section we describe a performance estimator that computes a *cost function*. This function estimates the run time of a parallelized program for a fixed data distribution. Given the performance estimator, we describe in this section how a suitable data distribution for the arrays can be found that minimizes the communication costs for the given sequential program.

12.5.1 Basic Approach

Clearly, inspecting all possible data distributions will be far too expensive. By giving up the strict separation of choosing a data distribution and estimating the run time we can reduce the amount of the analysis.

We use a branch–and–bound algorithm that is based on a *decision tree* to compute a data distribution. Each node of this tree represents the decisions for the distribution of *one* array a of the program. Each level of the tree consists of nodes for one array. Each path $a_1 \rightarrow \ldots \rightarrow a_n$ in the tree from the root to a leaf represents a complete data distribution that consists of data distributions for all arrays $a_1, \ldots, a_n$ on the path. The edges of the tree are decorated with estimated costs for the communication instructions that are provided by the performance estimator.

It is not necessary to keep the complete tree in the main memory. It is not even necessary to build the entire decision tree. Instead, we can build the tree incrementally by storing at most two paths of the tree from a leaf to the root at a time and aborting expensive paths as early as possible. The two paths that are stored are the path P_c that is currently being examined, and the cheapest complete path P_{min} found so far. The costs of the current path P_c are increasing with each edge added to the path. If the costs of P_c exceed the cost of P_{min}, we can abort the examination of P_c. If the costs of P_c are smaller than the costs of P_{min} when P_c has been constructed completely, we substitute P_{min} by P_c.

We define a set *DNSET* that contains a *distribution node* for each array of the source program. The nodes of the decision tree correspond to the distribution nodes in such a way that all nodes of the same tree level correspond to the same distribution node in *DNSET*. In section 12.5.3 we describe that further nodes may be added to *DNSET* that account for the redistribution of arrays. For each $dn_i \in DNSET$ we define the set of all possible distributions as

$$DISTRIBUTIONSET(dn_i) = \{(n_1, \ldots, n_d) \mid (n_1, \ldots, n_d) \text{ is a partition vector for the array corresponding to } dn_i\}$$

In the last section, we have mentioned that there is a call of an *exch()* statement for each read access of a source program statement S. The number of data items and thus the run time delay that is caused by an *exch()* statement is determined by the distribution of the corresponding array and the distribution of all arrays masking this instruction. We call the pair *(ra,msk)* of a read access *ra* to an array and the masking information *msk* of the access *ra* a *communication producer* (CP). The set of all communication producers is called *CPSET*.

Example 12.5.1

```
for i :=2 to 100 do
    for j := 1 to 99 do
        B[i,j] := B[i,j+1];
        C[i,j] := B[i,j];
        A[i,j] := A[i-1,j];
    od
od
```

In this case the set *DNSET* has three nodes for the three arrays A,B, and C:

$$DNSET = \{dn_A, dn_B, dn_C\}$$

and the set of all communication producers is

$$CPSET = \{((B, i, j + 1), (B, i, j)), ((B, i, j), (C, i, j)), ((A, i - 1, j), (A, i, j))\}.$$

In the following we use an abbreviation for the CP's: $((X, e_1, \ldots, e_{d_X}), (Y, e'_1, \ldots, e'_{d_Y}))$ is denoted by $X \rightarrow Y$ with the following meaning: elements of X are read to compute elements of Y. Using this notation, we can represent the communication producers for example 12.5.1 as

$$CPSET = \{B \rightarrow B, B \rightarrow C, A \rightarrow A\}.$$

12.5.2 Distribution Graph

Before we can calculate the communication delay of a single $cp \in CPSET$, we must know the current distribution of some of the arrays of the source program. We call these arrays *associated* with cp and collect them in the set $A(cp)$. To compute $A(cp)$, we must consider the following three facts.

(1) Each $cp \in CPSET$ represents a communication instruction caused by an use of an element of an array A. The distribution of A must be known, thus $A \in A(cp)$

(2) Furthermore the statement containing the read access of cp is usually masked. We must know the distribution of the arrays $B_1, \ldots, B_k$ in the mask to be able to compute the number of iterations in which the corresponding *exch* statement is executed. Thus $B_1, \ldots, B_k \in A(cp)$.

(3) A use of an array element can be involved in a loop carried dependence. In this case, the communication instruction to a communication producer cp_i may prevent concurrent execution of loop iterations. We call the loop carrying the dependence *sequentialized* by the related communication producer cp_i. The distribution of the arrays belonging to cp_i determines the amount of the sequentialization.

   In example 12.5.1, the CP $A \rightarrow A$ may sequentialize the i-loop: If array A is distributed by row, processor p_i must wait for p_{i-1} to complete its computations, before it can start working. Thus, no other communication instructions in the loop can operate concurrently. On the other hand, distribution by column does not affect any instructions in the loop, because the CP $A \rightarrow A$ causes no communication. Therefore, we must know the distribution of A to estimate the costs of any CP cp in the i–loop, i.e. $A \in A(cp)$.

   The information whether a loop is sequentialized can be computed by the usual data dependence tests (Banerjee test, GCD test, separability test, etc.), see [30].

The distributions that have to be known to compute the communication delay of a $cp \in CPSET$ are summarized in the sets

$$INFOSET(cp) = \{dn \in DNSET : \text{the array represented by } dn \text{ is associated to } cp \text{ by (1), (2) or (3)}\}$$

$$INFLUENCESET(cp) = \{cp_i \in CPSET : cp_i \text{ influences } cp \text{ acc. to (3)}\} \cup \{cp\}$$

These sets are computed for all $cp \in CPSET$. Using these sets, we define the distribution graph as follows:

Definition 12.5.1 *The* **distribution graph** *is a bipartite graph* $G = (V, E)$.

- $V = \text{CPSET} \cup \text{DNSET}$
- $E \subset \text{DNSET} \times \text{CPSET}$
  $E = \{(\text{dn}_j, cp_i) \in \text{DNSET} \times \text{CPSET} \mid \text{dn}_j \in \text{INFOSET}(cp_i)\}$

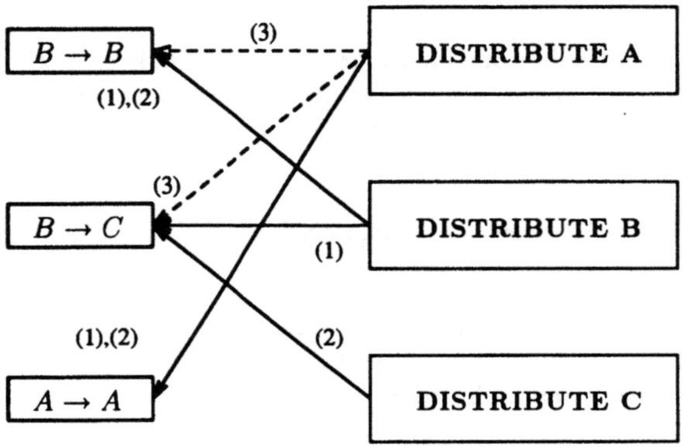

Figure 12.2 Distribution graph for example 12.5.1. The edges are labeled with numbers referring to the cases listed above.

An edge (dn_j, cp_i) in the distribution graph indicates that the distribution of the array corresponding to dn_j has to be fixed to compute the costs of communication producer cp_i. Figure 12.2 illustrates the distribution graph for example 12.5.1.

To reduce the run time of the analysis algorithm we try to abort the constructed paths in the decision tree as early as possible. Therefore we arrange the levels of the decision tree so that we can compute the costs of as many CPs as possible when adding a new node to the current path: With the information of the distribution graph we create a sorted list *DNLIST* of DNs implying the order of distribution decisions. We sort the $dn \in DNSET$ by the outdegree in the distribution graph, so that the arrays that influence more CPs than others are distributed first. This makes sure that a lot of cost computations can be executed as early as possible. This is performed by the procedure *create(DNLIST)*. We also determine for each $dn \in DNLIST$ the following set of CPs:

$$COSTSET(dn) = \{cp_j \in CPSET \mid \text{the costs of } cp_j \text{ can be computed when the distribution decision of } dn \text{ is made and the computation was not possible before this decision}\}$$

Figure 12.3 shows the order of the CP's and the associated *COSTSET* for example 12.5.1.

The following algorithm 12.5.1 implements the described path construction by the recursive procedure *decide*. The algorithm uses for each $cp \in CPSET$ a value $CPCOST(cp)$ representing the run time delay of *cp*. $CPCOST(cp)$ is computed by the performance estimator as described in the next section. To consider the frequency of executions of the communication instruction, we multiply $CPCOST(cp)$ for each *cp* with a factor $weight_{cp}$. This factor is the product of factors f_i, each one representing a surrounding control structure. The computation of the f_i depends on the surrounding control structure:

- For loops with loop variables that are used in an access function of *cp*, we set $f_i = 1$. Iterations of these loops are already considered by the cost function.

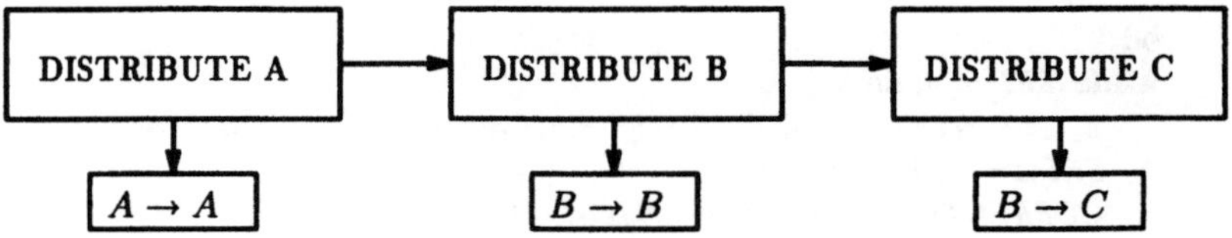

Figure 12.3 *COSTSETs* for example 12.5.1

- For loops with loop variables that are not used in an access function of *cp*, we set f_i to the number of loop iterations.
- For conditional statements, we set f_i to a value between 0 and 1 that represents the probability for the then or else part of the conditional to be executed. f_i can be obtained by profiling. If no profiling information is available, we assume that each part of a conditional statements is executed equally often and set f_i to 0.5.

Algorithm 12.5.1

```
var mincost: integer;
begin /* MAIN PROGRAM */
    var DNLIST: list of distribution nodes;
    create(DNLIST); /* see distribution graph */
    mincost := ∞;
    decide(0, DNLIST);
end
procedure decide(cost, LIST);
var cost: integer;
var LIST: list of distribution nodes;
begin
    var dn: distribution node;
    var SET: set of distribution vectors;
    var n⃗, n⃗_act: distribution vectors;
    var cp: communication producer;
    var CURRENTPATH, CHEAPPATH: subset of DNSET × DISTRIBUTIONSET(dn);
    if (LIST ≠ ∅)
        dn := head(LIST);
        SET := DISTRIBUTIONSET(dn);
        oldcost := cost;
        forall n⃗ ∈ SET do
            localcost_n⃗ := 0;
            forall cp ∈ COSTSET(dn) do
                localcost_n⃗ := localcost_n⃗ + weight_cp · CPCOST(cp);
```

od
od
while ($SET \neq \emptyset$) **do**
$\vec{n}_{act}$:= $select\_min(SET)$; /* selects the vector $\vec{n}$ with minimal $localcost_{\vec{n}}$ */
SET := $SET - \{\vec{n}_{act}\}$;
$CURRENTPATH$:= $CURRENTPATH \cup \{(dn, \vec{n}_{act})\}$;
$cost$:= $cost + localcost_{\vec{n}_{act}}$;
if ($cost \geq mincost$) /* ! abort expensive paths ! */
$cost := oldcost$;
else *decide(cost,tail(LIST))*; **fi**
$CURRENTPATH$:= $CURRENTPATH - \{(dn, \vec{n}_{act})\}$;
od
else /* ($LIST = \emptyset$) */
if ($cost < mincost$)
$CHEAPPATH = CURRENTPATH$;
$mincost := cost$;
fi
fi
end

Figure 12.4 shows the decision tree that is built by algorithm 12.5.1 for example 12.5.1 when using four processors. First A is distributed, because all $cp \in CPSET$ are influenced by this decision. For 4 processors, there are 3 possible distributions: by row, by block or by column. After A is distributed, we are able to compute $CPCOST(A \rightarrow A)$ for the different distributions of A. Because distribution by column causes no costs we follow this path. In the next step, B is distributed so that the costs of $B \rightarrow B$ can be calculated. We again follow the cheapest path which is distribution by row. In the last step we find that C should have the same distribution as B. By this, we have found a distribution that causes no communication and can stop analyzing the decision tree. If the distribution would cause communication, we would have to backtrack to the decision of B.

12.5.3 Redistribution during Program Execution

Redistribution of arrays during program execution is quite an expensive operation that causes a lot of communication. Nevertheless, for large input programs a redistribution of some of the arrays might result in a smaller overall communication. This is true, if for example an array is accessed differently in different parts of the program. Redistribution of arrays during the execution of the program can be considered, if we change the algorithm as follows: when building a new level of the decision tree, we not only consider the arrays not yet distributed, but also the arrays to be redistributed. The costs of the redistribution are added to the costs of the tree edges. The arrays that may be redistributed are added to the set *DNSET* and to the sorted list *DNLIST*. Note that the redistributions computed in this way are static and cannot be adapted to input data at run time.

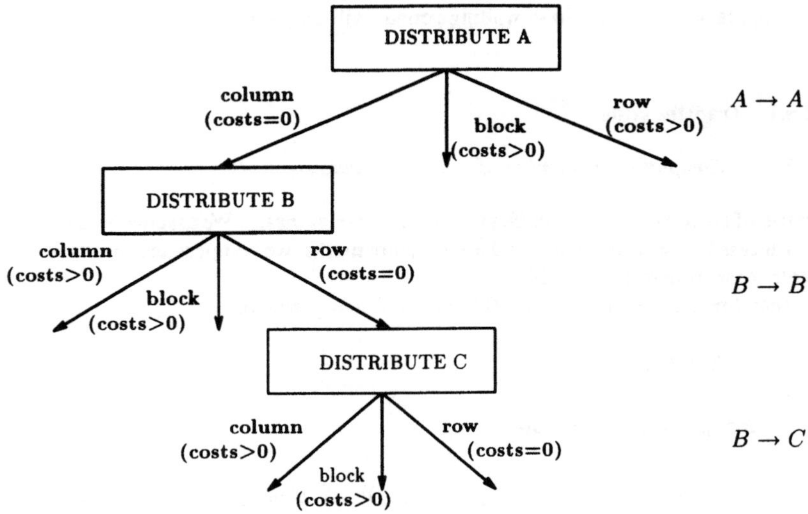

Figure 12.4 Decision tree for example 12.5.1 for 4 processors.

By allowing redistribution, the decision tree may get quite large. We can reduce the size by allowing array redistributions only at certain program points: For example, it surely makes no sense to redistribute an array within a basic block. In the current implementation, we only allow redistributions at the outermost loop level.

12.6 Performance Estimator

Algorithm 12.5.1 uses a cost function *CPCOST*() to estimate the run time delay caused by the communication instruction of a CP. We describe the cost function in this section. We assume that the loop bounds are constant and that the index functions are linear. Optimizations like constant propagation and profiling are used to reduce these restrictions. A communication instruction causes a run time delay in two different ways:

1. The access to an array element via network is much slower than a local access. Thus, the total number of array elements transferred through the net is significant for the delay. Subsection 12.6.1.1 describes the computation of this number. With respect to the restrictions for the loop bounds and the access functions we will be able to compute this number exactly.

2. Moreover, we have to estimate the effects of sequentializing communication instructions caused by data dependencies. Dependent on the distribution of the arrays

there may be time intervals during which some processors must wait for others. An approach to estimate these waiting periods will be given in subsection 12.6.2.

12.6.1 Transfer costs

12.6.1.1 Computing the number of transferred data elements

An use of an array element can be preceded by several masks. We assume here that each read access has only one mask. If there are more masks, we compose the results for each single mask as described in [14].
A general read access to an array B has the following structure:

for $i_1 := lb_1$ **to** ub_1 **do**
    ⋮
        for $i_m := lb_m$ **to** ub_m **do**
            ⋮
            $A[f_1(i_1,\dots,i_m),\dots,f_{d_A}(i_1,\dots,i_m)] \;:=\; B[g_1(i_1,\dots,i_m),\dots,g_{d_B}(i_1,\dots,i_m)];$
            ⋮
        od
    ⋮
od

Due to the restrictions above we assume that the index functions have the following form:

$$f_d(i_1,\dots,i_m) = a_d \cdot i_{j_d} + a_d^0, \qquad d \in [1,d_A], j_d \in [1,m]$$

$$g_d(i_1,\dots,i_m) = b_d \cdot i_{k_d} + b_d^0, \qquad d \in [1,d_B], k_d \in [1,m],$$

where d_X denotes the dimension of array X. We compute the number of the data transferred separately for each processor p. This computation requires two steps.

1. In the first step, we compute the elements of A that are defined by processor p. The index space is given by the bounds of the loop surrounding the access:

   $$INDEX = ([lb_1,ub_1],\dots,[lb_m,ub_m]),$$

   The array elements of A accessed by processor p are determined by the current distribution of A and the functions $f_1,\dots,f_{d_A}$: We get the part of the index space for which processor p executes the read access by solving the inequations

   $$lb_d^A \le f_d(i_1,\dots,i_m) \le ub_d^A, \qquad 1 \le d \le d_A$$

   where

$$A[lb_1^A : ub_1^A, \ldots, lb_{d_A}^A : ub_{d_A}^A]$$

is the part of A local to p. We denote the part of the index space of p by

$$RANGE_p = ([L_1, U_1], \ldots, [L_m, U_m]).$$

2. In the second step, we apply the index functions $g_1, \ldots, g_{d_B}$ to $RANGE_p$. Thus, we get the part of array B accessed by p. By intersecting this with the part of B owned by p we can easily compute the number of the elements received by p from other processors. We call this number $TRANS_p(cp)$.

We illustrate these computations by an example:

Example 12.6.1

```
var i, j, k: integer;
var A, B: array[1..32,1..32] of integer;
begin
    for i :=0 to 15 do
        for j := 4 to 10 do
            for k := 2 to 17 do
                A[2·i + 1, j − 3] := B[3·j, 2·k − 2];
            od
        od
    od
end
```

The index space is

$$INDEX = (\underbrace{[0,15]}_{i}, \underbrace{[4,10]}_{j}, \underbrace{[2,17]}_{k})$$

Figure 12.5 shows the assumed distribution of A and B.
The computation for processor $p = 5$ results in

$$RANGE_5 = ([8,15],[4,10],[2,17])$$

The accessed part of B is

$$B[12 : 30, 2 : 32].$$

Processor 5 owns

$$B[17 : 25, 1 : 17],$$

thus it must receive the 88 elements that are in the first set but not in the second. Processor 5 must receive in each iteration of the i–loop 88 elements of array B.

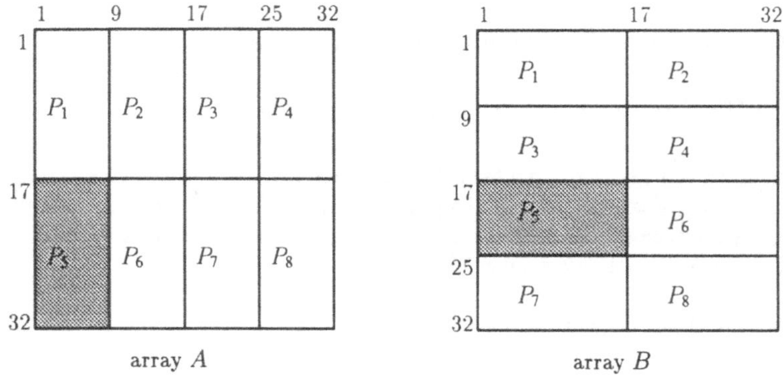

Figure 12.5 Distributions for example 12.6.1

12.6.1.2 Computing the number of messages

Communication instructions can be vectorized so that several elements are transferred by a single message. To estimate the total communication amount of a CP, we need to know the number of transferred data elements and the number of messages required for the transfer. Vectorization of communication leads to a better performance, because the data transfer time for one message of length n in our programming model refers to the following equation:

$$Transfertime(n) = SU + n \cdot BTFT$$

SU ist the startup time for a message, $BTFT$ is the time to transfer one byte. Each processor p receives $TRANS_p(cp)$ elements from other processors. $TRANS_p(cp)$ is the sum of all elements received by other processors $q \neq p$. q sends $TRANS_p^q(cp)$ array elements to p, where

$$TRANS_p(cp) = \sum_{q \neq p} TRANS_p^q(cp).$$

Vectorization of the communication instruction allows to put several array elements in a single message so that each q sends $M_p^q(cp)$ messages to p. To determine the number of the required *communication startups* we add the number of messages passed to p.

$$SN_p(cp) = \sum_{q \neq p} M_p^q(cp)$$

Thereafter we can calculate the costs for a cp to:

$$COST_p(cp) = SN_p \cdot SU + TRANS_p(cp) \cdot typesize(cp) \cdot BTFT,$$

where $typesize(cp)$ is a function that returns the size of an array element related to cp in bytes.

12.6.2 Combining the transfer costs

Now we are able to calculate for a given CP the number of bytes and the number of messages a processor p must receive. These informations are not sufficient to estimate the run time delay of a CP. Some processors may work in parallel, whereas other processors are delayed by data dependencies. To illustrate our approach for combining the $COST_p(cp)$ we examine the following example.

Example 12.6.2

```
var i, j: integer;
var A, B: array[1..32,1..32] of integer;
begin
    for i := 1 to 32 do
        for j := 1 to 32 do
            B[i,j] := i·j;
            A[i,j] := B[i,j];
        od
    od
end
```

We assume A to be distributed by block and B by row to 4 processors. According to section 12.6.1.1, each processor receives 32 elements from other processors. A more detailed analysis shows the following behaviour:

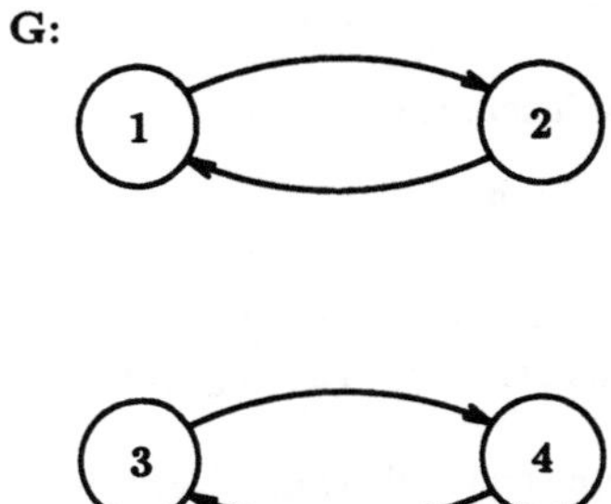

Figure 12.6 Dependencies of the processors for example 12.6.2

P_1 exchanges elements with P_2 and P_3 exchanges elements with P_4. These two groups of processors can work in parallel, so that we can express the $COST_p(cp)$ as

$$\max(COST_1(cp) + COST_2(cp), COST_3(cp) + COST_4(cp)).$$

We generalize this idea by introducing the data transfer graph in the next section.

12.6.3 Data Transfer Graph

To estimate the delay times of processors caused by data dependencies we need information about the interprocessor communication behaviour. Therefore, we describe the data transfer between processors by a graph, whose nodes represent processors. Our aim is to combine the $TRANS_p(cp)$ for a given $cp \in CPSET$ in a useful way.

Definition 12.6.1 *A* **data transfer graph DTG** *is a graph* $G_{cp} = (V, E)$*, where*

- $V = \{P_1, \ldots, P_n\}$ *is the set of processors*
- $E \subset V \times V$ *with*

$$(P_i, P_j) \in E \Leftrightarrow \exists cp_k \in INFLUENCESET(cp), \text{ which causes } P_i \text{ to send data to } P_j$$

Processors involved in cycles in the DTG usually cannot work in parallel because data dependencies cause mutual communication of processors. That's why we add all $TRANS_p(cp)$ of all processors p in one *strongly connected component* (SCC) of the **DTG**. We define the acylic data transfer graph:

Definition 12.6.2 *Let* $G_{cp} = (V, E)$ *be a* **DTG** *of a cp. Then* $AG_{cp} = (AV, AE)$*, where*

- $AV = \{s_1, \ldots, s_m\}$ *is the set of the SCC's of the graph* G_{cp}.
- $AE = \{(s_x, s_y) \mid x \neq y \wedge \exists P_i \in s_x, P_j \in s_y \text{ with } (P_i, P_j) \in E\}$

AG_{cp} *is called the* **acyclic data transfer graph** *ADTG of cp.*

Now we can define a cost function for SCC's:

$$COST_{scc}(cp) = \sum_{p \in scc} COST_p(cp)$$

Let us return to example 12.6.2. If we change the two accesses to B to $B[i+1, j]$ or $B[i-1, j]$, respectively, we obtain two pairs of graphs shown in figure 12.7 and figure 12.8.

If we examine the communication behaviour of these two examples in more detail, we make the following observations:

Example (i) (figure 12.7)

P_3 and P_4 start their work by sending their first row of data elements of array B to P_1 and P_2. After this, the two groups of processors can work concurrently. Due to this fact we can ignore the edge in the ADTG.

Example (ii) (figure 12.8)

P_3 and P_4 cannot start working until P_1 and P_2 have finished their work and have sent their last rows to P_3 and P_4. This means that the edge in the ADTG causes a *sequentialization*. The global costs are obtained by summing the costs of the SCC's.
This suggests to distinguish two kinds of edges in the ADTG of a *cp*.

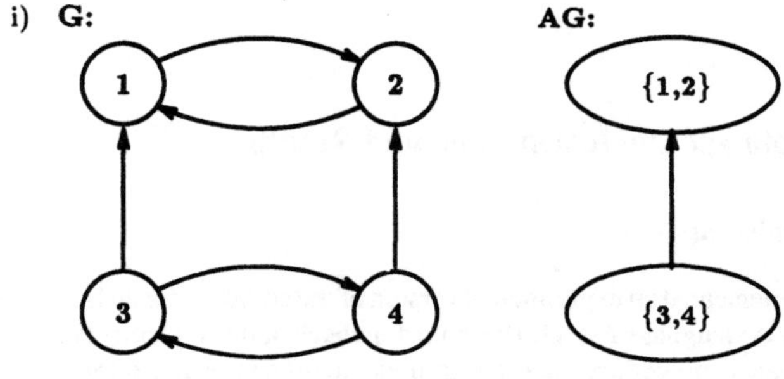

Figure 12.7 DTG and ADTG according to access $B[i+1,j]$

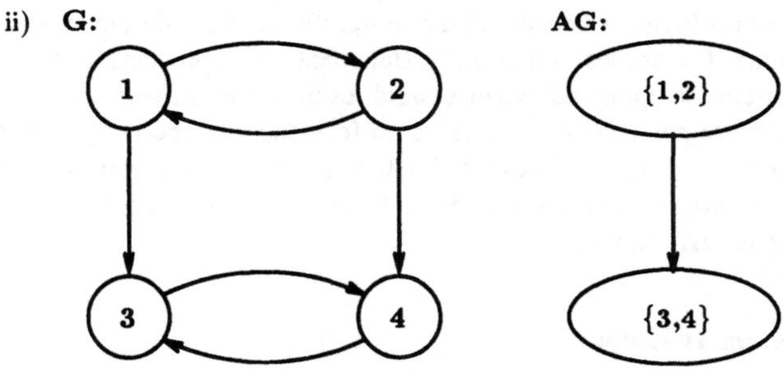

Figure 12.8 DTG and ADTG according to access $B[i-1,j]$

1. **Delay edges** force the destination processor of the edge to wait until the source processor has completed its work. Delay edges have the direction of the outermost loop, i.e. a delay edge represents a true data dependence carried by the outermost loop of the current loop nest. Data dependencies in inner loops do not cause a processor to wait until another processor has completely finished its work. An example is given in section 12.7.3.

2. **Parallel edges** cause data transfer, but sender and receiver can work in parallel.

A formal definition of delay edges and parallel edges can be found in [14]. Because parallel edges cause no data transfer, we can eliminate them from the ADTG AG_{cp}. This leads to a graph $AG'_{cp} = (AV', AE')$. With this graph we define the following functions:

$$CPCOST_{s_i}(cp) = COST_{s_i}(cp) + \max_{(s_i,s_j)\in AE'} CPCOST_{s_j}(cp)$$

$$CPCOST(cp) = \max_{s\in AV'} CPCOST_s(cp)$$

CPCOST(*cp*) is used by algorithm 12.5.1 to estimate the cost of a data distribution for all arrays.

12.7 Prototype Implementation and Results

12.7.1 Implementation

We have implemented an experimental version of the compiler for an Intel iPSC/860 with 32 nodes for the language Pascal. The main drawback of the implementation is that it is not yet able to handle procedure calls. The implementation is designed for easy modification for other languages such as C or Fortran. The transformations that are described in section 12.4 are applied to the intermediate representation of the program, and the resulting parallel program are emitted in C. The emitted program is then compiled with the standard compiler of the iPSC/860, thus giving an object program for the iPSC/860. There is a loss in efficiency because of the straightforward translation of the intermediate representation to C that uses a lot of `goto` statements. This prevents the C compiler from applying most of the optimizations that could result in a better performance. Depending on the source program, we determined a performance reduction by a factor that lies between 1 and 4. A more careful translation that tries to reconstruct the control structures of the original program like loops and conditional statements could eliminate most of this decrease in performance.

12.7.2 Livermore Loops

To evaluate the prototype implementation, we made tests for different types of applications. Table 12.1 shows the results of applying the compiler to the Livermore kernels that have been widely used to evaluate the performance of computer systems. Written originally in Fortran, the benchmarks were converted in Pascal for this test. These tests determine that 16 of the kernels were parallelized by the compiler. The speedup decrease for some of the kernels for 32 processors is caused by the fact that the problem size is not increased with the number of processors. For the affected kernels, the decrease in the computation time that is reached by using more processors is overbalanced by the increase in communication time that is caused by the fact, that more data has to be communicated to a larger number of processors, thus increasing the number of messages. Examination of the failed cases showed that some were not parallelizable, even by hand. In other cases, the kernel could be parallelized by rewriting it, e.g. kernel 6 or 17. Table 12.2 shows for one of the largest kernels that the number of nodes of the decision tree that are really built is usually quite small. Tests with other input programs confirm this observation.

To emphasize the effect of different distributions on the run time of a parallelized program we give some concluding examples dealing with relaxation of two dimensional arrays.

nr.	name	Speedup for x processors 2	4	8	16	32
1	Hydrodynamics	1.9	3.6	6.0	9.2	12.5
2	Incomplete Cholesky	not parallelized				
3	Inner product	1.7	2.3	2.6	2.5	1.5
4	Banded linear equations	not parallelized				
5	Tridiagonal elimination	0.2	0.3	0.5	0.8	1.2
6	Recurrence elimination	not parallelized				
7	Equation of state	1.9	3.8	7.5	13.6	23.5
8	ADI	1.9	3.7	6.7	11.6	17.9
9	Numerical Intregration	1.9	3.5	6.1	9.7	13.5
10	Numerical Differentiation	1.9	3.5	6.4	10.1	14.1
11	Finite sum	0.1	0.2	0.4	0.6	0.9
12	Finite difference	2.0	3.8	7.3	13.3	15.8
13	2D particle in cell	not parallelized				
14	1D particle in cell	not parallelized				
15	Prime example	1.9	3.9	7.5	13.9	23.9
16	Monte Carlo	not parallelized				
17	Conditional computation	not parallelized				
18	2D Hydrodynamics	1.8	2.9	4.1	4.7	3.9
19	Linear recurrence relation	not parallelized				
20	Discrete ordinates transport	0.4	0.7	1.2	2.2	3.9
21	Matrix product	1.9	3.6	6.5	12.0	19.7
22	Planck distribution	2.0	4.0	7.9	15.7	30.9
23	2D implicit Hydrodynamics	1.5	2.6	4.8	8.3	12.9
24	Minimization	1.6	2.0	2.0	1.7	1.1

Table 12.1 Results of applying the compiler to the Livermore Loops

n_p	n_d	n_v
2	32	12
4	243	21
8	1024	32
16	3125	45
32	7776	60

Table 12.2 Run time of the data distribution tool for kernel 15 that uses 5 two–dimensional arrays. n_p is the number of processors, n_d is the number of nodes of the decision tree, n_v is the number of nodes of the decision tree that are visited by the algorithms.

12.7.3 Gauss–Seidel Relaxation

The computational kernel of Gauss–Seidel relaxation consists of the following loop nest:

Example 12.7.1

for L := 1 **to** LP **do**
  for i := 2 **to** $N-1$ **do**
    for j := 2 **to** $N-1$ **do**

```
            a[i,j] := a[i,j] + a[i-1,j] + a[i,j-1] + a[i,j+1] + a[i+1,j];
        od
    od
od
```

We ran a parallelized version of this program on an iPSC/860 with 32 nodes. The number of iterations LP was set to 1000 and the size of array a was $N = 100$.

Table 12.3 shows the speedups for different distributions running the program on 8 processors.

npd–vector	8,1	4,2	2,4	1,8
Speedup	2.4	0.4	0.3	0.5

Table 12.3 Speedups for example 12.7.1 with 8 processors

Our decision algorithm chooses the *npd*–vector $(8, 1)$. Table 12.3 shows that this is the best distribution. In this case the data dependencies carried by the inner j–loop causes no communication. Concerning the i–loop, processor P_i must wait for P_{i-1} to fininsh its iterations, but after P_i has started its work, P_{i-1} begins to work on the next iteration of the outermost L–loop so that the load is nearly balanced. Table 12.4 shows the speedups resulting when distributing by row for different numbers of processors.

# processors	2	4	8	16	32
speedup	0.9	1.5	2.4	3.5	4.4

Table 12.4 Speedups for example 12.7.1

12.7.4 Jacobi Relaxation

Jacobi relaxation differs from Gauss–Seidel relaxation by the use of two arrays, so that there are no data dependencies concerning the two innermost loops. This makes the parallelization easier.

Example 12.7.2

```
for L := 1 to LP do
    for i := 2 to N - 1 do
        for j := 2 to N - 1 do
            a[i,j] := b[i,j] + b[i-1,j] + b[i,j-1] + b[i,j+1] + b[i+1,j];
        od
    od
    for i := 2 to N - 1 do
```

```
        for j := 2 to N − 1 do
            b[i,j] := a[i,j];
        od
    od
od
```

Different distributions of the arrays a and b differ only in the amount of communication. Therefore, all distributions with a and b distributed in the same way, yield good results. Tables 12.5 and 12.6 show the speedup values.

npd-vector	8,1	4,2	2,4	1,8
Speedup	5.2	5.3	5.2	5.0

Table 12.5 Speedups for example 12.7.2 (Jacobi relaxation) for 8 processors.

# processors	2	4	8	16	32
speedup	1.8	3.2	5.3	7.5	17.7

Table 12.6 Speedups for example 12.7.2 (Jacobi relaxation)

12.8 Conclusions and Further Research

The presented compiler automatically parallelizes sequential programs for a distributed memory computer. The compiler computes a data distribution for the source program automatically and parallelizes the program according to this distribution. The compiler can be applied to all programs having reference patterns that can be analyzed at compile time.

Although the compiler works well on a large class of applications, it is limited to the computation of data distribution for arrays. Future research may address the problem of distributing other data structures like lists, tree, graphs, and so on.

We could also optimize the existing algorithm for the distribution of arrays in some ways. Currently, it allows only regular block distributions for the arrays. Allowing more general distributions could result in a better performance of the parallelized programs. The resulting increase in the run time of the distribution tool might be outbalanced by not always computing an optimal distribution but to include the option that a suboptimal solution is sufficient. The number of input programs parallelizable by the compiler could be increased quite easy by including a tool that applies normalization transformations like induction variable substitution or scalar forward substitution to the input program.

12.9 Acknowledgements

The authors would like to thank Prof. Dr. R. Wilhelm, Prof. Dr. W. Paul, Christoph Keßler, Martin Alt, and Christian Ferdinand for their helpful support.

References

[1] G.R. Andews, R.A. Olsson, M. Coffin, I. Elshoff, K. Nilsen, T. Purdin, and G. Townsend. An Overview of the SR Language and Implementation. *ACM Transactions on Programming Languages and Systems*, pages 51–86, 1988.

[2] H.E. Bal, J.G. Steiner, A.S. Tanenbaum. Programming Languages for Distributed Computing Systems. *ACM Computing Surveys*, pages 261–322, 1989.

[3] V. Balasundaram, G. Fox, K. Kennedy, U. Kremer. An Interactive Environment for Data Partitioning and Distribution. Proceedings of the 5th Distributed Memory Computing Conference, 1990.

[4] B. Chapman, H. Herbeck, H. Zima. Automatic Support for Data Distribution. Technical Report ACPC/TR 91-14, Austrian Center for Parallel Computation, July 1991.

[5] B. Chapman, H. Herbeck, H. Zima. Knowledge–based Parallelization for Distributed Memory Systems. Technical Report ACPC/TR 91-11, Austrian Center for Parallel Computation, April 1991.

[6] B. Chapman, P. Mehrotra, and H. Zima. Programming in Vienna Fortran. In *Third Workshop on Compilers for Parallel Computers*, pages 121–160, 1992.

[7] A. Dierstein. Parallelisierung mit automatischer Datenaufteilung für imperative Programmiersprachen – Teil 1: Parallelisierungsstrategie. Diplomarbeit, Universität des Saarlandes, 1993.

[8] J.A. Feldmann, C.C. Lim, F. Mazzanti. pSather monitors: Design, Tutorial Rationale and Implementation. Technical Report TR-91-031, International Computer Science Institut Berkeley, CA, 1991.

[9] J.A. Feldmann, C.C. Lim, T. Rauber. The shared–memory language pSather on a distributed–memory multiprocessor. In Second Workshop on Languages, Compilers, and Run-Time Environments for Distributed Memory Multiprocessors, Boulder, CO, 1992.

[10] N.H. Gehani and W.D. Roome. Concurrent C. *Software – Practice and Experience*, pages 821–844, 1986.

[11] H.M. Gerndt. Automatic Parallelization for Distributed Memory Multiprocessing Systems. Dissertation, University of Bonn, 1989.

[12] M. Gerndt, H.P. Zima. Superb: Experiences and Future Research. Technical Report ACPC/TR90-5, Austrian Center for Parallel Computation, October 1990.

[13] M. Gupta and P. Banerjee. Automatic Data Partioning on Distributed Multiprocessors. University of Illinois, Technical Report CRHC-90-14, 1990.

[14] R. Hayer: Parallelisierung mit automatischer Datenaufteilung für imperative Programmiersprachen – Teil 2: Automatische Datenaufteilung. Diplomarbeit, Universität des Saarlandes, 1993.

[15] S. Hiranandani, K. Kennedy, C.W. Tseng. Compiler Support for Machine–Independent Parallel Programming in Fortran–D. Technical Report Rice COMP TR91-149, Rice University, March 1991.

[16] K. Ikudome, D. Fox, A. Kolawa and J. Flower. An Automatic and Symbolic Parallelization System for Distributed Memory Parallel Computers. Proceedings of the 5th Distributed Memory Computing Conference, IEEE, pages 1105–1114, 1990.

[17] INMOS Ltd. OCCAM Programming Manual. Prentice Hall, Englewood Cliffs, NJ, 1984.

[18] K. Kennedy, U. Kremer. Automatic Data Alignment and Distribution for Loosely Synchronous Problems in an Interactive Programming Environment. Technical Report COMP TR91-155, Rice University, April 1991.

[19] C.W. Keßler: Knowledge–Based Automatic Parallelization by Pattern Recognition. This volume.

[20] J. Li and M. Chen. Index Domain Alignment. Yale University, 1989.

[21] M. Metcalf. *Fortran 90 Explained.* Oxford Science Publications. Oxford University Press, 1990.

[22] R. Mirchandaney, J.H. Saltz, R.M. Smith, D.M. Nichol, K. Crowley. Principles of Runtime Support for Parallel Processors. In Proceedings of the ACM, 1988.

[23] Parasoft Co. EXPRESS user manual. Parasoft Co., 1989.

[24] Reference Guide for iPSC/860. Intel, 1990.

[25] K. Pingali, A. Rogers. Compiler Parallelization of SIMPLE for a Distributed Memory Machine. In *Languages, Compilers and Run–Time Environments for Distributed Memory Machines*, pages 63–78. Elsevier, 1992.

[26] R. Sawdayi, G. Wagenbreth, J. Williamson. MIMDizer: Functional and Data decomposition. In *Compilers and Runtime Software for Scalable Multiprocessors*. Elsevier, 1991.

[27] D. Scales, M. Rinard, M. Lam, J. Anderson. Hierachical Concurrency in Jade. 4th International Workshop on Languages and Compilers for Parallel Computing. Santa Clara, CA, August, 1991, Springer LNCS 589.

[28] User's Guide for iPSC/860. Intel, 1990

[29] J. Wexler. Concurrent Programming in Occam-2. Wiley, 1989.

[30] H. Zima and B. Chapman. Supercompilers for Parallel and Vector Computers, ACM Press Frontier Series, Addison–Wesley, 1990.

A Trademarks

Some of the supercomputer or software names occuring in this book are (registered) trademarks. We give a list of trademarks and corresponding companies and apologize if we should have some omitted or acknowledged incorrectly. Names that do not occur in this list can not be concluded not to be (registered) trademarks.

Ada is a trademark of U.S. Government Ada Joint Program Office.
Computing Surface is a trademark of Meiko Scientific Ltd.
Connection Machine, CM-2 and **CM-5** are trademarks of Thinking Machines Corporation.
CM Fortran (CMF) and **CMMD** are trademarks of Thinking Machines Corporation.
Cray 1 is a trademark of Cray Research Incorporated.
Express is a trademark of Parasoft Incorporated.
FORGE is a trademark of Applied Parallel Research.
FX-2800 is a trademark of Alliant Computer Systems Corporation.
GC is a trademark of Parsytec GmbH.
i860 is a trademark of Intel Corporation.
iPSC is a trademark of Intel Corporation.
Jade is a trademark of Jade Simulations International Corp..
KSR-1 is a trademark of Kendall Square Research Corporation.
Linda is a trademark of Scientific Computing Associates.
MIMDizer is a trademark of Applied Parallel Research.
MIPS is a trademark of MIPS Computer Systems.
MP1 is a trademark of MasPar Computer Corporation.
nCUBE, nCUBE-1 and **nCUBE-2** are trademarks of nCUBE Corporation.
Occam is a trademark of Inmos Limited.
OSF/Motif is a trademark of the Open Software Foundation Inc.
Paragon XP/S is a trademark of Intel Corporation.
Perfect Benchmarks is a trademark of the University of Illinois.
Silicon Graphics is a trademark of Silicon Graphics Inc.
SGI is a trademark of Silicon Graphics, Inc.
SP1 is a trademark of IBM Corporation.
Sun and **X11** are trademarks of Sun Microsystems, Inc.
Touchstone is a trademark of Intel Corporation.
Transputer, T414, T212, T800 and **T9000** are trademarks of Inmos Limited.
VP-100 is a trademark of Fujitsu Limited.
UNIX is a trademark of AT&T.
X-Windows is a trademark of Massachusetts Institute of Technology.
Windows-NT is a trademark of Microsoft.

Index

GPSR Compliance

The European Union's (EU) General Product Safety Regulation (GPSR) is a set of rules that requires consumer products to be safe and our obligations to ensure this.

If you have any concerns about our products, you can contact us on ProductSafety@springernature.com

In case Publisher is established outside the EU, the EU authorized representative is:

Springer Nature Customer Service Center GmbH
Europaplatz 3
69115 Heidelberg, Germany

Batch number: 10577919

Printed by Printforce, the Netherlands